From Pixels to Play - The Art and Science of Video Games

Edited by Tibor Guzsvinecz

Published in London, United Kingdom

From Pixels to Play - The Art and Science of Video Games
http://dx.doi.org/10.5772/intechopen.1008008
Edited by Tibor Guzsvinecz

Contributors
Ahmad Azadvar, Ahmed Adam Kada, Arun K. Kulshreshth, Ava Fatah gen. Schieck, Dariusz Myszor, Faiza Benfdil, Francisca Escudeiro, Józef P. Cyran, Krzysztof A. Cyran, Marats Kicikovs, Martin Traunmueller, Maxim Filin, Márcia Campos Gouveia, Nicholas Fisher, Nikola Peric, Nisrine EL Arrouf, Paula Escudeiro, Petros Koutsolampros, Qianhui Ni, Remi Poivet, Szabolcs Felszeghy, Tibor Guzsvinecz, Tieh-Huai Chang, Zhenan Tian

First published in London, United Kingdom, 2026 by IntechOpen
IntechOpen is the global imprint of INTECHOPEN LIMITED, registered in England and Wales, registration number: 11086078, 167-169 Great Portland Street, London, W1W 5PF, United Kingdom

For EU product safety concerns: IN TECH d.o.o., Prolaz Marije Krucifikse Kozulić 3, 51000 Rijeka, Croatia, info@intechopen.com or visit our website at intechopen.com.

British Library Cataloguing-in-Publication Data
A catalogue record for this book is available from the British Library

From Pixels to Play - The Art and Science of Video Games
Edited by Tibor Guzsvinecz
p. cm.
Print ISBN 978-1-83635-364-5
Online ISBN 978-1-83635-363-8
eBook (PDF) ISBN 978-1-83635-365-2

Meet the editor

Tibor Guzsvinecz is an Associate Professor at the Faculty of Information Technology, University of Pannonia, Hungary. He earned his Ph.D. in Information Science in 2021. His research focuses on data science, gamification, HCI, spatial ability, and virtual reality. He has published 124 scientific works, including 40 journal articles and 64 conference papers, and has edited three books on video game research. His Hirsch index is 12. He has received eight scholarships, a Best Paper Award, and an IEEE Section Chair Award. He serves on the organizing committees of two IEEE conferences (IEEE International Conference on Cognitive InfoCommunications and IEEE International Conference on Cognitive Aspects of Virtual Reality). He has been an IEEE member since 2023.

Contents

Preface

Nowadays, video games are complex, multidimensional systems that support cognitive, social, and technological development. Since they have evolved beyond recreational activities, this book offers an insight into game design, education, and digital technologies. The book is structured into four sections, which provide a deeper understanding of the role of video games.

The first section, titled "Game Mechanics, Player Experience, and Design", focuses on three main topics. In the first chapter, "Dynamic Difficulty Adjustment in Games: Concepts, Techniques, and Applications" by Nicholas Fisher and Arun K. Kulshreshth, the authors investigate gameplay mechanics that dynamically adapt gameplay to the player's performance. The next chapter, "Pathways to Mastery: A Taxonomy of Player Progression Systems in Commercial Video Games" by Tibor Guzsvinecz, introduces a model of progression systems that illustrates what motivates players and how feedback loops are structured. Lastly, the chapter "Crafting Virtual Characters for Games: A Player-Centered Approach" by Remi Poivet examines the psychological and affective aspects of avatar and NPC design.

The second section, titled "Socio-Cultural Aspects of Gaming", investigates gaming as a medium for social behavior and narrative construction. The first chapter, "Games as a Social-Cultural Medium: Motivation, Community, and Disruptive Behavior" by Ahmad Azadvar and Qianhui Ni, analyzes motivational profiles and behavioral phenomena in multiplayer video games. In the following chapter, "Environmental Storytelling in Video Games: Crafting Narratives beyond Words", Józef Cyran, Dariusz Myszor, and Krzysztof A. Cyran examine non-verbal narrative techniques, emphasizing spatial and symbolic communication in video games.

The third section is titled "Games and Learning: Educational Approaches through Play". It presents applications of games in educational settings. In the first chapter, "A Brief Discussion on Research Experiences in Games and Learning: A Predecessor of a Community of Practice Approach in Taiwan" by Tieh-huai Chang, institutional and cultural influences on game-based learning are examined. In the second chapter, titled "Enhancing Case-Based Serious Games in Dental Education with AI: A Comparative Study of Manual vs. AI-Driven Development" by Ahmed Adam Kada et al., the manual and AI-driven development of serious games is investigated. Finally, "Play with Purpose: Serious Games for Inclusion and Sustainability" by Paula Escudeiro et al. presents game-based approaches to promote equity and sustainable thinking.

The final section, titled "Technological Innovations in Gaming", covers both hardware and software paradigms. In the first chapter, titled "Exploring the Effect of Size on Viewers' Perception of Augmented Reality Objects on Mobile Devices" by Zhenan Tian et al., the design of AR interfaces is explored. Then, in the following chapter, titled "Internet-of-Things Integration: Sensor-Driven Gameplay on WowCube", Nikola Perić et al. present a tactile gaming platform that integrates IoT devices.

Overall, the chapters in this book present video games from multiple perspectives. I want to express my sincere gratitude to the authors for their rigorous work. With their contributions, the scientific value of this book has significantly increased.

Tibor Guzsvinecz
Department of Information Technology and its Applications,
University of Pannonia,
Zalaegerszeg, Hungary

Section 1

Game Mechanics, Player Experience, and Design

Chapter 1

Dynamic Difficulty Adjustment in Games: Concepts, Techniques, and Applications

Nicholas Fisher and Arun K. Kulshreshth

Abstract

Modern video games face the challenge of maintaining player engagement across a wide range of skills, experiences, and motivations. Traditional fixed difficulty settings often fail to meet this need, leading to early frustration for new players and boredom for experienced ones. Dynamic difficulty adjustment provides a flexible alternative by adapting gameplay in real-time based on player performance or emotional state. Grounded in concepts such as Flow Theory and Self-Determination Theory, adaptive systems seek to align challenge with player ability and psychological needs. This chapter reviews the historical development of difficulty systems, outlines performance-based, emotion-based, and hybrid adjustment methods, and examines a case study comparing five difficulty strategies within a custom first-person shooter game. Results show that while difficulty levels and perceived stress varied across methods, players' engagement, excitement, and enjoyment remained consistent, suggesting that adaptive systems can help maintain an optimal experience across diverse player profiles. The chapter concludes by discussing the limitations of dynamic adjustment, including the importance of transparency, the risk of undermining player competence, and the need to consider different motivations for play beyond the pursuit of challenge.

Keywords: dynamic difficulty adjustment, gameplay metrics, physiological sensors, player engagement, affective computing

1. Introduction

Video games today face a delicate challenge: how to keep players engaged without overwhelming or boring them. This balance is especially tricky because players come with vastly different skill levels, gaming experience, and even daily moods. A game that's too easy might feel dull; too hard, and it quickly becomes frustrating. Traditionally, game designers address this with fixed difficulty settings—"easy," "medium," or "hard"—but these one-size-fits-all approaches rarely capture the full range of player needs.

For some players, especially those new to gaming, even the "easy" setting can feel overwhelming. They may be unfamiliar with controls, core mechanics, or genre conventions, and often do not play long enough to adapt. Many non-gamers try a game once, feel lost or frustrated, and never return. This early drop-off can prevent them from reaching the positive feedback loop of skill development, increased confidence, and eventual mastery that keeps players engaged long term. On the opposite end of the spectrum are experienced or competitive players who may find even the hardest setting insufficiently challenging, resulting in boredom rather than engagement.

Designing for these outliers—novices and experts alike—requires flexible systems that respond to individual needs. Dynamic Difficulty Adjustment, or DDA, offers a promising solution. Rather than locking players into a fixed challenge level, DDA systems adjust the game in real time based on how a player performs—or even how they feel. By tailoring difficulty to each individual, DDA can help more players find their way into the game and stay engaged, whether they are picking up a controller for the first time or seeking a new level of challenge.

In this chapter, we explore the foundations of DDA, review key approaches, including performance-based and emotion-based systems, and share insights from a study that compared several difficulty adjustment strategies. This highlights how adaptive design can shape player experience and broaden a game's reach.

2. Origins of game difficulty

The idea of adapting difficulty based on the player's performance is not new. In fact, it can be traced back to the earliest arcade games of the 1970s and 1980s. These games often featured reactive mechanics that adjusted challenge on the fly, not out of player empathy, but for commercial reasons. As players survived longer, games like Space Invaders, Tetris, and Galaga increased the speed or complexity of their enemies. These adjustments kept the gameplay from becoming monotonous and nudged players toward a quicker end, encouraging repeat plays and, ideally, another coin in the machine.

Although primitive by today's standards, these early systems introduced a key idea: challenge can and should respond to player behavior. This real-time reactivity laid the seeds for modern adaptive systems, even if it was initially driven more by monetization than by user experience.

As games transitioned from arcades to home consoles and PCs, the model shifted. Developers began offering fixed difficulty settings—Easy, Medium, Hard—as a way to give players more control. Without the pressure to push players into game-over states for profit, games could offer longer, more narrative-driven experiences. But while this new model reduced pressure, it also assumed players knew how hard the game would be and how skilled they were before even starting. That assumption would prove limiting, especially for new players or those whose skill developed significantly over time.

3. Why fixed difficulty falls short

Despite their widespread use, fixed difficulty settings introduce significant limitations for both players and developers. While they were a logical evolution from the reactive mechanics of arcade-era design, fixed settings rely on the assumption that players can accurately assess their skill level and predict how challenging a game will be before they have even begun. In reality, this often leads to mismatches: players may underestimate themselves and breeze through the game with little engagement, or overestimate and hit a wall of frustration early on.

These decisions are often made before players have a clear understanding of the situation. New players, in particular, may be unfamiliar with the game's mechanics, pacing, or difficulty curve. Being asked to choose a challenge level before even touching the controls can feel alienating, especially when that choice directly shapes the entire experience.

For developers, fixed difficulty adds another layer of complexity. Designing multiple tiers that feel distinct, fair, and fun requires a deep understanding of player psychology and broad testing across varied skill levels. Despite best efforts, these tiers are rarely one-size-fits-all. Launching with fixed difficulty tiers that are too rigid or poorly tuned can result in mismatches between player ability and challenge, leading to frustration, disengagement, or uneven reviews. Even when multiple settings are available, they may fail to adapt to players whose skill develops over time or whose preferences shift across sessions. And while post-launch patches can tweak balance, they often come too late to recover lost player interest.

Another key issue is that fixed settings do not account for player improvement. As players progress, they often become more skilled, mastering mechanics, recognizing patterns, and refining their strategies. A difficulty level that once felt appropriate may become too easy over time, resulting in boredom during key narrative or climactic moments.

A more flexible solution is needed: one that evolves alongside the player. DDA addresses this gap by responding in real-time to performance or even emotional state. Instead of locking players into a single challenge level, DDA systems personalize the experience moment to moment, helping maintain engagement across a broader spectrum of player ability.

4. Foundations of adaptive difficulty

While fixed difficulty settings offer a simple solution to balancing challenge, they often fall short in addressing the diverse and evolving needs of players. DDA has emerged as a promising alternative. However, its development is not just a technical shift. It is grounded in longstanding design practices and psychological theories. Understanding these foundations helps explain why adaptive systems are more than reactive mechanics; they are rooted in principles of engagement, learning, and motivation. This section examines the historical origins of adaptive design and the theoretical models, such as Flow Theory, that continue to influence the understanding and implementation of DDA today.

4.1 Flow theory in dynamic systems

One of the most influential frameworks behind DDA is psychologist Mihaly Csikszentmihalyi's Flow Theory [1]. Flow describes a mental state of deep immersion, marked by intense focus, a sense of control, and intrinsic enjoyment in the activity itself. In games, flow occurs when the challenge posed by the game is well-matched to the player's abilities, a balance that fosters engagement without tipping into boredom or anxiety.

According to Csikszentmihalyi, if a task is too easy for the player's current skill level, it results in apathy or boredom; if the task is too difficult, it induces worry, frustration, or even anxiety. Flow emerges in the narrow channel between these extremes, where players are stretched just enough to stay immersed and motivated. This balance is illustrated by the challenge-skill model in **Figure 1**, which visually represents how an optimal experience arises when task difficulty aligns with individual capability.

A well-tuned DDA system aims to preserve this equilibrium by continuously adapting gameplay conditions in real time, responding to fluctuations in player skill, focus, and emotional state. Rather than relying on static difficulty settings, such systems adjust challenge dynamically to keep the player within the optimal "flow zone."

This principle is foundational to both performance-based and emotion-based adaptive systems. The phenomenon of being "in the zone" reflects this state of flow, often characterized by heightened arousal, sustained concentration, and a diminished awareness of time and self. While flow is frequently associated with high arousal and positive valence, these are distinct emotional dimensions—arousal refers to the intensity of the emotional state, while valence indicates its pleasantness or unpleasantness. By supporting this optimal state through real-time adaptation, DDA can lead to more engaging, personalized gameplay experiences.

4.2 Beyond flow: Motivation, feedback, and personalization

Beyond Flow, adaptive gameplay connects to broader ideas in motivation, learning, and player psychology. Games are often described as "systems of feedback"—they reward progress, signal failure, and provide clear goals. When this feedback is timely, relevant, and matched to the player's actions and abilities, it promotes a satisfying loop of effort and reward.

Motivation theories such as Self-Determination Theory (SDT) highlight three psychological needs that drive engagement: autonomy, competence, and relatedness [3]. Adaptive difficulty directly supports the need for competence by adjusting challenges to align with player skill, helping players feel capable and successful. This reinforcement loop, where a player attempts a task, receives feedback, and either advances or tries again with better information, is essential for maintaining both engagement and learning.

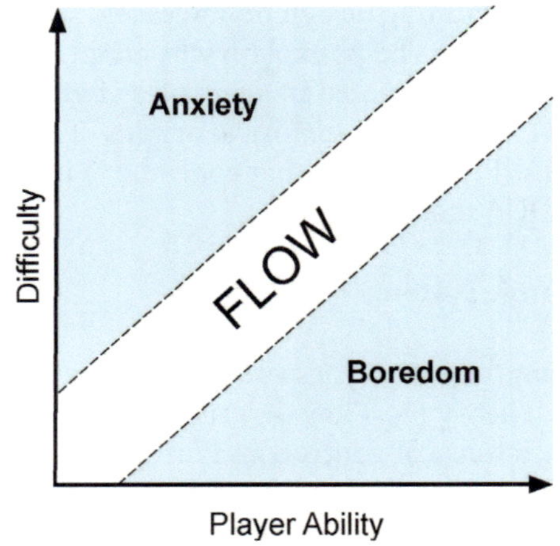

Figure 1.
Flow state is achieved when challenge matches player skill. Too much challenge causes anxiety; too little leads to boredom (Reproduced with permission from [2]).

This balance is not only motivational but also cognitive. According to Cognitive Load Theory [4], learners (and players) have a finite capacity for processing information. Adaptive difficulty can help regulate this load, reducing complexity when the player is overwhelmed and increasing it when the player is under-challenged, to ensure that the experience remains mentally manageable and engaging.

Feedback also plays a crucial role in how players perceive their own improvement. Systems that offer too little challenge risk making the player feel uninvested, while systems that are too punishing can lead to discouragement. Adaptive difficulty systems help maintain a motivational sweet spot, offering tasks that are just hard enough to promote effort, without overwhelming the player. This idea parallels scaffolding in educational design, where instruction adapts to a learner's needs to support growth.

Personalization amplifies these effects. In educational and entertainment contexts, research has shown that personalized systems—those that adapt to a user's preferences, pace, or performance—lead to better retention, deeper engagement, and longer play sessions. Adaptive systems that respond to emotional cues (e.g., frustration, boredom) or physiological signals (e.g., heart rate, gaze behavior) take this even further, potentially allowing for real-time difficulty tuning that meets the player exactly where they are.

By going beyond static levels and tailoring the experience to the individual, adaptive systems can meet the player's needs across multiple dimensions: cognitive, emotional, and motivational. This personalization helps create a gameplay experience that feels responsive, rewarding, and tailored to each player.

5. Dynamic difficulty adjustment types

DDA systems can be categorized by the types of data they use to assess the player's state and determine how to adjust gameplay. While the core goal remains the same—aligning challenge with player ability or experience—the methods used to achieve this vary widely. Some systems monitor performance metrics, while others assess emotional or physiological cues; many modern implementations combine multiple inputs to deliver more personalized and context-aware adjustments.

The following subsections outline three major types of DDA approaches: performance-based systems, emotion-based systems, and hybrid systems that combine both.

5.1 Performance-based systems

Performance-based DDA is the most common form of adaptive difficulty. These systems monitor the player's performance by tracking metrics such as accuracy, reaction time, win-loss ratio, and remaining health. Based on this data, the game dynamically adjusts the difficulty, for example, by increasing enemy speed, spawn rate, or AI behavior when the player is succeeding, or by reducing obstacles and offering assistance when they are struggling.

This approach is attractive because it directly responds to observable gameplay outcomes. It allows for real-time adjustment without requiring player input, and can be finely tuned to match specific design goals. Because performance is relatively easy to measure and interpret, these systems are among the most widely implemented in both commercial and experimental games.

Performance-based systems are especially well-suited to fast-paced or competitive games. A well-known commercial example is *Left 4 Dead*, where the game's AI Director adjusts enemy waves in real time based on team performance. Another frequently cited case is *Resident Evil 4*, which features a hidden difficulty adjustment system that modifies enemy behavior, damage, and item drops in response to player performance—creating a smoother experience without explicitly informing the player.

Academic research on performance-based DDA encompasses a range of genres and platforms. Early work explored dynamic challenge scaling in first-person shooters [5, 6], with subsequent studies focusing on balancing player experience through in-game performance metrics [7]. This approach has been extended to Massively Multiplayer Online environments through dynamic enemy tuning based on real-time data [8], and to the Multiplayer Online Battle Arena genre by adapting the challenge based on both team and individual performance [9].

More recent implementations have incorporated machine learning and novel interaction contexts. One study used deep learning to classify player skill and dynamically adjust difficulty in an arcade shooter, enhancing engagement and immersion [10]. Another application of DDA is to Virtual Reality (VR) exercise games, where procedurally generated environments are adapted to players' physical capabilities [11]. A separate model tailored difficulty in a 2D platformer using static danger zones and enemy behavior patterns [12].

Because performance metrics alone cannot capture the full range of player experience, researchers began exploring emotion-based systems—an approach intended to address not just external performance, but internal factors such as arousal, stress, and attentional engagement. While these systems are often described in affective terms, many rely on physiological indicators that primarily reflect emotional intensity (arousal), rather than emotional valence.

5.2 Emotion-based systems

While performance-based DDA adapts gameplay based on observable behavior, it does not always reflect how the player is feeling. A player may perform well but still experience stress, boredom, or cognitive overload. To address this limitation, emotion-based systems attempt to model the player's affective state and use that information to inform the adjustment of difficulty. These systems aim to support a more comprehensive understanding of the player's experience, capturing not only what the player is doing but also how they are emotionally responding to the game.

Emotion-based DDA systems rely on signals from the body to estimate how a player is feeling during gameplay. These systems use biosensors to detect emotional states such as stress, excitement, boredom, or fatigue. Common tools include heart rate monitors, skin conductance sensors, and brainwave measurement devices, such as electroencephalogram (EEG) headsets. However, most emotion-based systems focus on a specific signal to detect a single target emotion, such as using EEG to detect anxiety or heart rate variability (HRV) to infer stress. In practice, especially within affective computing and machine learning, these emotional states are often modeled as singular scalar values (e.g., "engagement" or "stress" scores from 0 to 100), rather than decomposed into independent dimensions like arousal and valence. These signals are then used to trigger adjustments in gameplay, such as modifying pacing, enemy density, or UI complexity. While these systems do not typically attempt to measure all emotional variables simultaneously, they can still offer targeted adaptation that enhances player comfort and engagement within specific gameplay contexts.

For example, researchers have used EEG to detect anxiety and mental focus in various types of games [13–15]. In contrast, others have explored excitement and arousal as key signals for adjusting difficulty in multiplayer settings [16]. Techniques like functional near-infrared spectroscopy have also been tested to measure mental workload [17], and HRV is often used to identify moments of stress or cognitive strain [18–21]. Skin conductance, measured through galvanic skin response, remains a popular method for tracking emotional arousal and has been widely applied in game adaptation research [22–24].

By gauging emotional cues such as stress, excitement, boredom, or fatigue, emotion-based systems can dynamically adjust the difficulty or gameplay elements in real-time. For instance, if the system detects signs of cognitive overload or frustration, it may lower the challenge or simplify interactions. If boredom or low arousal is detected, it may introduce new enemies, time pressure, or other stimulating events to counteract it. The goal is to create a more empathetic and responsive experience that adapts to both the player's internal state and their performance.

Although emotion-based DDA is still a growing area of research, a few commercial games have explored its potential. *Nevermind* uses heart rate sensors to detect player stress and dynamically adjusts the horror elements of its environment. *Deep*, a meditative VR experience, responds to diaphragmatic breathing to promote relaxation through gameplay. While not widespread in mainstream development, these games demonstrate how affective input can be used to shape both challenge and atmosphere, offering a glimpse into the future of emotionally adaptive design.

Despite its promise, emotion-based DDA presents challenges. Biosignals are often noisy, individual differences in emotional expression can be substantial, and interpreting affect in real-time remains a complex task. Moreover, while emotion-based systems offer a more human-centered lens on adaptation, they still represent only one side of what is required to sustain a flow state. These systems aim to support a more comprehensive understanding of the player's experience, capturing not only what the player is doing but also how they are emotionally responding to the game—typically through signals linked to emotional arousal rather than valence. Just as performance-based systems fall short by excluding emotion, emotion-based systems fall short by excluding ability. This limitation has led to a growing interest in hybrid approaches—systems that combine behavioral and physiological data to create a more comprehensive and adaptive gameplay experience.

5.3 Hybrid approaches

Hybrid DDA systems combine both behavioral and physiological data to inform adjustments to the difficulty level. By blending what the player is doing with how they might be feeling, these systems aim to form a more complete understanding of the player experience. Rather than relying on a single stream of input, such as performance metrics or emotional arousal alone, hybrid approaches integrate both to adapt gameplay in more nuanced and context-aware ways.

For example, a hybrid system might detect that a player is performing well, consistently landing shots, or completing objectives. Yet, physiological signals, such as elevated heart rate or skin conductance, indicate stress. Instead of raising the difficulty further, the system could maintain the current challenge level but ease the pressure by reducing time constraints or simplifying the interface. On the other hand, a player struggling with performance but showing signs of calmness or disengagement might trigger a gentle increase in challenge to re-engage their attention.

This dual-channel approach is particularly promising in the context of Flow Theory, which emphasizes the need for balance between challenge and skill, but also implicitly requires that players feel emotionally engaged, neither overwhelmed nor under-stimulated. By simultaneously accounting for both performance and affective cues, hybrid systems are well-positioned to maintain the conditions necessary for achieving a state of flow. In doing so, they can help sustain player engagement over longer sessions, support a wider range of player preferences, and create more meaningful, personalized experiences.

Hybrid systems are naturally more complex to develop. They require the fusion of multiple data streams, calibration across individuals, and often the use of machine learning models to classify affect and interpret gameplay context. Still, the payoff is a richer, more empathetic gameplay experience—one that responds to both what the player is capable of and how they are experiencing the game.

Recent studies have begun exploring these hybrid approaches in greater depth, combining performance data with physiological signals to refine adaptive difficulty techniques [2, 22, 25]. This integration aims to address the limitations of relying solely on one type of data, marking a promising direction for future research and application in the field. As the field continues to evolve, hybrid systems represent a compelling step toward more adaptive, emotionally aware, and skill-sensitive game experiences.

6. Case study: Exploring adaptive difficulty in a first-person shooter

Understanding the real-world challenges of adaptive difficulty systems requires examining how different adjustment strategies influence the player experience. This case study investigates a custom-built first-person shooter designed to compare five difficulty adjustment methods: Fixed Difficulty, Player-Selected Difficulty, Performance-Based Adaptation, Emotion-Based Adaptation, and a Hybrid approach. Rather than seeking to determine a superior method, the study explores how these strategies affect player engagement, enjoyment, perceived challenge, and emotional response. By analyzing gameplay metrics, physiological signals, and self-reported experience, the study offers insights into how adaptive systems can support stable and satisfying gameplay across diverse players (**Figure 2**).

6.1 Study overview

This study draws on previously published research [2] that examined the impact of dynamic difficulty adjustment on player experience in a custom-designed first-person shooter. Five difficulty adjustment strategies—Fixed, Player-Selected, Performance-Based, Emotion-Based, and Hybrid—were compared in terms of their effects on perceived difficulty, engagement, stress, excitement, and enjoyment.

Participants played under all five conditions, with gameplay order randomized to control for sequence effects. The study focused on whether different adaptive methods would meaningfully alter emotional responses linked to arousal, or maintain engagement across varying gameplay conditions.

6.2 Experimental setup

Thirty-one Participants completed preliminary questionnaires on gaming habits and immersive tendencies, then were fitted with electroencephalography and heart

Figure 2.
Screenshot from the custom FPS game used in the study, designed to evaluate five different difficulty strategies. Reproduced with permission from [2].

rate sensors. After a brief training session to familiarize them with game controls, baseline physiological signals were recorded.

Each participant then played five short gameplay sessions, each using a different difficulty adjustment method. Sessions lasted up to 3 minutes or ended when the player's character was defeated. After each session, participants rated their perceived stress, focus, excitement, enjoyment, and difficulty. Throughout gameplay, performance metrics (e.g., accuracy, survival time) and physiological signals (e.g., engagement, stress) were continuously recorded.

For adaptive systems (Performance-Based, Emotion-Based, Hybrid), a 40-second moving average was used to smooth dynamic difficulty adjustments and avoid abrupt changes in challenge.

6.3 Difficulty adjustment methods

The five difficulty strategies varied in how they responded to player input, performance, or emotional state:

- *Fixed difficulty*: A constant, medium difficulty level served as a baseline comparison.

- *Player-selected*: Players chose their preferred difficulty (1–7) before starting. This allowed self-adjustment based on perceived skill or mood.

- *Performance-based*: Difficulty scaled using gameplay metrics such as accuracy, survival time, and objectives completed. High performance triggered increased challenge.

- *Emotion-based*: Difficulty adapted based on physiological signals. Affective data from EEG and heart rate sensors were used to maintain players in an optimal arousal range, aligned with Flow Theory, thereby avoiding boredom and overload.

- *Hybrid*: Combined both performance and emotional signals, with greater weight (0.6) given to emotion-based data, based on pilot testing that suggested emotional alignment had greater influence on player engagement.

6.4 Key findings

EEG-Derived Metrics. Physiological analysis focused on electroencephalography-derived metrics aligned with Flow Theory: Focus, Engagement, and Stress. Objective difficulty levels assigned by each system were also compared.

As shown in **Table 1**, mixed-effects modeling confirmed significant differences in assigned difficulty levels ($p < .001$), while experiential EEG metrics such as Focus, Engagement, and Stress remained largely stable across conditions. Although the model suggested subtle effects for some measures, none survived Bonferroni correction, reinforcing the interpretation that player engagement was broadly maintained across different adaptive strategies.

As shown in **Figure 3**, Emotion-Based adaptation consistently assigned higher difficulty levels (mean 5.93 on a 7-point scale), while Fixed and Performance-Based methods produced moderate difficulty. Player-selected conditions exhibited the greatest variability, reflecting individual differences in initial preference.

Self-Reported Experience. Participant self-reports mirrored objective difficulty trends. Stress and perceived difficulty ratings differed significantly across conditions, with higher difficulty corresponding to greater perceived stress. However, ratings of excitement, focus, and enjoyment remained statistically similar across methods (**Table 2**).

These patterns are further illustrated in **Figure 4**, which shows that the Emotion-Based adaptation was perceived as the most difficult on average, while Fixed and Performance-Based methods were rated as moderately challenging. Emotion-based adaptation was perceived as the most difficult (mean 5.34 out of 7), closely followed by the Hybrid approach. Fixed and Performance-Based strategies clustered around moderate difficulty ratings (approximately 4.0). Player-selected difficulty again showed the widest range, underscoring the variability in player self-assessment.

Overall, our results did not reveal one difficulty strategy as consistently superior in terms of player enjoyment, focus, or engagement. However, this lack of divergence may be meaningful in itself. Despite varying challenge levels—some systems adapting to stress, others to performance—players across all conditions reported similar

Metric	**Mixed Model p -value**
Difficulty	$<.001$
Focus	.034
Excitement	.144
Interest	.280
Engagement	.029
Stress	.040
Relaxation	.363

Table 1.
Summary of mixed-effects model results across difficulty adjustment methods. Difficulty reflects the actual in-game challenge level; all other metrics are derived from EEG signals. Only Difficulty remained significant after Bonferroni correction ($\alpha = .0071$).

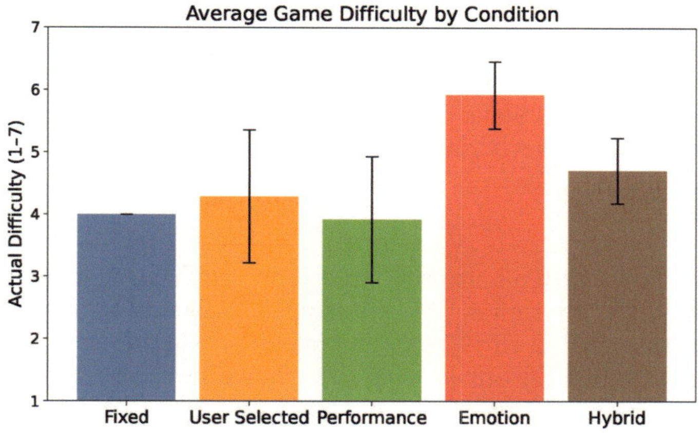

Figure 3.
Mean difficulty level assigned during gameplay, grouped by difficulty adjustment method. Bars represent the average setting applied by the system, with error bars showing standard deviation. The Emotion-Based system consistently assigned higher difficulty levels, while the Fixed and Performance-Based methods centered on moderate challenge. User-selected difficulty showed the widest variation across participants.

Question	Friedman Test
Please rate your average stress level while playing this iteration of the game	χ^2 (4) = 23.135, $p < .001$
Please rate your average excitement level while playing this iteration of the game	χ^2 (4) = 4.215, $p = .378$
Please rate your average focus level while playing this iteration of the game	χ^2 (4) = 2.675, $p = .614$
How much fun did you have playing the game this iteration?	χ^2 (4) = 4.098, $p = .393$
How difficult would you rate this iteration of the game?	χ^2 (4) = 21.766, $p < .001$

Table 2.
Friedman test results for selected post-questionnaire items comparing perceived experience across difficulty adjustment methods.

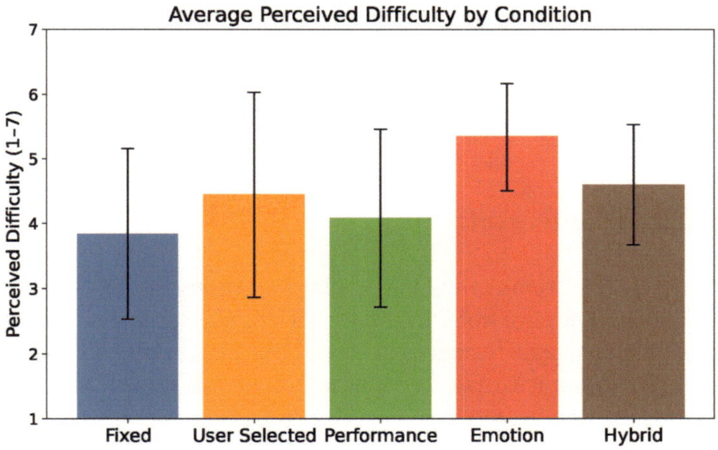

Figure 4.
Average perceived difficulty rating for each difficulty adjustment method, based on post-condition questionnaire responses. Bars represent the mean reported difficulty (1–7), with error bars indicating standard deviation. Participants rated the Emotion-Based condition as the most difficult on average, while Fixed and Performance conditions were perceived as more moderate. User-selected difficulty showed the greatest variability across participants.

emotional states based on Emotiv's predefined affective metrics. Both EEG signals and self-reports suggest that engagement was broadly sustained, regardless of how difficulty was tuned. This stability may reflect a core strength of adaptive systems: rather than amplifying emotional differences, they help ensure a consistent and playable experience across a diverse player base.

6.5 Design implications

Adaptive difficulty systems are often expected to produce highly personalized experiences; however, our findings suggest that their role may be more stabilizing than transformative. Across all adjustment strategies—whether based on performance, emotion, or a hybrid—players reported similar levels of enjoyment, focus, and excitement. This consistency highlights a key strength of adaptive design: its ability to maintain engagement across a diverse player base, even when gameplay conditions differ behind the scenes.

Rather than viewing this uniformity as a shortcoming, it may reflect successful alignment between challenge and ability. Flow Theory posits that engagement peaks when difficulty matches skill, and our results suggest that each system achieved this balance in its own way. Players remained emotionally invested, regardless of the method used to tune difficulty, suggesting that adaptation can support immersion without drawing attention to itself.

At the same time, our data challenges the assumption that all players want to be optimally challenged. The broad range of difficulty selections in the User-Selected condition points to varied motivations. Some participants may have been seeking mastery or competition, while others may have preferred a relaxed or exploratory experience. These findings reinforce the idea that adaptive systems should consider not just performance, but intent. Player-centered adaptation means supporting different play styles—not simply pushing everyone toward high difficulty, but tailoring the experience based on what the player wants out of the session.

Finally, the convergence across physiological signals, gameplay telemetry, and self-report lends confidence to these conclusions. While no single metric revealed dramatic differences, together they painted a coherent picture of stable engagement. This suggests that the value of adaptation may lie less in creating extreme highs and lows, and more in offering gameplay that remains steady, immersive, and responsive across a wide spectrum of player experiences.

7. Limitations of adaptive difficulty

Although adaptive systems can help stabilize player engagement across diverse gameplay conditions, they are not without tradeoffs. The same mechanisms that allow for smooth and responsive experiences can also create unintended consequences, particularly when players are unaware of, or uncomfortable with, how and when adaptation occurs.

One key concern is the impact on perceived competence. From the lens of Self-Determination Theory, players derive motivation from overcoming meaningful challenges. If a system quietly reduces difficulty to prevent failure, it may undermine the sense of achievement that comes from mastering a task. Even if players remain engaged, they may question whether their progress is truly earned, which can weaken the emotional payoff of success.

DOI: http://dx.doi.org/10.5772/intechopen.1011703

Similarly, adaptive systems that raise difficulty in lockstep with player improvement may obscure growth. Without visible markers of advancement, such as increased scores or tangible skill mastery, players may feel as if they are treading water, unable to track their development or feel a sense of momentum.

Transparency is especially critical in this context. While adaptive features are often framed as subtle or seamless, our findings suggest players are attuned to changes in difficulty, even when not explicitly informed. If those changes feel arbitrary or hidden, they risk undermining trust. This is particularly problematic in competitive or high-stakes settings, where fairness is of paramount importance. Perceptions of "invisible punishment," such as suspected skill-based matchmaking penalties, can damage player confidence even if the system is functioning as intended.

Lastly, many adaptive systems are guided by Flow Theory, which assumes players benefit most from maintaining a state of optimal challenge. But our findings and prior research suggest this model may not suit all playstyles. Some players engage for relaxation, while others do so for narrative, social connection, or curiosity. If systems rigidly aim to push players toward high challenge, they may misalign with those broader motivations.

These motivational mismatches, along with concerns about transparency and perceived competence, have behavioral consequences that extend beyond moment-to-moment experience. The Theory of Planned Behavior [26] suggests that players' intentions—and ultimately their behavior—are shaped by their attitudes toward the system, social context, and perceived control. If players feel that difficulty adjustments occur without their knowledge or input, or that they reflect negative evaluations of their skill, this can erode trust and reduce willingness to continue playing.

Beyond these experiential concerns, adaptive systems raise ethical questions. Because DDA can subtly influence player behavior, it could be exploited to serve design goals that benefit developers more than players—for instance, encouraging longer sessions or increased spending on microtransactions. When adaptation is used in this way without transparency or consent, it risks becoming manipulative rather than supportive.

Together, these limitations highlight the need for adaptive systems that go beyond performance metrics and skill matching. Truly player-centered adaptation requires not only flexibility and responsiveness, but also transparency, ethical boundaries, and an understanding of the diverse reasons players engage with games.

8. Conclusion

Dynamic difficulty adjustment offers significant promise for creating tailored gameplay experiences, but realizing that promise will require careful attention to both technical constraints and the evolving psychological expectations of modern players. However, despite its potential, several limitations still require attention for broader application. Technical constraints, such as the accuracy and reliability of physiological signals in emotion-based systems, present notable hurdles. Performance-based systems, while more straightforward, often neglect critical emotional and psychological dimensions of player experience, potentially limiting their ability to sustain engagement over time.

Hybrid systems, which integrate both physiological and performance metrics, align closely with principles from Flow Theory and offer a compelling direction for future research. Yet their practical application remains constrained by complexity, cost, and the challenge of achieving seamless, real-time integration of diverse data streams. In addition to technical hurdles, psychological factors must be considered carefully. Adaptive systems must preserve player autonomy, perceived fairness, and trust; transparent adaptation practices and user-centered design will be crucial for maintaining long-term satisfaction.

Looking forward, dynamic adaptation has the potential to evolve beyond simply adjusting difficulty along a traditional easy–medium–hard continuum. Rather than assuming that all players seek optimal challenge at all times, future systems could embrace adaptive profiles that align with the player's intent for the gaming session. Options such as "challenge-focused," "relaxation-focused," or "story-driven" experiences would allow players to express their goals more directly, with adaptation tuning itself accordingly.

To truly align with players' goals and expectations, future adaptive systems must account not only for real-time data but also for the psychological factors that drive continued engagement. As discussed earlier, behavioral models such as the Theory of Planned Behavior highlight the importance of perceived control and player attitudes—factors that are essential to fostering trust and long-term satisfaction. By considering not just performance metrics but also behavioral intentions and player experience, dynamic systems can overcome the limitations not only of traditional difficulty models but even of Flow Theory itself, recognizing that sustaining engagement sometimes means challenging the player, and other times means supporting exploration, immersion, or rest.

Acknowledgements

This material is based upon work supported by the Louisiana Board of Regents under contract No. LEQSF(2022-2025)-RD-A-24.

Conflict of interest

The authors declare no conflict of interest.

Abbreviations

2D	two-dimensional
3D	three-dimensional
DDA	dynamic difficulty adjustment
EEG	electroencephalography
FPS	first-person shooter
HRV	heart rate variability
SDT	self-determination theory
UI	user interface
VR	virtual reality

DOI: http://dx.doi.org/10.5772/intechopen.1011703

Author details

Nicholas Fisher* and Arun K. Kulshreshth
School of Computing and Informatics, University of Louisiana at Lafayette, Lafayette, United States

*Address all correspondence to: fisher.nicholas@gmail.com

References

[1] Csikszentmihalyi M. Flow: The Psychology of Optimal Experience. Harper & Row; 1990

[2] Fisher N, Kulshreshth AK. Exploring dynamic difficulty adjustment methods for video games. Virtual Worlds. 2024;**3**(2):230-255. Available from: https://www.mdpi.com/2813-2084/3/2/12

[3] Deci EL, Ryan RM. Intrinsic Motivation and Self-Determination in Human Behavior. New York, NY: Springer Science and Business Media; 2013

[4] Sweller J, van Merrienboer JJG, Paas FGWC. Cognitive architecture and instructional design. Educational Psychology Review. 1998;**10**(3):251-296. DOI: 10.1023/A:1022193728205

[5] Hunicke R, Chapman V. AI for dynamic difficulty adjustment in games. In: Proceedings of the Challenges in Game Artificial Intelligence Workshop, AAAI; 2004 Jul 25-29; San Jose, CA, USA. Menlo Park, CA: AAAI Press; 2004. pp. 91-96

[6] Hunicke R. The case for dynamic difficulty adjustment in games. In: Proceedings of the 2005 ACM SIGCHI International Conference on Advances in Computer Entertainment Technology. Valencia Spain: ACM; 2005. pp. 429-433. Available from: https://dl.acm.org/doi/10.1145/1178477.1178573

[7] Hristova D. Dynamic Difficulty Adjustment (DDA) in First Person Shooter (FPS) Games. 2017. Available from: https://www.academia.edu/4921794/

[8] Pfau J, Smeddinck JD, Malaka R. Enemy within: Long-term motivation effects of deep player behavior models for dynamic difficulty adjustment. In: Proceedings of the 2020 CHI Conference on Human Factors in Computing Systems. Honolulu HI USA: ACM; 2020. pp. 1-10. Available from: https://dl.acm.org/doi/10.1145/3313831.3376423

[9] Silva MP, Silva VN, Chaimowicz L. Dynamic difficulty adjustment on MOBA games. Entertainment Computing. 2017;**18**:103-123. Available from: https://www.sciencedirect.com/science/article/pii/S1875952116300350

[10] Romero-Mendez EA, Santana-Mancilla PC, Garcia-Ruiz M, Montesinos-López OA, Anido-Rifón LE. The use of deep learning to improve player engagement in a video game through a dynamic difficulty adjustment based on skills classification. Applied Sciences. 2023;**13**(14):8249. Available from: https://www.mdpi.com/2076-3417/13/14/8249

[11] Huber T, Mertes S, Rangelova S, Flutura S, Andre E. Dynamic difficulty adjustment in virtual reality exergames through experience-driven procedural content generation. In: 2021 IEEE Symposium Series on Computational Intelligence (SSCI). Piscataway, NJ: IEEE; 2021. DOI: 10.1109/SSCI50451.2021.9660086

[12] Francillette Y, Tremblay H, Bouchard B, Lescieux S, Rozon M, Linard J. Automated difficulty assessment model for platformer games: A comprehensive approach. In: 2023 IEEE Gaming, Entertainment, and Media Conference (GEM); 2023 Nov 27-30; St. Michael, Barbados. Piscataway, NJ: IEEE; 2023. pp. 1-6

[13] Liu C, Agrawal P, Sarkar N, Chen S. Dynamic difficulty adjustment in

computer games through real-time anxiety-based affective feedback. International Journal of Human-Computer Interaction (Abingdon, UK: Taylor & Francis). 2009;**25**(6):506-529. Available from: http://www.tandfonline.com/doi/abs/10.1080/10447310902963944

[14] Park S, Sim H, Lee W. Dynamic game difficulty control by using EEG-based emotion recognition. International Journal of Control and Automation. 2014;**7**(3):267-272. Available from: http://article.nadiapub.com/IJCA/vol7_no3/26.pdf

[15] Fernandez BHD, Mikami K, Kondo K. Adaptable game experience based on player's performance and EEG. In: In: 2017 Nicograph International (NicoInt). Kyoto: IEEE; 2017. pp. 1-8. Available from: https://ieeexplore.ieee.org/document/8047384/

[16] Stein A, Yotam Y, Puzis R, Shani G, Taieb-Maimon M. EEG-triggered dynamic difficulty adjustment for multiplayer games. Entertainment Computing. 2018;**25**:14-25. Available from: https://linkinghub.elsevier.com/retrieve/pii/S1875952117301325

[17] Afergan D, Peck EM, Solovey ET, Jenkins A, Hincks SW, Brown ET, et al. Dynamic difficulty using brain metrics of workload. In: Proceedings of the SIGCHI Conference on Human Factors in Computing Systems. CHI '14. New York, NY, USA: Association for Computing Machinery; 2014. pp. 3797-3806. DOI: 10.1145/2556288.2557230

[18] Kim HG, Cheon EJ, Bai DS, Lee YH, Koo BH. Stress and heart rate variability: A meta-analysis and review of the literature. Psychiatry Investigation. 2018;**15**(3):235-245. Available from: http://psychiatryinvestigation.org/journal/view.php?doi=10.30773/pi.2017.08.17

[19] Taelman J, Vandeput S, Spaepen A, Van Huffel S. Influence of mental stress on heart rate and heart rate variability. In: Magjarevic R, Nagel JH, Vander Sloten J, Verdonck P, Nyssen M, Haueisen J, editors. 4th European Conference of the International Federation for Medical and Biological Engineering. Vol. 22. Berlin, Heidelberg: Springer Berlin Heidelberg; 2009. pp. 1366-1369. Available from: http://link.springer.com/10.1007/978-3-540-89208-3_324

[20] Salahuddin L, Cho J, Jeong MG, Kim D. Ultra short term analysis of heart rate variability for monitoring mental stress in mobile settings. In: 2007 29th Annual International Conference of the IEEE Engineering in Medicine and Biology Society; 2007 Aug 22-26; Lyon, France. Piscataway, NJ: IEEE; 2007. pp. 4656-4659

[21] Moschovitis P, Denisova A. Keep calm and aim for the head: Biofeedback-controlled dynamic difficulty adjustment in a horror game. IEEE Transactions on Games. 2023;**15**(3):368-377. Available from: https://ieeexplore.ieee.org/document/9787784/

[22] Rosa MPC, Dos Santos EA, De Moraes ILR, Silva ETBP, Sarmet MM, Castanho CD, et al. Dynamic difficulty adjustment using performance and affective data in a platform game. In: Stephanidis C, Soares MM, Rosenzweig E, Marcus A, Yamamoto S, Mori H, et al., editors. HCI International 2021 - Late Breaking Papers: Design and User Experience. Vol. 13094. Cham: Springer International Publishing; 2021. pp. 367-386. Available from: https://link.springer.com/10.1007/978-3-030-90238-4_26

[23] Nguyen D. Improving Game Experience Using Dynamic Difficulty Adjustment Based on Physiological Signals [PhD Thesis]. Master Thesis. Technical University of Denmark, DTU Compute; 2014

[24] Karavidas L, Apostolidis H, Tsiatsos T. Usability evaluation of an adaptive serious game prototype based on affective feedback. Information. 2022;**13**(9):425. Available from: https://www.mdpi.com/2078-2489/13/9/425

[25] Darzi A, McCrea SM, Novak D, et al. User experience with dynamic difficulty adjustment methods for an affective exergame: Comparative laboratory-based study. JMIR Serious Games. 2021;**9**(2):e25771. Publisher: JMIR Publications Inc., Toronto, Canada

[26] Ajzen I. The theory of planned behavior. Theories of Cognitive Self-Regulation. 1991;**50**(2):179-211. Available from: https://www.sciencedirect.com/science/article/pii/074959789190020T

Chapter 2

Pathways to Mastery: A Taxonomy of Player Progression Systems in Commercial Video Games

Tibor Guzsvinecz

Abstract

Player progression systems are a central design element in digital games that shape how players experience growth, mastery, and engagement over time. This chapter proposes a taxonomy of the following six progression types: skill-based, XP-based, item-based, narrative, social, and hybrid. Special emphasis is placed on the transformative role of artificial intelligence (AI) that enables adaptive, personalized, and procedurally generated progression structures. Through structured SWOT analyses and detailed examples from representative games, the chapter provides information for researchers and developers seeking to analyze or construct progression systems. Future trends, which include meta-progression across platforms, AI-driven narrative generation, emotion-aware design, and ethical regulation, are also explored. By providing a framework, this taxonomy can serve as a reference for game designers, researchers, and industry professionals who seek to understand and optimize progression mechanics in video games.

Keywords: game design, intrinsic motivation, player progression, reward structures, taxonomy, video game

1. Introduction

Player progression is an important component of video game design that can directly influence how players interact with mechanics, experience growth, and remain engaged over time. While progression is not the sole contributor to an engaging gameplay experience, it serves as a critical scaffolding mechanism that shapes long-term motivation and a sense of achievement [1–3]. However, its implementation varies between different types of games [4]. In action games, progression might emphasize skill acquisition and reflex mastery, while in role-playing games (RPGs), it often hinges on numerical growth, narrative milestones, or social standing. Therefore, it is necessary to contextualize progression not as a monolithic construct, but as a multifaceted design strategy tailored to genre-specific goals.

This chapter focuses on player progression in entertainment-focused digital video games, mainly those spanning single-player and multiplayer genres such as RPGs, action-adventure games, open-world experiences, and competitive online games. While some theoretical studies may draw from formal game theory, the scope of this taxonomy is limited to empirical and practical game design models. The taxonomy does not apply to abstract, mathematical games (e.g., zero-sum games, coordination games) discussed in economic or decision theory literature.

Progression systems perform multiple psychological and functional roles in games. They provide players with goals, structure the gameplay experience, and regulate challenges. Cognitive Load Theory shows that well-designed progression systems reduce information overload by sequencing difficulty and content. Thus, they enable sustained engagement and learning [5]. Self-determination theory suggests that progression systems are most effective when they support psychological needs such as competence and autonomy [6–8]. Relatedness may also play a role, particularly in socially driven games, although its applicability is genre-dependent [9]. To further understand progression, Flow Theory illustrates how optimal challenge-skill balance can lead to deep immersion [10]. Operant Conditioning underpins many reward systems as players respond to structured incentives such as experience points (XP), loot, or achievements [2, 11, 12]. However, an overreliance on extrinsic rewards may promote compulsive behaviors rather than meaningful engagement [13]. It can also lead to prolonged play sessions [14].

Recent trends have added new dimensions to progression systems with the use of artificial intelligence (AI), procedural generation, and live-service models. AI enables adaptive difficulty, personalized content, and dynamic progression paths [15]. Procedural content generation and engagement-based reward systems have also changed how games sustain player interest across multiple sessions [16, 17]. Consequently, a modern taxonomy of progression systems must account not only for traditional mechanics but also for technological innovations that reshape player experiences.

Despite the existence of progression systems in commercial video games, a comprehensive, academically grounded taxonomy has not been widely established. This chapter aims to fill that gap by categorizing player progression into six key types: skill-based progression, XP-based numerical growth, item-based systems, narrative progression, social progression in multiplayer environments, and hybrid models that integrate multiple approaches. Each category is contextualized with historical evolution, design challenges, and best practices, with an emphasis on psychological, technological, and structural considerations.

By offering a taxonomy for understanding progression systems, this chapter serves as a resource for researchers, designers, and developers aiming to analyze or optimize progression mechanics in video games. The chapter is structured as follows: Section 2 provides a historical overview of progression systems; Section 3 presents the taxonomy and its six categories; Section 4 discusses AI integration; Section 5 speculates on future trends; and Section 6 concludes the results.

2. The evolution of player progression systems in video games

Player progression systems have undergone significant transformation since the early days of digital games. In the late 1970s and early 1980s, progression was rudimentary. It was mainly based on score accumulation and increased difficulty levels. Arcade games like Pac-Man (1980) and Donkey Kong (1981) had skill-based progression where continued survival and higher scores indicated mastery. These early systems did not retain player achievements between sessions. Consequently, this showed a transient and linear form of progression coupled with player reflexes and pattern recognition [8].

A paradigm shift occurred with the advent of RPGs, particularly those influenced by tabletop systems such as Dungeons and Dragons (1974). Titles like Final Fantasy (1987) introduced XP as a persistent metric for character development. XP-based progression became synonymous with RPGs that enabled players to level up their characters, allocate skill points, and unlock new abilities over time. This structured numerical growth provided clear and satisfying feedback loops, reinforcing behaviors aligned with in-game objectives [2].

By the late 1990s and early 2000s, progression systems became more diverse. Western RPGs such as Baldur's Gate (1998) and The Elder Scrolls III: Morrowind (2002) merged XP accumulation with narrative branching and player choice. These titles expanded the scope of progression to include not just character stats but also storyline advancement, world exploration, and player agency. Simultaneously, item-based progression systems became prominent in games like Diablo II (2000), where randomized loot served as both a reward mechanism and power progression.

The increasing popularity of multiplayer games in the 2000s added a new dimension: social progression. Titles such as World of Warcraft (2004), League of Legends (2009), and Overwatch (2016) introduced ranking systems, guild structures, and persistent reputation mechanics. Progression in these contexts extended beyond individual achievement and reflected status within the community.

Hybrid models soon became the norm that integrated multiple progression systems to accommodate diverse player motivations. For example, The Witcher 3: Wild Hunt (2015) combined XP-based leveling, narrative progression, item acquisition, and skill customization. Genshin Impact (2020) even incorporated all major types: skill, XP, item, social, and narrative. These hybrid systems can mainly be found in open-world and live-service games where personalization and longevity are key design goals [17].

Recent advancements in AI and procedural content generation have further influenced progression mechanics. Games like Left 4 Dead (2008) and No Man's Sky (2016) used AI to dynamically adjust difficulty and generate content based on player behavior. These systems enable adaptive progression paths that ensure sustained engagement without requiring static leveling curves or handcrafted content [15, 16].

Thus, the evolution of progression systems reflects a shift in game design from transient, reflex-driven challenges to persistent, complex experiences tailored to individual player preferences. As technological capabilities expand and player expectations evolve, progression systems are increasingly designed to support dynamic, player-centric gameplay experiences.

3. The taxonomy of player progression systems

Player progression systems are central to shaping user experience, mainly in how games structure long-term engagement and reward mechanisms. Drawing on genre conventions, psychological theories, and player typologies, this section presents a taxonomy consisting of six major progression types: skill-based, XP-based, item-based, narrative, social, and hybrid systems. Each subtype is examined with its definition, common usage contexts, key examples, design implications, and a SWOT analysis. The following subsections present these six progression types.

3.1 Skill-based progression

Skill-based progression refers to systems where advancement is tied to the player's improvement regarding game mechanics. In these systems, progression reflects player learning, reaction, and strategic decision-making. While numerical upgrades or rewards can be present in this progression system, the emphasis is on skill. Skill-based progression is common in competitive and difficult games where challenge is a core part of the experience. Unlike RPGs where progression requires "grinding" (doing tasks multiple times to accumulate XP to get stronger), skill-based games require players to refine their abilities through trial and error.

- Typical genres: Platformers, fighting games, puzzle games, soulslikes, competitive shooters.
- Example games: Celeste, Street Fighter II, Dark Souls, Counter-Strike: Global Offensive, Super Meat Boy.
- Required skills (depending on the game): Creative problem-solving, logical reasoning, pattern recognition, enemy AI adaptation, tactical positioning, aiming accuracy, perfect dodging, timing, memorizing level layouts, and combos.

Table 1 shows the SWOT analysis of skill-based progression systems.

Based on the SWOT analysis, the following design guidelines were formed for skill-based progression systems:

- Introduce a gradual and adaptive difficulty curve;
- Deliver actionable feedback that supports learning;
- Ensure fair and consistent challenge scaling.

3.2 XP-based progression systems

XP-based progression is one of the most common progression systems in video games. In this case, players earn XP by completing certain actions. These can be combat encounters, exploration, quest completion, or other achievements. By accumulating XP, players can increase their level or rank. Consequently, they can improve their stats, learn new abilities, or receive expanded customization options. Unlike

Strengths	**Weaknesses**
High replayability due to mastery mechanics	Can frustrate new or casual players
Sense of achievement through skill growth	Requires precise balancing of difficulty
Opportunities	**Threats**
Enables deep skill expression and competition	Risk of steep learning curve causing player churn
Long-term engagement for expert players	Perceived unfairness if mechanics are not transparent

Table 1.
The SWOT analysis of skill-based progression systems.

skill-based progression, XP-based systems create a numerical representation of growth. This approach can appeal to players who enjoy measurable progress that provides clear indicators of advancement. This type of progression is effective because it is similar to the Operant conditioning principles [2, 11, 12]: players are rewarded at regular intervals that reinforces dopamine-driven feedback. This cycle keeps players engaged and motivated to continue playing. This also makes this system effective in RPGs and live-service games.

- Typical genres: RPGs, strategy games, massively multiplayer online (MMO) games, live-service titles.
- Example games: Final Fantasy, Pokémon, The Division, World of Warcraft.
- **Figure 1** shows a summary of XP-based progression systems. Note that not all XP sources and rewards are mentioned, only the most common ones are presented.

Table 2 presents the results of the SWOT analysis of XP-based progression systems.

Based on the SWOT analysis, the following design guidelines were formed for XP-based progression systems:

- Diversify XP sources to support different playstyles;
- Avoid grind loops that hinder pacing;
- Link XP gain to meaningful in-game choices.

3.3 Item-based progression systems

Item-based progression refers to player advancement through gathering, crafting, or upgrading items such as weapons, armor, or other types of tools. Instead of relying

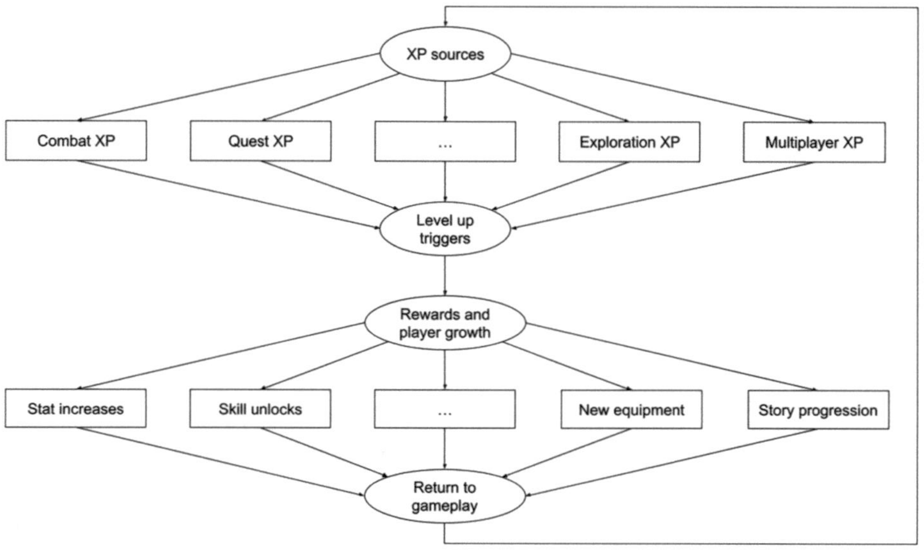

Figure 1.
A summary of XP-based progression systems.

Strengths	Weaknesses
Clear, quantifiable progress	Can devolve into grinding
Structured reward system	Can reduce skill-based agency
Opportunities	**Threats**
Appeals to goal-oriented players	Stat inflation and artificial difficulty scaling
Easy to track and balance	Repetitiveness if XP sources lack variety

Table 2.
The SWOT analysis of XP-based progression systems.

on XP accumulation or skill mastery, item-based progression grants power and new abilities through objects obtained in the world of the video game. Item-based progression uses reward anticipation and the loot drop dopamine effect. It also has variable reward systems, focuses on player agency, and motivates exploration due to hidden gear. Item-based progression follows random reinforcement schedules that make rewards exciting but unpredictable. Unlike XP-based progression, this type offers choices since players can decide which weapons to craft, upgrade, or prioritize.

- Typical genres: Action RPGs, survival games, looter shooters.
- Example games: Monster Hunter: World, The Legend of Zelda, Diablo II, Borderlands.

It should be also noted that this type of progression system can have subcategories:

- Tool-based progression: Players acquire key items that unlock new areas or abilities;
- Loot-based progression: Players acquire randomized gear, with rarity tiers and stat improvements;
- Crafting-based progression: Players gather materials and craft weapons, armor, and tools.

To better understand how such systems work, **Figure 2** shows a summary of item-based progression systems.

Table 3 details the results of the SWOT analysis of item-based progression systems.

Based on the SWOT analysis, the following design guidelines were formed for item-based progression systems:

- Combine random and deterministic item acquisition;
- Offer meaningful differences between equipment types;
- Balance rarity, utility, and accessibility.

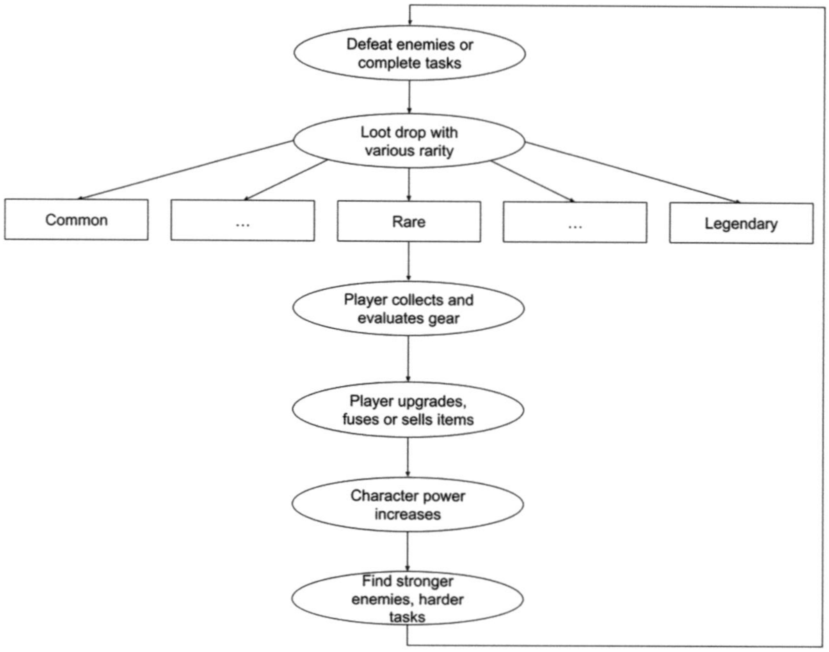

Figure 2.
A summary of item-based progression systems.

Strengths	**Weaknesses**
Tangible, immediate power increases	Random number generation (RNG) can frustrate progression
Supports diverse builds and playstyles	Complexity can overwhelm players
Opportunities	**Threats**
Supports exploration and player agency	Grind or imbalance in loot systems
Promotes replayability	Pay-to-win risks in monetized systems

Table 3.
The SWOT analysis of item-based progression systems.

3.4 Narrative progression systems

In these types of progression systems, player advancement occurs through story events, character development, and branching decisions instead of numerical stats or skill mastery. Progress is measured by how far a player has moved through a game's storyline rather than by XP or gear upgrades. Thus, these types of systems focus on story engagement and character-driven decisions. These systems are mainly common in RPGs and adventure games since choices shape the game world and influence the experience of the players. Due to this, many games also offer multiple paths in the story. Interaction with non-playable characters (NPCs) also affects relationships, quests, and even endings. These types of progression systems have emotional engagement and decision-making psychology. For example, branching choices make players feel like they are co-authors of the story. Meanwhile, meaningful decisions create stronger emotional connections with the characters in the games. These progression systems also enhance the curiosity of the players since they replay narrative-driven games to see different outcomes of the story.

- Typical genres: Story-driven RPGs, adventure games, visual novels.
- Example games: The Witcher 3: Wild Hunt, Life is Strange, Detroit: Become Human.

For an example of narrative storytelling, we should think of a hypothetical scenario which is illustrated in **Figure 3**.

A mysterious stranger arrives in the town of the player character. He proposes the following deal for the player: "Find an ancient magic scroll, then bring it back to me or face my wrath". Depending on the choice of the player, the following can happen: if the player declines this offer, the stranger calls his army and they destroy the hometown of the player character, resulting in a bad ending. If the player accepts, a new questline starts. Then, the player finds the scroll, but it is guarded by an ancient dragon. The game allows the player to fight the dragon or negotiate with it, and both decisions can yield two outcomes. The player can either be victorious or defeated. These two outcomes can consequently save the player character's town or result in its destruction, respectively. Naturally, this hypothetical scenario is simplified since these narrative decision trees can be much more complex in today's video games, and more than two endings can be reached.

To better understand these types of progression systems, a SWOT analysis was conducted. Its results can be seen in **Table 4**.

Based on the SWOT analysis, the following design guidelines were formed for narrative progression systems:

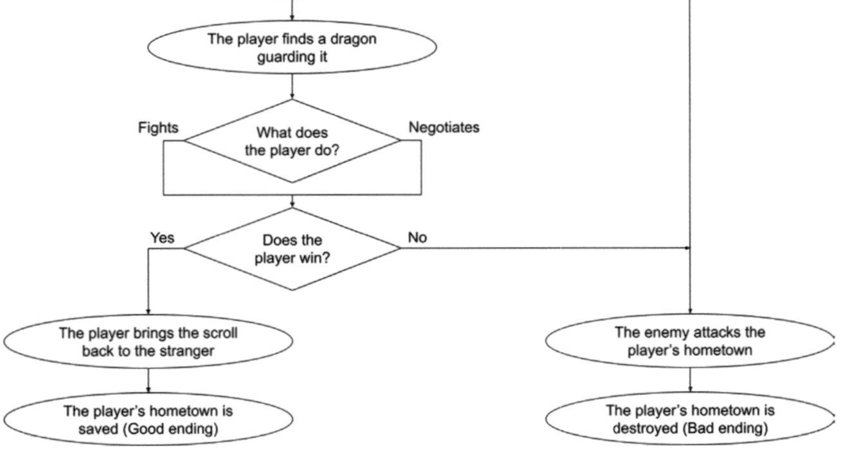

Figure 3.
A summary of narrative progression systems.

Strengths	**Weaknesses**
Deepens emotional engagement	Illusion of choice if poorly designed
Encourages exploration and agency	Limited appeal for action-focused players
Opportunities	**Threats**
High replay value *via* branching paths	High development costs and narrative complexity
Enhances immersion	Risk of dissonance between story and mechanics

Table 4.
The SWOT analysis of narrative progression systems.

- Ensure choices influence both the plot and game world;
- Balance nonlinearity with narrative coherence;
- Reflect player decisions through world and character responses.

3.5 Social progression systems

In the case of social progression systems, players advance through interactions with other players, reputation systems, multiplayer ranking, and community-driven achievements. Unlike the previous player progression systems, social progression is tied to the status and social influence of the player while engaging in cooperative or competitive tasks in the world of the game. These progression systems are most frequently found in multiplayer games, MMO games, and other, live-service titles. Here, the player's growth is measured by their standing in the community. This standing can consist of ranking in competitive play or contribution to cooperative goals. Furthermore, unlike progression in single-player games, social progression persists beyond individual play sessions with evolving leaderboards and guild hierarchies.

- Typical genres: MMOs, competitive online games, live-service games.
- Example games: League of Legends, Fortnite, Call of Duty: Warzone, EVE Online.

Table 5 shows the SWOT analysis of social progression systems.

Based on the SWOT analysis, the following design guidelines were formed for social progression systems:

- Reward collaborative behavior and sportsmanship;
- Balance competition with inclusivity;
- Design transparent and fair progression metrics.

Strengths	**Weaknesses**
Drives community engagement and competition	Toxic behavior and elitism
Encourages teamwork and cooperation	Harder for new players to join established hierarchies
Opportunities	**Threats**
Creates persistent progression loops	Social pressure may discourage some players
Enables community-driven content	Requires constant moderation and balancing

Table 5.
The SWOT analysis of social progression systems.

Strengths	Weaknesses
Supports diverse player motivations	May overwhelm new players
Flexible and customizable systems	Requires delicate balancing
Opportunities	**Threats**
Increases replayability and depth	Risk of feature bloat or redundancy
Enables personalized experiences	Uneven emphasis on different progression tracks

Table 6.
The SWOT analysis of hybrid progression systems.

3.6 Hybrid progression systems

These types of progression systems combine two or more aforementioned progression types to create a more dynamic and engaging experience. Instead of relying on a single method of advancement, these systems offer multiple paths for player growth. Consequently, these allow individuals to engage with the game mechanics that suit their playstyle since diverse player preferences require flexible and layered progression systems [18, 19]. For example, based on player types, achievers engage with XP-based leveling, item rewards, and rank progression; explorers can benefit from open-ended progression systems; socializers prefer faction reputation, guild ranks, and social influence-based growth; and competitors focus on skill-based mastery and ranked leaderboards.

- Typical genres: Open-world games, modern RPGs, sandbox games.
- Example games: The Witcher 3 (Narrative + XP + Skill), Elden Ring (Skill + XP + Item + Narrative), Destiny 2 (Item + XP + Social), Final Fantasy VII (XP + Item + Narrative).

Table 6 presents the results of the SWOT analysis of hybrid progression systems.

Based on the SWOT analysis, the following design guidelines were formed for hybrid progression systems:

- Ensure synergy between different progression systems;
- Avoid feature overload by streamlining redundant mechanics;
- Let players prioritize progression paths that suit their playstyle.

4. Artificial intelligence in player progression

The integration of AI into player progression systems has influenced the evolution of modern game design. No longer limited to static structures such as fixed XP thresholds, linear narrative branches, or predetermined loot drops, progression mechanics can now be customized in real-time based on individual player behavior, cognitive load, and emotional state. The convergence of machine learning, procedural generation, and player modeling enables games to deliver adaptive and personalized progression systems that continuously respond to the player's learning curve and engagement profile.

This section explores how AI technologies are currently being used in-game progression through six focal areas: dynamic difficulty adjustment (DDA), procedural content generation (PCG), personalized learning systems, reward system optimization, and ethical considerations.

4.1 AI-driven dynamic difficulty adjustment

Dynamic difficulty adjustment is one of the earliest and most impactful applications of AI in games. Rather than offering static difficulty levels selected at the outset of a game, DDA allows for in-the-moment recalibration of gameplay variables based on player performance metrics such as reaction time, accuracy, success-to-failure ratio, or input frequency. These adaptations may occur invisibly or be communicated explicitly through in-game feedback systems [20]. For example, in Resident Evil 4 (both in the original and its remake), the AI dynamically adjusts enemy density and item drops to maintain a balanced experience. Valve's Left 4 Dead series created the "AI Director," which modulates environmental tension, spawn rates, and item placements to maximize player immersion and team coordination [21].

Table 7 details the results of the SWOT analysis of AI-driven DDA.

AI-based DDA systems have been shown to increase retention and satisfaction in both novice and expert players [22]. However, the literature shows that balance is the key if the system reduces difficulty too aggressively, players may feel their skill is undervalued. Conversely, poorly tuned increases can lead to frustration. Player modeling techniques such as behavior trees, fuzzy logic, and Bayesian inference are often used to make DDA more robust. For instance, Yannakakis and Hallam demonstrate how real-time adaptation mechanisms can dynamically adjust gameplay parameters such as challenge and curiosity to enhance player engagement [23]. Their work on the Bug Smasher game showed that even a simple gradient-ascent-based controller and player interaction data (e.g., response time, pressure variance, and input frequency) could significantly improve the entertainment value of a game. Moreover, their results indicate that maladaptive parameter changes correlate with decreased player preference. This shows the importance of precision in DDA design.

Strengths	**Weaknesses**
Enables personalization without requiring extensive user input or manual configuration	Risks undermining player agency and perceived skill mastery if adjustments are overly intrusive or opaque
Supports accessibility by adapting to diverse cognitive and motor skill levels	Relies on accurate, interpretable player modeling; errors in prediction can lead to maladaptive responses
Opportunities	**Threats**
Applicability extends beyond entertainment to domains such as education, rehabilitation, and training simulations	Privacy and ethical concerns regarding the collection and use of player data, mainly in the context of minors or biometric tracking
Potential for long-term adaptive profiles across platforms, enhancing cross-game personalization	Risk of misalignment between adaptive difficulty goals and commercial incentives (e.g., engagement vs. monetization)

Table 7.
The SWOT analysis of AI-driven DDA.

Recent advancements in AI-driven DDA have highlighted its evolution from heuristic-based systems to personalized mechanisms that enhance player engagement. For instance, Rahimi et al. introduced a continuous reinforcement learning-based DDA approach in a visual working memory game [24]. This improved player experience and performance compared to traditional rule-based methods. Similarly, Kristensen et al. used factorization machines to predict personalized game difficulty that enabled more accurately customized challenges to individual players [25]. Furthermore, adaptive systems using Monte Carlo Tree Search (MCTS) algorithms have been developed to adjust game difficulty based on predicted player affective states, such as challenge and flow, enhancing overall player experience [26]. These developments illustrate that effective DDA is not merely about matching difficulty to performance metrics but involves a complex understanding of player behavior, preferences, and emotional states. As AI continues to advance, DDA systems are poised to become more responsive and personalized. Consequently, they contribute to more immersive and satisfying gaming experiences.

4.2 Procedural content generation in progression

Procedural content generation involves using algorithms to generate game assets such as maps, levels, enemies, and quests. With the use of AI, PCG can also incorporate player preferences, progress history, and behavior patterns to produce content that evolves alongside the user [27]. For example, No Man's Sky uses a mathematical model and seeded randomness to generate over 18 quintillion planets with unique flora, fauna, and atmospheric conditions [28]. Roguelikes like Hades or Dead Cells use PCG to create dungeon layouts that adjust in difficulty and complexity as the player progresses.

Recent approaches in PCG *via* machine learning (PCGML) have allowed for the generation of levels that adapt not only structurally but also semantically. In other words, the content serves specific learning objectives or engagement patterns [16]. Reinforcement learning, generative adversarial networks (GANs), and Markov decision processes (MDPs) are among the key techniques enabling these innovations. For instance, Khalifa et al. introduced PCGRL that is a framework that uses reinforced learning to train level-designing agents [29]. This enables the creation of game levels that adapt to player performance and preferences. Meanwhile, Liu et al. provided a survey on the use of deep learning for procedural content generation while highlighting methods like convolutional neural networks and recurrent neural networks for generating complex game elements [30]. These innovations signify a shift toward more intelligent and adaptive content generation in games. By integrating machine learning techniques, PCG systems can produce content that not only varies structurally but also aligns with the semantic and experiential aspects of gameplay, offering personalized and engaging experiences for players. As research in this area continues to evolve, we can anticipate even more sophisticated PCG systems that seamlessly blend algorithmic generation with player-centric design principles.

4.3 Personalized progression paths through AI

One of AI's most promising contributions is in supporting individualized player journeys. AI can segment players based on behavioral telemetry such as movement patterns, combat preferences, and exploration tendencies and provide progression paths that match these patterns [31]. This is not just difficulty scaling; it allows for changes in narrative delivery, mission objectives, upgrade paths, and even the emotional tone of gameplay. The Nemesis system of Middle-earth: Shadow of Mordor is a prime example. In that system, AI-generated enemies evolve in personality and tactics based on previous encounters. In educational games, intelligent tutoring systems can adjust challenge levels to align with Bloom's taxonomy of cognitive skills that results in higher learning retention and flow [32].

Furthermore, the role of AI in player segmentation has been important in understanding and predicting player behavior. By analyzing in-game actions and preferences, developers can create more engaging and personalized experiences. This approach not only enhances player satisfaction but also informs game design decisions to cater to diverse player profiles. Zhu and Ontañón present a player-centered framework of AI for game personalization as they identify open problems and emphasize the need for collaboration between technological advancement and player experience design [33].

Overall, the integration of AI into game design paves the way for the creation of personalized progression paths that adapt to individual player behaviors and preferences. By leveraging behavioral telemetry, procedural content generation, and adaptive learning frameworks, AI enables dynamic and engaging experiences that evolve with the player. This marks an important shift from static game design to responsive, player-centric models.

4.4 The use of AI in reward systems

AI also transforms how players are rewarded by optimizing the timing, frequency, and type of feedback. Unlike traditional fixed-reward schedules (e.g., get 10 XP for every kill), AI-driven systems use engagement prediction models to identify when a player is at risk of disengaging and deploy appropriate incentives. These might include offering bonus objectives, providing rare loot, or introducing surprise narrative content [34]. For example, Destiny 2 dynamically adjusts loot drops based on a player's recent reward history to prevent monotony or "loot fatigue." Machine learning models trained on user retention metrics can detect when players are likely to churn and introduce corrective mechanisms such as progression boosts, narrative reminders, or social incentives.

Importantly, these mechanisms require careful calibration to avoid creating manipulative or addictive loops. While reinforcement learning and behavioral modeling are powerful, designers must be cautious not to exploit player vulnerabilities in pursuit of engagement metrics. To address these concerns, researchers advocate for the integration of ethical frameworks within AI systems. By incorporating machine ethics into reinforcement learning, developers can ensure that AI agents make decisions aligned with human values and norms. Thus, they can promote responsible and sustainable gaming practices [35].

4.5 Ethical considerations in AI-driven progression

The use of AI in progression systems raises critical ethical issues. A well-designed AI system should empower players. However, concerns arise when AI is used to impose artificial barriers such as slowing progression or manipulating challenge levels to steer players toward monetized options like microtransactions or paid boosters. Opacity is another issue as players are often unaware that an AI system is shaping their experience. Without transparency, trust in the system may erode, particularly in competitive environments where fairness is of crucial importance. The black-box nature of some AI systems makes it difficult for players to understand how decisions are made. This can further increase concerns about fairness and accountability.

Best practices suggest giving players visibility and control over AI-driven systems, including the ability to opt out of personalization or toggle transparency modes. Game designers must also navigate data privacy concerns, especially when integrating biometric or affective feedback systems into progression logic. The principles of explainable AI (XAI) and human-in-the-loop (HITL) design are becoming increasingly relevant in games to ensure that progression systems remain comprehensible and ethically sound [36]. Furthermore, data privacy is an important concern, mainly when AI systems use biometric or affective feedback to inform progression logic. Ensuring that players have control over their data and the ability to opt out of personalization features is essential to maintain ethical standards and comply with data protection regulations [37].

5. The possible future of player progression systems

Player progression systems have undergone significant transformation over the past decades, evolving from rudimentary XP mechanics and static skill trees to sophisticated, AI-driven models that offer dynamic and personalized experiences. Emerging technologies such as AI, machine learning ML, blockchain, cloud computing, and virtual reality (VR) are poised to further revolutionize these systems. This enables more immersive and adaptive gameplay [38]. Historically, progression in video games was linear and predefined that required players to follow fixed leveling curves and rigid upgrade paths. In contrast, contemporary developments have introduced dynamic progression models that afford greater player agency, adaptability, and persistent engagement across multiple platforms and game ecosystems.

This section examines how these AI-driven mechanics could affect player progression in the coming years. It discusses AI-powered adaptive difficulty, meta-progression across platforms, AI-generated quests and storylines, as well as the ethical challenges of progression design in an era of live-service models.

5.1 The shift toward AI-driven progression

Artificial intelligence is increasingly integral to the structuring and delivery of player progression. Moving beyond static skill trees and predefined leveling systems, future games are anticipated to use AI to create adaptive and personalized experiences. AI-driven progression systems can analyze player behavior in real time, adjusting skill recommendations, challenge levels, and rewards to align with individual playstyles. This paradigm shift from fixed RPG character development to adaptive progression models ensures that each player's experience is unique. For instance, an AI assistant in a role-playing game could learn from a player's combat style, preferred weapons, and movement patterns. Thus, it provides real-time suggestions that evolve alongside the player's behavior. If a player frequently utilizes ranged attacks but struggles in melee combat, the AI could recommend ranged perks, suggest strategies, or adjust enemy behavior to accommodate the player's strengths and weaknesses.

However, ethical considerations must be addressed in the design of such systems. AI-driven progression should enhance player agency rather than diminish it. Overly deterministic AI-generated suggestions may undermine the sense of accomplishment and personal investment, leading to a diminished gaming experience. Therefore, it is imperative to balance AI adaptability with meaningful player choices to maintain engagement and satisfaction.

5.2 Meta-progression and cross-game continuity

The transition toward cloud-based ecosystems and live-service models has elevated the relevance of meta-progression. These are progression systems that persist beyond a single game session, platform, or even franchise. Instead of restarting character growth with each new game, future progression models may enable players to maintain a persistent progression profile that carries over across multiple games. This concept was exemplified in the Mass Effect series (2007–2012), where players could transfer saved games between titles, allowing previous narrative choices to influence subsequent storylines. Looking forward, the development of interconnected universes could facilitate similar continuity on a broader scale.

An emerging and contentious area of in-game progression is blockchain-based persistence, wherein player-owned progression assets such as skills, ranks, and digital items exist independently of specific game servers. In theory, blockchain technology could enable ownership of in-game progression elements, cross-game asset transfers, and decentralized progression tracking. This approach could enhance player autonomy by allowing assets to retain value across different gaming environments. However, it also raises concerns regarding monetization, accessibility, and potential exploitation. The risk of pay-to-win economies necessitates careful consideration of the ethical implications of integrating blockchain into progression systems.

5.3 Procedural and AI-generated story progression

AI-driven narrative design is expected to redefine the nature of progression in story-rich games. Procedural quest generation, previously limited to fetch quests or randomized events is becoming more sophisticated through natural language processing (NLP) and large language models (LLMs) [39, 40]. These systems can dynamically generate branching story arcs, context-sensitive dialog, and evolving world states based on player actions.

In future games, the decisions of the players could not only shape immediate outcomes but also generate new plotlines and character relationships in real-time. Progression in such systems would be less about completing pre-authored content and more about co-creating narrative paths that reflect the unique playstyle, values, and history of the individual player.

5.4 Gamification beyond entertainment

The principles of player progression are increasingly being applied outside of entertainment in areas such as education, workplace training, mental health, and civic engagement. Serious games and gamified applications already use progression systems to motivate learning and behavior change [41]. With the support of AI, these systems can become more adaptive and impactful. For example, educational platforms may use procedural skill trees to guide students through personalized curricula. Fitness apps can deploy AI to recommend workout goals and dynamically adjust difficulty based on past performance. Even civic apps can track social contributions or sustainable behavior through progression metaphors like leveling or badges.

In these contexts, progression becomes a tool for long-term behavior reinforcement, but it must also preserve intrinsic motivation and avoid excessive gamification that may trivialize real-world issues.

5.5 Ethical considerations in future progression systems

As progression systems become more complex, persistent, and data-driven, they must adhere to evolving standards of digital ethics and regulation. Regulatory frameworks such as the General Data Protection Regulation (GDPR) in Europe already impact how games handle player data, especially in AI-driven personalization [42]. Designers and developers will need to establish best practices for fairness, transparency, and explainability. Player autonomy must remain a central design goal, particularly when progression systems adapt based on biometric or behavioral data.

Moreover, there is a growing demand for ethical AI audits and third-party validation of adaptive systems in games, especially those involving vulnerable populations such as minors. The future of player progression will depend not only on technological capabilities but also on the industry's commitment to responsible innovation.

Overall, the following can be stated:

- AI should be used to enhance progression, not throttle XP gain artificially to encourage microtransactions.
- Games must ensure that progression remains rewarding rather than a grind that feels endless with no meaningful payoffs.
- AI-driven skill recommendations must suggest and not force progression paths. This can allow players to experiment and find their own playstyle.

6. Conclusions

Player progression systems serve as the backbone of long-term engagement in video games, shaping not only the player's moment-to-moment actions but also their broader sense of development, mastery, and identity. This chapter has provided a taxonomy of six key player progression types: skill-based, XP-based, item-based, narrative, social, and hybrid. By formalizing these systems, designers, and researchers can be offered a common vocabulary for analyzing and constructing progression mechanics.

Moreover, the integration of AI has redefined what progression can mean in a digital game context. From dynamic difficulty adjustment and procedural content generation to emotionally responsive and personalized progression paths, AI has enabled systems that adapt to the player's style, preferences, and performance. These developments not only enhance player satisfaction but also present novel challenges in ethical design, transparency, and regulatory compliance.

Looking ahead, progression systems are poised to expand beyond individual games and even the entertainment domain itself. Persistent meta-progression across ecosystems, AI-generated narratives, and biometric feedback mechanisms all point toward increasingly sophisticated and immersive player journeys. Simultaneously, the adoption of gamified progression structures in education, health, and civic technologies highlights the versatility of these systems and the importance of designing them with care and responsibility.

As games continue to evolve as cultural, economic, and technological artifacts, player progression systems must remain both innovative and accountable. This requires collaboration between designers, data scientists, ethicists, and players themselves to ensure that progression mechanics serve diverse audiences, respect user autonomy, and foster meaningful engagement.

In summary, progression is not merely a structural element. It is a dynamic, multidimensional tool for shaping how players grow, both within and beyond the game world. Thoughtfully designed progression systems, especially those augmented by AI, have the potential to create not just better games, but better human experiences.

Acknowledgements

This work has been implemented by the TKP2021-NVA-10 project with the support provided by the Ministry of Culture and Innovation of Hungary from the National Research, Development and Innovation Fund, financed under the 2021 Thematic Excellence Programme funding scheme.

Conflict of interest

The author declares no conflict of interest.

Appendix A: Methodology for SWOT Analyses

The SWOT analyses shown in this chapter were developed using a structured qualitative method designed to ensure practical relevance. The process combined expert input, targeted literature review, and comparative game analysis to derive a balanced set of evaluations for each progression system. They had the following four steps:

- Step #1: For each progression type, 3–5 influential or genre-defining games were selected as reference points. The selection prioritized titles that are widely recognized in the academic literature, have detailed postmortems or developer insights available (e.g., through GDC talks), and exhibit progression systems representative of their category.

- Step #2: Academic sources were consulted to identify theoretical advantages and drawbacks associated with each progression system. These included:

- Game studies literature on player motivation and engagement (e.g., SDT, Flow Theory)

- Technical design texts (e.g., Game Analytics, AI, and Games)

- Empirical studies and player behavior analyses

- Step #3: For each progression type, results from the literature and game examples were categorized into:

- Strengths: Elements that increase player engagement, satisfaction, or retention
- Weaknesses: Limitations that may reduce accessibility, depth, or balance
- Opportunities: Design possibilities for future innovation or genre expansion
- Threats: External or internal risks, including monetization pitfalls or design complexity
- Each table was reviewed for balance to avoid overgeneralization and ensure that SWOT entries reflected diverse player experiences and use cases.

Step #4: After the initial tables were drafted, they were refined through internal peer feedback during the manuscript preparation. Adjustments were made to avoid overlap, sharpen definitions, and align terminology with current discourse in game design scholarship. This structured approach ensures that the SWOT analyses serve as both a pedagogical tool for taxonomy and a practical guide for game development and evaluation.

Appendix B: Game titles referenced by progression type

The following list includes the primary games analyzed to support the taxonomy and SWOT analyses in this chapter. Titles were selected based on their influence within their genre, innovative use of progression mechanics, and availability of developer commentary or academic discussion. Each game demonstrates the core characteristics of one or more progression types. This list is not exhaustive but reflects the core examples used to illustrate the variety and complexity of progression systems analyzed throughout the chapter.

- Skill-based progression: Celeste (2018), Dark Souls (2011), Super Meat Boy (2010), Street Fighter II (1991), Counter-Strike: Global Offensive (2012).
- XP-based progression: Final Fantasy series (1987–present), Pokémon series (1996–present), World of Warcraft (2004), Tom Clancy's The Division (2016)
- Item-based progression: Diablo II (2000), Monster Hunter: World (2018), The Legend of Zelda: Breath of the Wild (2017), Borderlands 2 (2012)
- Narrative progression: The Witcher 3: Wild Hunt (2015), Life is Strange (2015), Detroit: Become Human (2018), Mass Effect series (2007–2012)
- Social progression: League of Legends (2009), EVE Online (2003), Call of Duty: Warzone (2020), Fortnite (2017)
- Hybrid progression: Destiny 2 (2017), Elden Ring (2022), Final Fantasy VII Remake (2020), The Witcher 3: Wild Hunt (2015)

Author details

Tibor Guzsvinecz
Department of Information Technology and its Applications, Faculty of Information Technology, University of Pannonia, Zalaegerszeg, Hungary

*Address all correspondence to: guzsvinecz.tibor@zek.uni-pannon.hu

References

[1] Juul J. A Casual Revolution: Reinventing Video Games and their Players. Cambridge, Massachusetts, London, England: MIT Press; 2012

[2] Gee JP. What video games have to teach us about learning and literacy. Computers in Entertainment. 2003;**1**(1):1-4. DOI: 10.1145/950566.950595

[3] Sweetser P, Wyeth P. GameFlow: A model for evaluating player enjoyment in games. Computers in Entertainment. 2005;**3**(3):1-24. DOI: 10.1145/1077246.1077253

[4] Przybylski AK, Rigby CS, Ryan RM. A motivational model of video game engagement. Review of General Psychology. 2010;**14**(2):154-166. DOI: 10.1037/a0019440

[5] Sweller J. Cognitive load during problem solving: Effects on learning. Cognitive Science. 1988;**12**(2):257-285. DOI: 10.1207/s15516709cog1202_4

[6] Deci EL, Ryan RM. Intrinsic Motivation and Self-Determination in Human Behavior. 1985th ed. New York, NY: Springer; 1985

[7] Ryan RM, Rigby CS, Przybylski A. The motivational pull of video games: A self-determination theory approach. Motivation and Emotion. 2006;**30**(4):344-360. DOI: 10.1007/s11031-006-9051-8

[8] Salen, Tekinbas K, Zimmerman E. Rules of Play: Game Design Fundamentals. Cambridge, Massachusetts, London, England: MIT Press; 2003

[9] Gee J. Glued to games: How video games draw us in and hold us spellbound. American Journal of Play. 2012;**4**(4):510-511

[10] Csikszentmihalyi M. Flow: The Psychology of Optimal Experience. New York, USA: Harper & Row; 1990

[11] Skinner BF. Operant conditioning. The Encyclopedia of Education. 1971;7:29-33

[12] Yee N. The gamer motivation profile: What we learned from 250,000 gamers. In: Proceedings of the 2016 Annual Symposium on Computer-Human Interaction in Play. New York, NY, USA: ACM; 2016. p. 2

[13] King DL, Delfabbro PH. Video game monetization (eg,'loot boxes'): A blueprint for practical social responsibility measures. International Journal of Mental Health and Addiction. 2019;**17**(1):166-179. DOI: 10.1007/s11469-018-0009-3

[14] Anderson CA, Dill KE. Video games and aggressive thoughts, feelings, and behavior in the laboratory and in life. Journal of Personality and Social Psychology. 2000;**78**(4):772-790. DOI: 10.1037/0022-3514.78.4.772

[15] Yannakakis GN, Togelius J. Artificial Intelligence and Games. 1st ed. Cham, Switzerland: Springer International Publishing; 2018. DOI: 10.1007/978-3-319-63519-4

[16] Summerville A, Snodgrass S, Guzdial M, Holmgard C, Hoover AK, Isaksen A, et al. Procedural content generation via machine learning (PCGML). IEEE Transactions on Games. 2018;**10**(3):257-270. DOI: 10.1109/tg.2018.2846639

[17] El-Nasr MS, Nguyen T-HD, Canossa A, Drachen A. Game Data

Science. London, England: Oxford University Press; 2021

[18] Bartle R. Hearts, clubs, diamonds, spades: Players who suit MUDs. Journal of MUD Research. 1996;**1**(1):1-27

[19] Yee N. The demographics, motivations, and derived experiences of users of massively multi-user online graphical environments. Presence (Camb). 2006;**15**(3):309-329. DOI: 10.1162/pres.15.3.309

[20] Andrade G, Ramalho G, Santana H, Corruble V. Challenge-sensitive action selection: An application to game balancing. In: IEEE/WIC/ACM International Conference on Intelligent Agent Technology. Compiegne, France: IEEE; 2006. pp. 194-200. DOI: 10.1109/IAT.2005.52

[21] Booth M. The ai systems of left 4 dead. In: Artificial Intelligence and Interactive Digital Entertainment Conference at Stanford. Palo Alto, California, USA: AAAI Press; 2009

[22] Hunicke R. The case for dynamic difficulty adjustment in games. In: Proceedings of the 2005 ACM SIGCHI International Conference on Advances in Computer Entertainment Technology. New York, NY, USA: ACM; 2005. pp. 429-433. DOI: 10.1145/1178477.1178573

[23] Yannakakis GN, Hallam J. Real-time game adaptation for optimizing player satisfaction. IEEE Transactions on Computational Intelligence in AI and Games. 2009;**1**(2):121-133. DOI: 10.1109/tciaig.2009.2024533

[24] Rahimi M, Moradi H, Vahabie A-H, Kebriaei H. Continuous reinforcement learning-based dynamic difficulty adjustment in a visual working memory game. arXiv. 2023:1-6. DOI: 10.48550/arXiv.2308.12726

[25] Kristensen JT, Guckelsberger C, Burelli P, Hämäläinen P. Personalized game difficulty prediction using factorization machines. In: Proceedings of the 35th Annual ACM Symposium on User Interface Software and Technology. New York, NY, USA: ACM; 2022. pp. 1-13. DOI: 10.1145/3526113.3545624

[26] Moon J, Choi Y, Park T, Choi J, Hong J-H, Kim K-J. Diversifying dynamic difficulty adjustment agent by integrating player state models into Monte-Carlo tree search. Expert Systems with Applications. 2022;**205**(117677):117677. DOI: 10.1016/j.eswa.2022.117677

[27] Shaker N, Togelius J, Nelson MJ. Procedural Content Generation in Games. 1st ed. Cham, Switzerland: Springer International Publishing; 2016. DOI: 10.1007/978-3-319-42716-4

[28] Parkin S. No man's sky: The game where you can explore 18 quintillion planets. The Guardian. 2015. Available from: https://www.theguardian.com/technology/2015/jul/12/no-mans-sky-18-quintillion-planets-hello-games

[29] Khalifa A, Bontrager P, Earle S, Togelius J. PCGRL: Procedural content generation via reinforcement learning. Proceedings of the AAAI Artificial Intelligence and Interactive Digital Entertainment Conference. 2020;**16**(1):95-101. DOI: 10.1609/aiide.v16i1.7416

[30] Liu J, Snodgrass S, Khalifa A, Risi S, Yannakakis GN, Togelius J. Deep learning for procedural content generation. Neural Computing and Applications. 2021;**33**(1):19-37. DOI: 10.1007/s00521-020-05383-8

[31] Paraschos PD, Koulouriotis DE. Game difficulty adaptation and

experience personalization: A literature review. International Journal of Human Computer Interaction. 2023;**39**(1):1-22. DOI: 10.1080/10447318.2021.2020008

[32] Smith AM, Nelson MJ, Mateas M. LUDOCORE: A logical game engine for modeling videogames. In: Proceedings of the 2010 IEEE Conference on Computational Intelligence and Games. Copenhagen, Denmark: IEEE; 2010. pp. 91-98. DOI: 10.1109/ITW.2010.5593368

[33] Zhu J, Ontañón S. Player-centered AI for automatic game personalization: Open problems. In: International Conference on the Foundations of Digital Games. New York, NY, USA: ACM; 2020. pp. 1-8. DOI: 10.1145/3402942.3402951

[34] Holmgard C, Green MC, Liapis A, Togelius J. Automated playtesting with procedural personas through MCTS with evolved heuristics. IEEE Transactions on Games. 2019;**11**(4):352-362. DOI: 10.1109/tg.2018.2808198

[35] Vishwanath A, Dennis LA, Slavkovik M. Reinforcement learning and machine ethics: A systematic review. arXiv. 2024:1-9. DOI: 10.48550/arXiv.2407.02425

[36] Tsiakas K, Murray-Rust D. Using human-in-the-loop and explainable AI to envisage new future work practices. In: The15th International Conference on PErvasive Technologies Related to Assistive Environments. New York, NY, USA: ACM; 2022. pp. 388-394. DOI: 10.1145/3529190.3534779

[37] Seif El-Nasr M, Kleinman E. Data-driven game development: Ethical considerations. In: International Conference on the Foundations of Digital Games. New York, NY, USA: ACM; 2020. pp. 1-10. DOI: 10.1145/3402942.3402964

[38] Mehta N. The role of AI in game development and player experience. SSRN Electronic Journal. 2025:1-13. DOI: 10.2139/ssrn.5101269

[39] Kumaran V, Rowe J, Mott B, Lester J. SceneCraft: Automating interactive narrative scene generation in digital games with large language models. Proceedings of the AAAI Artificial Intelligence and Interactive Digital Entertainment Conference. 2023;**19**(1):86-96. DOI: 10.1609/aiide.v19i1.27504

[40] Chung JJY, Kim W, Yoo KM, Lee H, Adar E, Chang M. TaleBrush: Sketching stories with generative pretrained language models. In: CHI Conference on Human Factors in Computing Systems. New York, NY, USA: ACM; 2022. pp. 1-19. DOI: 10.1145/3491102.3501819

[41] Hamari J, Koivisto J. "Working out for likes": An empirical study on social influence in exercise gamification. Computers in Human Behavior. 2015;**50**:333-347. DOI: 10.1016/j.chb.2015.04.018

[42] Tsamados A, Aggarwal N, Cowls J, Morley J, Roberts H, Taddeo M, et al. The ethics of algorithms: Key problems and solutions. In: Philosophical Studies Series. Cham: Springer International Publishing; 2021. pp. 97-123. DOI: 10.1007/978-3-030-81907-1_8

Chapter 3

Crafting Virtual Characters for Games: A Player-Centered Approach

Remi Poivet

Abstract

This chapter investigates how player experience is influenced by virtual characters. Virtual characters in video games include both player avatars and non-player characters (NPCs). These two types serve distinct functions in shaping gameplay and narrative engagement. Avatars represent the player's embodiment within the virtual environment, while NPCs act as social agents that populate and structure that environment. Both are essential for creating believable, emotional, and engaging game experiences. The first section focuses on avatars. It compares predefined and customizable forms, examining how each influences player identification, which refers to the psychological connection between player and character. It also explores how avatars affect social representation, inclusion, and emotional engagement. The second section addresses NPCs and their role in shaping player experience. It explains how visual design influences player expectations and how behavior shapes perceptions of intelligence, coherence, and credibility. This section also discusses how recent developments in artificial intelligence are enabling more adaptive and expressive NPC behavior. The chapter concludes by analyzing the relationship between avatars and NPCs. It outlines how their roles differ while contributing to the overall experience. It ends with practical recommendations for researchers and designers who aim to align character design with player psychology and expectations.

Keywords: virtual character, psychology, user research, game design, avatar, NPC

1. Introduction

This chapter discusses the challenges video game developers face when creating virtual characters that are appealing and engaging. It focuses on two main types of virtual characters: avatars, which are controlled by the player, and non-player characters (NPCs), which are controlled by the game. While avatars and NPCs differ in their functions, both are essential to how players interact with and emotionally invest in the game environment [1]. Conversely to characters in other media, virtual characters in video games respond to player input, translating their intention into the virtual environment [2]. This dynamic, where virtual characters adapt to and reflect the player's intention and decisions, is crucial to shaping emotions, immersion, and decision-making in games [3, 4]. Therefore, considering players' minds during the creative process benefits virtual characters' design.

Historically, technological and game design advancements have driven the evolution of avatar design. Early arcade games like Pong (1972) and Space Invaders (1978) featured avatars that were simple shapes, designed to represent players in the virtual environment instead of conveying narrative meaning [2]. Super Mario Bros. (1985) marked a significant advancement by introducing Mario, a fully animated, anthropomorphic avatar. Mario could run, jump, and transform through power-ups, offering a more dynamic and immersive experience [3]. Mario's introduction marked a significant shift from the static characters of earlier games like Space Invaders. His movement, influenced by gravity and momentum, provided players with a greater degree of control. His animations and consistent visual identity helped establish an emotional connection between the player and the character [2]. As 3D technology developed, avatars became more detailed and played more significant narrative roles. Characters like Solid Snake in Metal Gear Solid (1998) navigated 3D spaces and appeared in cinematic sequences that revealed their thoughts, feelings, and social context [5]. This shift from 2D to 3D design marked a significant change in avatar development, turning them from basic gameplay tools into complex, psychologically engaging figures. From 2010 to 2020, avatars became more customizable, appearing as virtual representations of players in open-world role playing games (RPGs) or fully voiced protagonists in narrative-driven games like The Last of Us Part II (2020). As avatars grew more complex, so did player expectations. Visual fidelity and responsive controls were no longer enough. Players began to expect emotional depth, consistent personality, and alignment with the game's narrative and thematic tone [4, 6, 7].

On the other hand, virtual characters controlled by the game, referred to as NPCs, have also evolved significantly over time. Early examples, like the ghosts in Pac-Man (1980), followed simple, scripted behaviors that provided challenges but lacked narrative depth. By the late 1990s, games like Ultima V (1988) and Half-Life (1998) introduced NPCs with daily schedules and reactive dialog to provide a richer game experience [5]. Today, NPCs can serve as dynamic companions, such as Atreus in God of War (2018), emotional anchors like Clementine in The Walking Dead (2012), or complex agents with memory and autonomy, like the villagers in Animal Crossing: New Horizons (2020). Some NPCs, such as those in Middle-earth: Shadow of Mordor (2014) or The Elder Scrolls V: Skyrim (2011), use advanced systems like the Nemesis mechanic or Radiant AI to create the illusion of individual agency and long-term relationships with the player [7]. Hence, designing these characters requires more than programming behavior or writing dialog. It requires understanding how players interpret NPC actions and infer traits like intelligence, loyalty, or empathy from subtle cues in behavior, animation, and pacing [2]. Poorly designed NPCs can break immersion and frustrate players, while well-designed ones can foster empathy, support player agency, and enhance the narrative [4].

Both NPCs and avatars are developed with similar consideration during game production. The two virtual characters contribute to creating a believable and, therefore, immersive game experience. Their design involves technical, narrative, and psychological challenges. As players engage with characters, they bring their own cognitive schemas, social expectations, and heuristics into the game world. Consequently, it influences how players interpret characters' appearance and behavior, which shapes their evaluation of a character's believability and emotional depth. Therefore, understanding how players interpret virtual characters is essential. This chapter is organized into two main sections. First, we examine avatars as embodied virtual characters, focusing on how they transcend gameplay functions to become anchors of identity and psychological engagement. We analyze their role in shaping player experiences, with an emphasis on body, gender, and representation. The second section explores NPCs, tracing their evolution from simple, scripted entities to social agents. We analyze how NPC appearance impacts player perception, how behavior affects believability and player expectations, and how recent advances in AI are making NPCs more dynamic and conversational. Throughout, we explore the psychological dimensions of character design and how avatars and NPCs shape the overall player experience.

2. Avatars as embodied virtual characters: Identity, representation, and player psychology

In modern video games, the avatar is more than a tool for connecting the player to the system. It is an embodied figure where identity, narrative, and agency converge. As players navigate rich virtual environments, their avatars act as psychological, cultural, and narrative anchors. These avatars shape how players interact and how they perceive themselves within the game space [3]. Whether predefined by developers or sculpted through player-driven customization systems, avatars embody social cues and affordances that influence player identification, self-perception, and behavior [8]. Far from being neutral or interchangeable, these virtual characters convey symbolic meaning. They invite players to project, perform, or contest facets of identity through the act of play [9].

This section explores the psychological and experiential dimensions of avatar embodiment. It begins with the player's avatar as an anchor of narrative empathy and self-representation, then examines its visual and symbolic features, including body, gender, and race. Finally, it discusses how these design choices reflect and reproduce broader cultural logics [10]. Through this lens, avatars are seen both as virtual characters and as deeply meaningful figures within the interactive grammar of games [7].

2.1 Avatar: A tool for identification

In video game design, avatars are not just tools for interaction but also virtual characters through which players project, experiment with, or even transform aspects of their identity. The extent to which players identify with their avatars emotionally, cognitively, or behaviorally varies depending on whether the avatar is predefined or fully customizable. Predefined avatars, such as Mario in Super Mario Bros. or Nathan Drake in the Uncharted series, are characters with fixed appearances, personalities, and narrative arcs. These avatars are integrated into the game's storytelling and aim to deliver a narrative experience similar to film or television. In these cases, player identification is primarily narrative-based. Players engage empathically with the avatar's emotions and motivations but do not perceive the character as a reflection of themselves. Instead, the avatar becomes a parasocial figure, a character the player forms an attachment to, much like a protagonist in a novel [11].

By contrast, fully customizable avatars, such as those in Skyrim, The Sims series, or Elden Ring (2022), allow players to control physical appearance, gender, race, clothing, voice, and sometimes moral alignment or personality traits. This level of personalization turns the avatar into a self-representational agent, blurring the line between the player and the character. Customization strengthens identification by activating both similarity identification and wishful identification [12]. In other words, players either create avatars that resemble themselves or idealized versions of who they wish to be. Customizable avatars tend to elicit greater self-investment. Players spend more time crafting a character that reflects their identity or aspirations [13, 14]. This investment increases immersion, making the game environment feel more like an extension of the player's self. However, the trade-offs between predefined and customizable avatars are not merely about control versus constraint. Predefined avatars offer narrative coherence and depth, often enabling rich character arcs, emotional pacing, and thematic consistency. Customizable avatars, while empowering for self-expression, often lack the predefined narrative depth necessary for emotional storytelling. This limitation can be overcome when games integrate emergent or player-driven narrative structures, as seen in Skyrim and Cyberpunk 2077 (2020), where the player's choices influence their avatar's appearance and the narrative.

The choice between predefined and fully customizable avatars can lead to potential ludonarrative dissonance. Hocking [15] defines this as a conflict between a game's narrative (story and characterization) and its gameplay (actions performed by players). Ludonarrative dissonance occurs when the ludic elements, such as gameplay sequences and narrative structures, fail to align, disrupting immersion and player identification [16, 17]. In Uncharted games, players are encouraged to empathize with Nathan Drake as a witty and morally complex hero. However, in gameplay, he casually dispatches hundreds of enemies, creating a gap between Drake's portrayal in narrative cutscenes and his behavior in gameplay. This mismatch can weaken identification with the character [18]. From a psychological perspective, ludonarrative dissonance introduces cognitive dissonance in the player-avatar relationship. The player may think, "I wouldn't have done that" during a cutscene when the character's actions seem inconsistent with the player's own values or prior actions. If the narrative paints the protagonist as compassionate but the gameplay necessitates brutality, this inconsistency can break the illusion of unity between the player and the character [19]. The result is emersion, the opposite of immersion, which reduces emotional engagement and pulls the player out of the experience. However, not all games suffer from ludonarrative dissonance. Recent titles such as God of War: Ragnarök (2022) align the protagonist's personal growth with the game mechanics, encouraging restraint and emotional depth in both narrative and action. In Ragnarök, Kratos's evolving emotional stance is reflected in systems that reward defensive timing over aggression, contextualize rage abilities within moral tension, and emphasize cooperative mechanics with Atreus that foster care and mentorship. This alignment reinforces the narrative arc and enhances ludonarrative harmony, maintaining player agency while deepening the emotional experience.

In summary, customizable and predefined avatars offer distinct possibilities for player identification. Custom avatars encourage projection and embodiment, allowing players to express or explore facets of their identity, while predefined avatars foster empathy through strong narrative design and character development. The psychological impact of each approach depends on the avatar's design and on how gameplay mechanics and narrative context are aligned. When this alignment is coherent, both types of avatars can facilitate deep emotional engagement and identification. When misaligned, dissonance may emerge and disrupt immersion. Yet beyond structural and narrative factors, avatar design also exerts a subtler, often unconscious, influence on player behavior and self-perception. How an avatar looks, its body type, gender, and racial markers can shape how players act, feel, and see themselves in-game and beyond. This psychological dynamic is encapsulated in what has come to be known as the Proteus Effect, which forms the foundation of the following section.

2.2 Body, gender, and representation

While player identification is enabled by structural elements such as customization and narrative framing, it is equally influenced by the features of the avatar itself, specifically its body type, gender, racial traits, and other visual cues. These embodied dimensions are not merely aesthetic choices. They carry social, cultural, and psychological values, shaping how players relate to themselves and others in virtual environments. Avatars are never neutral; their appearance conveys implicit norms about beauty, power, and desirability, often reflecting societal standards of race, gender, and class [9]. It can also influence how players perceive their own agency, competence, and identity in the virtual environment. In this section, we explore how the visual representation of the avatar, including its gendered, racialized, and physical traits, can affect player behavior, self-perception, and social attitudes, often in subtle but measurable ways. Central to this discussion is the Proteus Effect, a phenomenon that reveals how avatar embodiment can shape player psychology and behavior, even beyond the boundaries of the game [20]. Through this lens, we consider how both predefined and customizable avatars affect not just the characters players control but also how they perceive themselves.

2.2.1 The Proteus Effect and avatar influence

Coined by Yee and Bailenson [20], the Proteus Effect refers to the tendency of individuals in virtual environments to conform to the behavioral and psychological traits associated with their avatars. In their initial experiment, participants assigned to taller or more conventionally attractive avatars displayed greater confidence in negotiation tasks, both virtually and in subsequent face-to-face settings. This demonstrated that embodying a virtual self can influence real-world attitudes and behaviors.

This effect has since been replicated and extended across different identity dimensions. For instance, Fox et al. [21] showed that women using hypersexualized avatars in VR environments experienced increased self-objectification and body dissatisfaction. When avatars were customized to resemble the participants' own faces, it altered their body images outside of the virtual environment. Peck et al. [22] found that white participants embodying Black avatars in VR exhibited lower implicit racial bias during and after the experiments, suggesting that avatar embodiment can alter both self-perception and social attitudes. Outside of VR, Ratan et al. [23] explored how avatars' resemblance to players affects their gaming experience using Nintendo Mii characters. Participants played a tennis game in Wii Sports (2006), either with a self-created Mii that resembled them or a generic, pre-made Mii. To assess the cognitive load, participants were intermittently prompted to solve simple verbal math and word problems during gameplay. The study introduced two self-awareness conditions. In the virtual self-awareness condition, participants were told they were being recorded only within the game environment. In the real self-awareness condition, they were told they were recorded both in-game and in the physical room. Results showed that real self-awareness negatively affected performance, with participants demonstrating lower scores in both gameplay and cognitive tasks. This effect was likely due to increased self-consciousness and divided attention. However, this decline was mitigated for participants using self-created avatars. Across both conditions, they showed higher performance in the tennis game and in the cognitive tasks. This suggests that identifying with an avatar resembling oneself can foster greater engagement and reduce the cognitive demands of multitasking. These findings underline the potential of avatar customization in enhancing emotional involvement and facilitating cognitive processing during gameplay. Similarly, Li et al. [24] studied the Proteus Effect in the context of physical performance. In their experiment, overweight children were randomly assigned to play Wii Fit (2007) using either a normal-weight avatar, an overweight avatar, or a normal-weight avatar preceded by a stereotype threat related to obesity. This prime consisted of exposure to negative media messages about overweight individuals, subtly activating concerns about confirming weight-based stereotypes. The children then participated in a game task involving aerobic activity, and their game performance, motivation to exercise, and attitudes toward physical activity were measured. Those who used normal-weight avatars, without exposure to stereotype cues, demonstrated higher motivation, more positive attitudes, and significantly better performance outcomes than the other groups. These effects were attributed in part to wishful identification, as the children were more likely to engage in effortful behavior when embodying idealized avatars that reflected their aspirational self-image. This highlights the motivational power of customizable avatars in shaping in-game performance and real-world attitudes. Collectively, these studies show that the visual and symbolic traits of avatars, especially when aligned with self-perception, can influence more than just identification. They shape emotion, empathy, motivation, and performance.

2.2.2 Body and gender in avatar design

Avatar body type and gender representation are among the most visible and contested aspects of avatar identity. In many games, male avatars are still often portrayed as muscular, assertive, and dominant, while female avatars are frequently sexualized or designed for visual appeal. For instance, in the Tomb Raider series, the protagonist Lara Croft was initially depicted with exaggerated physical features, emphasizing her sexuality. However, the character has evolved to present a more realistic and empowered image, reflecting a shift in the industry's approach to female representation [25]. Despite this evolution, many portrayals in games still reinforce narrow, hegemonic norms about gender and desirability, which may alienate players whose real-life identities do not align with these archetypes. In contrast, games that enable broader customization of gender identity, body shape, and presentation provide richer opportunities for self-expression and identity affirmation. The Sims 4 (2014), for instance, allows players to mix and match gender attributes independently of assigned sex, including voice pitch, clothing preferences, and whether a character can become pregnant. Cyberpunk 2077 broke from traditional RPG conventions by detaching gender labels from body type and voice settings. However, it was also critiqued for limited body diversity and a lack of authentic non-Western representations, demonstrating that increased customization does not always equate to meaningful inclusion.

Research has underlined the psychological and experiential stakes of these design choices. Han and Ho [26] investigated how players engage with avatar customization systems as a means of exploring and expressing gender identity. Through semi-structured interviews with 20 participants of diverse gender backgrounds, the researchers identified three key functions of avatar design: navigating and negotiating gender norms, symbolizing self-identity, and enabling safe gender experimentation. Their findings suggest that even within systems constrained by binary options, players find creative ways to embody a range of identities. These insights highlight the potential of avatar customization as both a technical feature and a psychologically meaningful tool for identity work. Further supporting this view, Morgan et al. [27] conducted a mixed-method study to explore how transgender and gender-diverse (TGD) young people use avatars in video games to explore and affirm their gender identities. Drawing on focus groups with TGD participants, the study found that avatar customization features, such as body shape, pronouns, clothing, and voice, played a central role in supporting emotional safety and identity expression. Participants reported greater enjoyment and comfort in games that allowed flexible representation, while restrictive or binary systems were associated with feelings of exclusion and dysphoria. These findings underline the importance of inclusive customization tools in promoting psychological well-being and self-affirmation.

These examples highlight a central tension in avatar design: while customization offers freedom, the constraints of design (i.e., what is made available or excluded) shape the range of identities players can express. When players are able to create avatars that reflect their lived or aspirational identities, particularly non-binary, queer, or gender-diverse avatars, they often report stronger identification, higher emotional safety, and more positive gaming experiences [9, 28]. Conversely, when customization tools reinforce normative aesthetics or exclude marginalized identities, they can lead to alienation, misrepresentation, or erasure.

2.2.3 Race, intersectionality, and cultural framing

These dynamics of inclusion and exclusion become more complex when considering race, ethnicity, and their intersections with other identity dimensions. While gender customization has made notable advancements, recent industry efforts have also started to focus on race and cultural identity. This shift is prompting a broader rethinking of how avatar design can better reflect diverse player experiences. However, many games still follow longstanding defaults in character representation, often centering white, male avatars as the normative baseline. As Nakamura [29] has argued, virtual characters are not neutral; they are coded constructs that reflect and reinforce societal structures of racial power and inequality. This is especially evident in role-playing games and fantasy titles, where darker skin tones are frequently linked to "tribal" or "monstrous" races. These portrayals reinforce associations of nonwhite bodies with exoticism or savagery. These aesthetic codes, though rarely explicit, are deeply embedded in design logic and continue to marginalize certain *identities*.

Even when customization options appear more inclusive, the underlying issue continues in more subtle ways. Leonard [30] coined the term "cosmetic diversity" to describe avatar options that provide superficial modifications, such as skin tone, but do not include corresponding facial features, hairstyles, or cultural markers. These missing elements prevent players of color from fully identifying with their avatars. This issue remains visible in contemporary titles like Elden Ring, which offers a wide range of skin tones in its character creator but provides a limited selection of hairstyles that predominantly reflect Eurocentric styles (see **Figure 1**). The absence of textured or Afro hair types exemplifies how certain identities are still not fully envisioned within the framework of character creation, even when representation appears to have advanced. Research into players' experiences confirms how these omissions impact identity expression. In a qualitative study of Australian gamers from diverse racial, gender, and sexual backgrounds, Phillips [31] describes how participants

Figure 1.
Limited representation of non-Eurocentric hairstyles in Elden Ring's avatar customization system.

reported not only aesthetic disappointments but also emotionally dissonant moments of erasure. Although individual identity traits might be available, their inability to be meaningfully combined often signals to players that some identities are not meant to coexist in the game's imagined world. This highlights one limit: customization systems claim to offer the freedom to "be anyone," yet they are constrained by what the system can visually and narratively support.

Intersectionality, as a design principle, remains largely underdeveloped in most games. While individual aspects of identity, such as race, gender, and body type, may now be available in character editors, the combinatory logic often privileges normative pairings. For example, feminine-coded avatars may be restricted to slim body types, or darker skin tones may not be accompanied by culturally appropriate features. These constraints are not merely technical oversights; they reflect deeper normative assumptions about which bodies are imagined as viable within game worlds. The illusion of freedom becomes apparent in such design choices, where the ability to express multifaceted identities is compromised by a default logic still anchored in whiteness, thinness, and heteronormativity. These dynamics make it especially important to examine how intentional representation can work differently. In Deathloop (2021), the decision to center two Black protagonists, Colt and Julianna, was not limited to skin tone or voice acting but extended to the narrative structure and characterization itself. This kind of design choice stands in contrast to cosmetic inclusion, signaling a shift toward more integrated and meaningful representation. Jarrell and Peillard [32] provides support for the value of such representation: in their study, participants played a short 2D game where they embodied avatars coded with marginalized, intersectional identities, including Black women. After gameplay, those participants were significantly less likely to exhibit racial or gender bias when evaluating a fictional job candidate. The researchers concluded that even brief interactions with diverse avatars can interrupt implicit biases and reshape social perception.

Representation in games has effects beyond visual recognition; it can reshape affective and cognitive orientations toward real-world others. When characters like Colt or Julianna are not just present but are well-developed and emotionally complex, they offer players more than diversity in the display. They provide opportunities for perspective-taking, identification, and potential shifts in empathy. In this regard, Deathloop reflects a design trend and exemplifies the kind of narrative and psychological engagement that research identifies as essential for dismantling bias. However, the fact that such gains remain the exception rather than the norm reflects an ongoing tension in game development between market-driven diversity and structural transformation. As Ruberg and Shaw [33] has argued, representation in games often begins and ends with visibility. Surface-level diversity, without changes to how characters function narratively, mechanically, or relationally, risks reinforcing existing hierarchies under the guise of inclusion. For true intersectional design, it is not enough to simply offer a wide array of identity traits; these traits must also shape the avatar's experience in the game environment. This includes influencing dialog, interactions, and gameplay mechanics, ensuring that representation is not just visible but meaningfully integrated into the game experience. This deeper form of inclusion is what Gray [34] documents in their ethnographic research on Black gamers. Many of these gamers engage with games critically and creatively. They push back against marginalizing structures by constructing their own forms of identity, performance, and community. Their work shifts the focus from developers to players. It highlights the ways in which marginalized communities create counter-narratives and affirming play practices in response to structural erasure.

The discussion of race, intersectionality, and cultural framing in avatar design reveals that inclusion in video games remains as much about structure as it is about visibility. While some titles acknowledge diversity, the continued presence of normative design defaults, coupled with limited support for intersecting identities, indicates that achieving true representational equity demands both aesthetic variation and systemic change. It is only through a more intersectional and culturally aware approach that avatar design can begin to reflect the full spectrum of player identities. The design choice between predefined and fully customizable avatars has significant consequences for how players engage emotionally, cognitively, and behaviorally with their digital counterparts. Fully customizable avatars invite projection and personalization, encouraging players to craft identities that resonate with who they are or who they wish to become. Studies on the Proteus Effect [20] have shown that these self-representations can influence player behavior and self-perception, subtly reshaping how individuals act within and beyond the game space. Conversely, predefined avatars offer curated, narratively rich experiences, where the player is invited not to embody the character but to empathize with them. While this can support deep emotional engagement, it can also lead to ludonarrative dissonance when the gameplay mechanics contradict the character's portrayed identity. In Uncharted, for example, the disjunction between Nathan Drake's charming vulnerability in cutscenes and his relentless violence during gameplay may weaken the player's identification, creating cognitive friction. However, when narrative and gameplay align, as seen in God of War: Ragnarök, where Kratos's emotional growth is mirrored in evolving combat systems and cooperative play, the result is a powerful sense of ludonarrative harmony. More than just a medium for play, the avatar stands at the heart of identification, projection, and meaning-making. Yet, this process of player engagement does not occur in isolation. It unfolds in an environment populated by other agents; some scripted, some reactive, and some emotionally expressive. To understand the full scope of how players experience virtual characters in games, we must now turn to those others: the non-player characters whose design, behavior, and presence shape how players interpret, navigate, and emotionally invest in virtual environments.

3. Non-player characters: From scripted props to social agents

NPCs have evolved from scripted virtual characters into dynamic agents that play a crucial role in the player's experience. In contemporary video games, NPCs do more than populate the environment. They contribute to world-building, drive narrative progression, serve as emotional and social mirrors to the player's journey, and even function as gameplay mechanics, as seen in the Shin Megami Tensei: Persona series. Their design, which includes appearance, behavior, and interactivity, significantly influences how players perceive the game environment and their place within it. NPCs, unlike avatars controlled by the player, are perceived as external entities whose roles and functions are determined through observation. Players do not inhabit NPCs but encounter them in a context where meaning arises from what they do, how they behave, and how they fit within the game's narrative and gameplay structure. These functions, whether narrative, mechanical, or social, shape how players interpret and emotionally engage with NPCs. An NPC's role as a mentor, threat, companion, or bystander shapes player expectations and guides their attention and behavior. For this reason, clarity and coherence in role-function signaling are essential to maintaining immersion. Designing NPCs is a distinct challenge from designing avatars. Avatars should enable identification and agency, while NPCs need to facilitate recognition, interpretation, and interaction. Their success depends on how convincingly they fulfill their role, how understandable their behavior is, and how consistent they appear within the logic of the game world. Poorly designed NPCs can disrupt immersion, confuse the player, or break narrative continuity. By contrast, well-conceived NPCs enrich the player experience by reinforcing the believability of the game environment, providing emotional depth, and supporting meaningful gameplay interactions.

This section explores the psychological and experiential dimensions of NPC design by focusing on two key design parameters: appearance and behavior. First, it examines how visual features influence players' immediate perceptions, expectations, and judgments of NPCs. Then, it analyzes how behavioral patterns, from scripted routines to advanced AI systems, shape believability, emotional engagement, and social interpretation. Finally, it considers how recent innovations in artificial intelligence are expanding the expressive range of NPCs, particularly through human-like nonverbal and verbal interactions.

3.1 NPCs visual design: Appearance and perception

In complex, densely populated virtual environments, players must continually discern which NPCs warrant attention and which serve merely as atmospheric background. Players often rely on mental models and stereotypes to form initial expectations and judgments about NPCs [35]. These cognitive frameworks, shaped by prior experiences and cultural conditioning, allow players to quickly categorize characters based on visual and contextual cues. The visual design of NPCs, such as their appearance, attire, and posture, activates these existing mental models, influencing players' expectations about their behaviors and roles within the game. This process allows players to allocate attention more efficiently and navigate the environment with greater fluency. However, these mental shortcuts can also perpetuate biases and reinforce stereotypes if not thoughtfully designed.

Warpefelt [35] conducted an experiment to investigate players' expectations of NPCs based on their appearance. Participants were shown static images of NPCs from various game genres and asked to assign each character a likely social function, such as merchant, guard, or antagonist, along with a rationale for their choice. Participants relied on visual attributes, such as apparel, facial expression, and body posture, to make these judgments. The results revealed a strong match between design intention and player expectation, emphasizing the role of visual-role congruence in supporting intuitive gameplay. When appearance and function align, players require less trial-and-error interaction, and the virtual environment becomes more legible as a social system. Additionally, Rogers et al. [36] proposed a framework to design NPCs' appearance, focusing on narrative roles such as mentor, companion, and enemy. Their study demonstrated that players can accurately identify these roles based on visual cues, highlighting the effectiveness of stereotypical visual design in conveying character function. However, the same perceptual shortcuts that support efficiency can also convey bias. Pradantyo et al. [37] explored how visual features, including body type, skin tone, and clothing, affect player evaluations of NPCs. Using a within-subjects design, participants were exposed to the appearance of multiple video game antagonists and then asked to evaluate each one using a morality questionnaire and to indicate which features influenced their ratings. The findings revealed significant stereotype-driven effects: age, skin color, skin conditions, and even tattoos were disproportionately perceived as markers of immorality or untrustworthiness, even in the absence of behavioral or narrative context. These results demonstrate that players bring culturally learned heuristics and biases into gameplay, meaning that visual design choices can unintentionally reinforce real-world stereotypes in virtual contexts. In a study by de Freitas et al. [38], players assessed how features from virtual characters' appearance influenced their perceptions in an interactive narrative game. Participants evaluated characters based on traits such as temper, clothing, and behavior. The study revealed that visual elements, like being well or poorly dressed, significantly influenced participants' perceptions of honesty and kindness. This underlines the importance of aligning character appearance with intended narrative roles to guide player judgments. In games, players are predisposed to form rapid judgments based on minimal visual input, a process that persists in virtual spaces, where interaction decisions must often be made instantly. These impression-forming mechanisms are shaped by the character's visual features as well as environmental cues, camera framing, and genre conventions [39, 40]. When an NPC's appearance matches its intended narrative or ludic function, such as a healer wearing robes surrounded by potions, players experience perceptual ease and narrative coherence. Conversely, a gap between appearance and function can create friction, momentarily interrupting immersion or producing hesitation.

Examples from open-world games illustrate the necessity of these design choices. In Assassin's Creed Unity (2014), densely populated historical settings contribute to visual richness, yet the abundance of visually similar NPCs dilutes the player's ability to intuit who can be interacted with (see **Figure 2**). This often requires reliance on interface prompts, which can disrupt immersion. In contrast, games like Skyrim and The Witcher 3 (2015) utilize a combination of attire, posture, and spatial anchoring to signal the importance of NPCs, facilitating a more seamless interpretive process. Guards stand in formation with weapons drawn, traders occupy well-marked stalls, and quest-givers adopt distinctive idle animations, all of which reinforce their gameplay roles. The visual design of NPCs works as a semiotic system that helps players interpret and act within the game environment. It provides immediate, surface-level cues about social function, emotional valence, and gameplay relevance. When thoughtfully constructed, this system enhances immersion and navigational efficiency. However, when visual tropes reflect unexamined stereotypes or when

Figure 2.
Navigating dense NPC crowds in Assassin's Creed Unity.

role-signaling is ambiguous, player understanding may falter or, worse, reinforce real-world biases. For this reason, appearance should be regarded as a tool of clarity, as well as a site of ethical and narrative responsibility.

3.2 NPCs' behavior: Believability, perceived intelligence, and emotion

3.2.1 Foundations of NPC behavior in video games

Early advancements in NPC behavior in video games primarily focused on improving player-NPC interactions, with a particular emphasis on enemy AI. Finite State Machines (FSMs) were among the first formal methods used to model NPC behaviors by defining discrete states and transitions triggered by player actions or game events. This approach laid the groundwork for more complex systems like behavior trees, which gained prominence in games such as Halo 2 (2004). Behavior trees organize NPC decision-making hierarchically, allowing for modular, flexible, and reusable behavior sequences that enhance the illusion of intelligence by making enemies appear more reactive and adaptive to player tactics. Building on this, the game F.E.A.R. (2005) introduced a significant technological breakthrough with Goal-Oriented Action Planning (GOAP). Unlike FSMs or behavior trees that rely on predefined states or sequences, GOAP enables NPCs to dynamically select actions based on changing tactical goals, such as taking cover, flanking, or forcing player movement with grenades. This adaptive decision-making allowed enemies to respond adequately or unpredictably to player behavior, creating a heightened sense of challenge, emotional engagement, and illusion of intelligence. While these early systems improved the quality of player-NPC interaction, NPC behaviors also needed to extend beyond direct player influence to sustain immersion within a believable virtual world. Players do not perceive the underlying AI systems themselves but experience the resulting sequences of actions. To maintain immersion, these actions must appear coherent, contextually appropriate, and believable, reflecting an internal logic that operates independently of the player's presence. Contemporary game design increasingly incorporates environment-oriented behaviors, where NPCs follow routines and respond to the virtual world around them. For example, in Skyrim, NPCs engage in daily cycles such as working, eating, and sleeping, contributing to a sense of embeddedness within a living ecosystem. In Red Dead Redemption 2 (2018), NPCs respond dynamically to environmental factors like weather and time of day while also adapting to player actions. These systems fluidly blend scripted routines with reactive states, supporting the illusion of intelligence and social consistency. By focusing on environment-driven behavior as well as player interaction, games encourage players to perceive NPCs not merely as functional components but as believable social agents inhabiting a coherent and evolving virtual world.

3.2.2 Player perception of NPCs: Believability and intelligence

Two associated dimensions shape how these behaviors are interpreted: believability and perceived intelligence. According to Poivet [41], building on a conceptual framework introduced by Gomes [42], believability reflects the alignment between a player's expectations and the observed behavior of an NPC. When this alignment is disrupted, such as when an NPC acts inconsistently with its social role, immersion can suffer. Perceived intelligence, as defined by Bartneck et al. [43], refers to a user's evaluation of an artificial agent's capacity to behave in a manner that appears competent, adaptive, and contextually appropriate. This includes both the logical coherence of the artificial agent's actions and their responsiveness to user input and environmental conditions. Poivet [41] expands on this definition in video games, linking perceived intelligence and believability to how players judge NPC behavior. In a broader context, Bartneck et al. [43] demonstrated that even minimal nonverbal cues influence how users assess an artificial agent's intelligence. In their study, robots that performed simple head or gaze movements were perceived as more competent and intentional than identical robots without such cues. Moussawi et al. [44] supported this view by showing that users' adoption of artificial agents depends strongly on perceived intelligence and anthropomorphism. Their work highlights that these attributions are not only based on technical complexity but also on whether the agent's behavior aligns meaningfully with users' expectations.

In video games, players tend to judge NPCs based on expectations shaped by genre conventions, character appearance, and personal stereotypes. As a result, NPCs may be perceived as unintelligent not due to a lack of underlying complexity, but because their behavior fails to align with the internal logic of the game as understood by the player. When NPCs behave in ways that appear inconsistent with the game world or unresponsive to player actions, they are often seen as rigid and unconvincing. Game designers have long worked empirically to enhance the illusion of intelligence in NPCs. Both technological advancements and design innovations have influenced how players evaluate NPC intelligence. For instance, Butcher and Griesemer [45] examined this phenomenon in the development of Halo 2, where enemy behavior was adjusted through game design parameters to increase perceived challenge. At the time, players commonly associated intelligence with difficulty and logical behavior. To test this, developers conducted playtests comparing two versions of the game: one in which enemies had lower health points and dealt less damage, and another where enemies had higher health and damage outputs. Participants in the latter condition consistently rated the enemies as more intelligent. These findings suggest that, within the context of player expectations at the time, increased difficulty was equated with greater competence and logic. Thus, the perception of intelligence was effectively reinforced through heightened challenge. Building on these insights, Poivet et al. [46] provided experimental evidence for how design parameter manipulation influences players' evaluation of NPCs. In a controlled study, enemy soldiers identical in appearance and weaponry were assigned different behavioral characteristics. Specifically, the researchers varied two parameters: shooting accuracy and mobility. Despite these being relatively simple adjustments, the changes led to marked differences in how players perceived the enemies. NPCs that pursued the player relentlessly, even when it put them at risk, were rated as more aggressive and hostile. These NPCs also provoked greater emotional responses, including heightened tension and fear. This study demonstrated that aggressiveness and threat can be effectively conveyed within expected enemy behavior boundaries without complex AI. Minor parameter changes alone can significantly influence affective engagement and perceived intelligence. Additionally, games like F.E.A.R. enhanced NPC communication through vocal cues, commonly called "barks," which provide players with direct indications of an NPC's current state or intent. These context-sensitive vocalizations help players anticipate enemy behavior and create a more immersive and believable experience by making NPCs appear more aware and reactive within the game world. Maintaining players' understanding of why and how an NPC chooses to perform an action is crucial for fostering both perceived intelligence and believability. When players can infer the intent behind NPC behaviors and recognize their logic, immersion is strengthened. Moreover, this transparency can itself become a powerful game mechanic, shaping player experience and emotional engagement. While perceived intelligence arises from inferred intent and responsiveness, believability depends primarily on behavioral coherence. As Poivet [41] notes, behaviors that violate visual or narrative expectations can disrupt immersion. However, not all such violations harm believability. In some cases, they support genre-specific goals. For instance, in Ready or Not (2023), a tactical SWAT-style shooter, an NPC with a civilian appearance may suddenly switch from passive to aggressive behavior. Although this violates conventional expectations of alignment between visual cues and roles, it reinforces the game's focus on tactical uncertainty. Within this context, unpredictability is not a flaw, but a mechanism designed to simulate the psychological stress of real-life interventions. The tension created by inconsistent behavioral signals enhances immersion, precisely because it forces players to stay alert and reevaluate situations dynamically.

3.2.3 Facial animation as emotional communication

Beyond functional actions, facial expressions convey affective and social signals that are crucial for shaping player interpretation, especially during verbal interactions. Amadou et al. [47] found that the realism of virtual agents' facial animation, particularly expressions and speech synchrony, influenced user perceptions of social presence and realism. Similarly, Fukayama et al. [48] demonstrated that subtle gaze behavior shapes user impressions and perceptions of attentiveness, reinforcing engagement during conversations. These kinds of nonverbal behaviors help establish a sense of presence and emotional depth, activating social heuristics in the player's mind. Further support for the impact of such cues comes from Kätsyri et al. [49], who found that dynamic nonverbal expressions, like facial configuration and head position, shaped participants' empathic responses and personality judgments, and Torre et al. [50], who showed that expressive virtual faces triggered neural responses similar to those elicited by real human expressions. While these studies were not conducted within traditional video game environments, their findings align with player expectations of believable character interaction in narrative-driven games. A notable application of this principle is L.A. Noire (2011), which incorporates facial animation as a central gameplay mechanic. Players are required to observe NPCs' micro-expressions and subtle facial movements to determine whether they are lying during interrogations, making expressive realism not just aesthetic but essential for gameplay progression (see **Figure 3**). Similarly, Baldur's Gate 3 (2023) uses facial motion capture and nuanced dialog animation to support emotionally engaging interactions. Each major character is rendered with a high degree of facial expression, allowing players to respond to cues like furrowed brows or averted gazes. Torre et al. [50] showed that expressive facial speech animation enhances the emotional clarity of virtual agents. In this context, players interpret NPCs as emotionally coherent social agents because facial behavior aligns with the narrative tone. Moser et al. [51] also found that expressive avatar faces increase neural activity in emotion-related brain areas, enhancing involvement. These findings suggest players may form deeper emotional connections when visual cues support continuous interpretations of intent and mood. As a result, even secondary characters in Baldur's Gate 3 often appear emotionally complex, reinforcing the perception of intelligence and depth. Ultimately, facial animation functions as a visual enhancement as well as a crucial mechanism for narrative immersion and psychological engagement.

NPC behavior is not solely a functional system but also a medium of psychological interpretation. Players assess virtual characters based on what they do, how and when they act, and whether those actions align with the game's narrative logic and interactive context. When behavior is coherent, expressive, and responsive, players are more inclined to attribute autonomy, emotional depth, and intelligence. When behavior is inconsistent or misaligned with the NPC's intended role, even highly detailed characters may be perceived as artificial or irrelevant. The design challenge lies in achieving a balance between behavioral complexity and interpretability. Systemically generated actions must work as intended, be comprehensible to the player, and be meaningful in the context of the game's diegetic world. As Poivet [41] argues, creating NPCs that are

Figure 3.
Facial animation is a core gameplay mechanic in L.A. Noire.

perceived as both believable and intelligent requires more than technical sophistication. It demands an understanding of player expectations and a careful orchestration of behavior that supports immersion, emotional engagement, and narrative coherence.

3.3 The AI revolution: Toward conversational and human-like NPCs

Recent advances in artificial intelligence are significantly reshaping how NPCs are designed and experienced. Moving beyond static, rule-based systems, modern AI techniques enable NPCs to exhibit context-sensitive, believable behaviors that enhance narrative depth and gameplay immersion. Two key dimensions: verbal and nonverbal behaviors, could benefit from these advancements. As discussed in the previous section, NPC behaviors contribute directly to their overall perceived intelligence and believability. In this section, we examine how cutting-edge AI tools and methods are enriching these two domains of NPC design.

3.3.1 Verbal behavior and dialog systems

Verbal interaction has seen significant improvements through natural language processing and generative models, which enable NPCs to engage in dynamic, context-aware dialog. Unlike traditional dialog trees that constrain player choice, large language models such as BERT and ChatGPT, in some cases, have shown possibilities to facilitate free-form interactions that feel responsive and natural. For instance, recent community-driven projects have demonstrated this potential: in Skyrim, the Herika mod integrates a language model to enable a companion NPC to engage in context-aware, spoken conversation; similarly, in Stardew Valley (2016) and Mount and Blade II: Bannerlord (2008), modders connected NPCs to OpenAI's API to support free-form dialog that reacts to player input in more natural and varied ways [52]. Feedback from the distinct game communities has been promising, highlighting the potential of integrating emotional context into AI dialog to enable NPCs to respond empathetically and appropriately to player input.

This emphasis on the potential benefits for NPCs to engage naturally with players is echoed in studies exploring user experiences with conversational agents. In a game context, the study of Poivet et al. [53] investigated how conversational agent roles and communication styles shape user experience. In a detective game setting, the researchers manipulated both the narrative role of the NPC (witness versus suspect) and their communication style (aggressive versus cooperative). While all conditions were rated as generally believable due to the fluent natural language, the alignment between role and style had a strong impact on player perception. Aggressive suspects were seen as engaging and believable, whereas aggressive witnesses created a sense of dissonance and irritation. This demonstrates that fluency alone is insufficient: verbal behavior must be coherent with narrative expectations to support immersion. The findings highlight that effective verbal AI depends on both language quality and emotional tone, narrative consistency, and sensitivity to player expectations.

3.3.2 Nonverbal behavior for human-like NPCs

The second axis of advancement focuses on nonverbal behavior, particularly relevant in competitive and cooperative multiplayer contexts, where NPCs or bots must perform actions that appear intentional, adaptive, and human-like. Traditional state machine AI often falls short of producing player-like movement and decision-making. In contrast, reinforcement learning and imitation learning allow agents to learn complex behavior patterns through trial and error or demonstration. Notably, OpenAI Five showcased how self-play could train bots to master Dota 2 (2013) at a high level, adapting strategies in real time to match shifting gameplay conditions.

Togelius et al. [54] argues that such adaptive AI can lead to more engaging and believable interactions, especially in dynamic environments where scripted behaviors fail to anticipate player creativity. The goal is not just functional competence but the appearance of situational awareness. This aligns with research demonstrating that players prefer bots that mimic human variability, including imperfections, over perfectly optimized, robotic counterparts. These bots are rated as more enjoyable and fairer, precisely because they feel like real opponents with unique personalities and strategies [55]. Gran Turismo 7 (2022) further illustrates this trend by using player data to generate AI "ghost" drivers that replicate individual driving styles, extending the illusion of presence even when friends are offline. This approach enhances both competition and immersion. As noted in studies on social presence in virtual agents, even subtle cues such as appropriate timing, emotional congruence, and turn-taking can signal social presence and intelligence in virtual agents. These behaviors are essential to both gameplay mechanics and the creation of emotionally resonant, human-like characters, which open up new opportunities for game mechanics [56].

Despite these advances, implementing AI in NPC design presents significant challenges. The technology is often computationally intensive, raising concerns about energy consumption and scalability. It also requires technical expertise and infrastructure that may be difficult to integrate into already-strained game production pipelines. Most critically, AI systems must be meaningfully aligned with game design goals to enhance rather than disrupt the player experience. However, as described above, navigating these constraints remains a challenge but a potential future breakthrough for the video game industry.

4. Conclusion

This chapter has examined how virtual characters contribute to player experience through the design of avatars and non-player characters. These characters are embedded in gameplay systems, narrative structures, and cultural contexts. Their impact depends on both technical implementation and how they align with players' expectations, emotions, and interpretations. Avatars function as self-representational agents shaped by customization, visual embodiment, and narrative framing. Identification can emerge through resemblance, aspiration, or narrative empathy. NPCs are experienced as external agents whose appearance and behavior guide players' attributions of intention, emotion, and social function. When appearance and function are aligned and behavior is coherent and responsive, players are more likely to perceive NPCs as believable and intelligent. Advances in artificial intelligence are further expanding the expressive range of NPCs while also raising challenges for narrative coherence and player interpretation.

Designing virtual characters requires anticipating how players perceive and respond to them. User research should be integrated throughout development to address usability and to investigate how players interpret predefined avatars, form mental models of NPCs, and emotionally engage with character behavior. This supports early identification of potential ludonarrative dissonance and helps ensure that character behavior aligns with narrative intent. A player-centered approach that combines psychological theory with iterative testing is essential to creating virtual characters that are both meaningful and believable. In parallel, virtual characters shape player experience and offer researchers valuable tools for investigating psychological and social processes. They provide a controlled yet dynamic environment for studying emotional engagement, the influence of appearance on perception, the persistence of social stereotypes, and the mechanisms of identification with artificial agents. Insights from such research can inform design practices and contribute to the broader understanding of human-computer interaction.

Future research should further explore how players' individual characteristics, such as gender, skin color, and cultural background, influence their perceptions and evaluations of virtual characters, particularly NPCs. While these factors have been extensively considered in the context of avatar customization and identification, their role in shaping expectations and interpretations of NPCs remains underexplored. Investigating these dynamics is essential for fostering inclusive and psychologically grounded character design. At the same time, emerging technologies are transforming how virtual characters are created and experienced. Generative AI, particularly in the form of image-based models, enables the creation of highly personalized avatars that can more accurately reflect players' identities and support stronger identification. These tools offer new possibilities for enhancing diversity and representation, but their psychological impact and user acceptance require careful study. Advances in photorealistic rendering, including techniques such as Gaussian splatting, add another dimension to this evolving landscape. By increasing visual realism, these methods may significantly influence immersion, emotional engagement, and cognitive responses to both avatars and NPCs. Games like *Detroit: Become Human* (2018) and the *Death Stranding* series have already shown how the use of real actors' likenesses can shape players' empathy and perceptions. As players begin to control photorealistic avatars modeled on celebrities or themselves, new research avenues emerge around topics such as parasocial relationships, social presence, and the boundaries between fiction and reality. These technological and psychological developments highlight the need for interdisciplinary approaches that integrate design practice, user research, and cognitive science. Understanding how players respond to increasingly realistic and personalized virtual characters will be essential for creating experiences that are emotionally compelling, socially responsible, and culturally meaningful.

Acknowledgements

This research was supported by Stage11. The author declares no conflict of interest.

Author details

Remi Poivet
Independent Researcher, Paris, France

*Address all correspondence to: remipoivet@yahoo.fr

References

[1] Schroeder R, Axelsson A-S, editors. Avatars at Work and Play: Collaboration and Interaction in Shared Virtual Environments. Dordrecht: Springer; 2006. DOI: 10.1007/1-4020-3898-4

[2] McMahan A. Immersion, engagement, and presence: A method for analyzing 3-D video games. In: Wolf MJP, Perron B, editors. The Video Game Theory Reader. New York: Routledge; 2003. pp. 67-86. DOI: 10.4324/9780203700457-4

[3] Yee N. The psychology of massively multi-user online role-playing games: Motivations, emotional investment, relationships and problematic usage. In: Schroeder R, Axelsson A-S, editors. Avatars at Work and Play: Collaboration and Interaction in Shared Virtual Environments. Dordrecht: Springer; 2006. pp. 187-207. DOI: 10.1007/1-4020-3898-4_9

[4] Vorderer P, Klimmt C, Ritterfeld U. Enjoyment: At the heart of media entertainment. Communication Theory. 2004;**14**(4):388-408. DOI: 10.1111/j.1468-2885.2004.tb00321.x

[5] Bartle RA. Designing Virtual Worlds. Indianapolis: New Riders; 2004. DOI: 10.5555/1196681

[6] Birk MV, Mandryk RL. Exploring emotional attachment to game characters. In: Proceedings of the Annual Symposium on Computer-Human Interaction in Play. New York: ACM; 2019. pp. 313-324. DOI: 10.1145/3311350.3347169

[7] Koster R. A Theory of Fun for Game Design. 2nd ed. Sebastopol: O'Reilly Media; 2013. DOI: 10.5555/2601678

[8] Lombard M, Ditton T. At the heart of it all: The concept of presence. Journal of Computer-Mediated Communication. 1997;**3**(2). DOI: 10.1111/j.1083-6101.1997.tb00072.x

[9] Shaw A. Gaming at the Edge: Sexuality and Gender at the Margins of Gamer Culture. Minneapolis: University of Minnesota Press; 2014. DOI: 10.5749/minnesota/9780816693153.001.0001

[10] Giddens A. Modernity and Self-Identity: Self and Society in the Late Modern Age. Stanford: Stanford University Press; 1991

[11] Klimmt C, Hefner D, Vorderer P. The video game experience as "true" identification: A theory of enjoyable alterations of players' self-perception. Communication Theory. 2009;**19**(4):351-373. DOI: 10.1111/j.1468-2885.2009.01347.x

[12] Van Looy J, Courtois C, De Vocht M, De Marez L. Player identification in online games: Validation of a scale for measuring identification in MMOGs. Media Psychology. 2012;**15**(2):197-221. DOI: 10.1080/15213269.2012.674917

[13] Turkay S, Kinzer CK. The effects of avatar-based customization on player identification. International Journal of Gaming and Computer-Mediated Simulations. 2014;**6**(1):1-25. DOI: 10.4018/ijgcms.2014010101

[14] Birk MV, Atkins C, Bowey JT, Mandryk RL. Fostering intrinsic motivation through avatar identification in digital games. In: Proceedings of the 2016 CHI Conference on Human Factors in Computing Systems; 7-12 May 2016; San Jose, CA. New York: ACM; 2016. pp. 2982-2995. DOI: 10.1145/2858036.2858062

[15] Hocking C. Ludonarrative dissonance in BioShock: The problem of what the game is about. Click Nothing Blog. 2007. Available from: https://clicknothing.typepad.com/click_nothing/2007/10/ludonarrative-d.html

[16] Seraphine F. Towards a ludonarrative model: Analyzing conflict in video game narrative. Game Studies. 2016;**16**(2). Available from: https://gamestudies.org/1602/articles/seraphine

[17] Dennin K, Burton A. Experiential play as an analytical framework: Empathetic and grating queerness in The Last of Us Part II. Game Studies. 2023;**23**(2). Available from: https://gamestudies.org/2302/articles/denninburton

[18] Matulef J. Uncharted 4: A thief's end review. Eurogamer. 2016. Available from: https://www.eurogamer.net/uncharted-4-a-thiefs-end-review

[19] Rusch DC. Mechanisms of the soul: Tackling the human condition in videogames. In: Proceedings of DiGRA 2009: Breaking New Ground: Innovation in Games, Play, Practice and Theory; 1-4 September 2009; London, UK. Tampere, Finland: DiGRA; 2009. DOI: 10.26503/dl.v2009i1.488

[20] Yee N, Bailenson J. The Proteus effect: The effect of transformed self-representation on behavior. Human Communication Research. 2007;**33**(3):271-290. DOI: 10.1111/j.1468-2958.2007.00299.x

[21] Fox J, Bailenson JN, Tricase L. The embodiment of sexualized virtual selves: The Proteus effect and experiences of self-objectification via avatars. Computers in Human Behavior. 2013;**29**(3):930-938. DOI: 10.1016/j.chb.2012.12.027

[22] Peck TC, Seinfeld S, Aglioti SM, Slater M. Putting yourself in the skin of a black avatar reduces implicit racial bias. Consciousness and Cognition. 2013;**22**(3):779-787. DOI: 10.1016/j.concog.2013.04.016

[23] Ratan RA, Santa Cruz M, Vorderer P. Multitasking, presence & self-presence on the Wii. In: Proceedings of the 10th Annual International Workshop on Presence (PRESENCE 2007); 25-27 October 2007; Barcelona, Spain. Cleveland, OH: International Society for Presence Research (ISPR); 2007. pp. 167-174

[24] Li BJ, Lwin MO, Jung Y. Wii, myself, and size: The influence of Proteus effect and stereotype threat on overweight children's exercise motivation and behavior in exergames. Games for Health Journal. 2014;**3**(1):40-48. DOI: 10.1089/g4h.2013.0081

[25] TIME. How Lara Croft became a feminist icon. Time Magazine. 2018. Available from: https://time.com/longform/lara-croft-feminist-icon/

[26] Han Y, Ho X. "More than just playing a character": Gender exploration and expression in avatar customization. Games Cult. 2024. pp. 1-23. DOI: 10.1177/15554120241307982

[27] Morgan H, O'Donovan A, Almeida R, Lin A, Perry Y. The role of the avatar in gaming for trans and gender diverse young people. International Journal of Environmental Research and Public Health. 2020;**17**(22):8617. DOI: 10.3390/ijerph17228617

[28] Gray KL. Race, Gender, and Deviance in Xbox Live: Theoretical Perspectives from the Virtual Margins. New York: Routledge; 2014. DOI: 10.4324/9781315721378

[29] Nakamura L. Cybertypes: Race, Ethnicity, and Identity on the Internet. New York: Routledge; 2002

[30] Leonard D. High tech blackface: Race, sports video games and becoming the other. Intelligent Agent. 2004;**4**(4.2):1-6. Available from: https://www.intelligentagent.com/archive/IA4_4gamingleonard.pdf

[31] Phillips MJ. Hiding in the shadows: A qualitative exploration of women gamers' identities and perceptions of the video gaming context. SN Social Sciences. 2025;**4**:181. DOI: 10.1007/s43545-024-00980-z

[32] Jarrell M, Peillard E. Using intersectional representation & embodied identification in standard video game play to reduce societal biases. In: Proceedings of the 2021 CHI Conference on Human Factors in Computing Systems. New York, NY: Association for Computing Machinery (ACM); 2021. pp. 1-13. DOI: 10.1145/3411764.3445161

[33] Ruberg B, Shaw A, editors. Queer Game Studies. Minneapolis: University of Minnesota Press; 2017

[34] Gray KL. Intersectional Tech: Black Users in Digital Gaming. Baton Rouge: Louisiana State University Press; 2020

[35] Warpefelt H. Cues and insinuations: Indicating affordances of non-player character using visual indicators. In: Proceedings of DiGRA 2015 Conference. Tampere, Finland: DiGRA; 2015. DOI: 10.26503/dl.v2015i1.713

[36] Rogers K, Subramonyam H, Leung R. Character design for narrative roles in games: An empirical approach. In: Proceedings of the 2018 CHI Conference on Human Factors in Computing Systems. New York, NY: Association for Computing Machinery (ACM); 2018. pp. 1-13. DOI: 10.1145/3173574.3173844

[37] Pradantyo HR, Nakamura A, Ichikawa D. Stereotypes in character design: The impact of visual appearance on moral judgment in video games. Entertainment Computing. 2021;**36**:100397. DOI: 10.1016/j.entcom.2020.100397

[38] de Freitas S, Rebolledo-Mendez G, Liarokapis F, Magoulas GD, Poulovassilis A. Experiential factors in player perception of character traits in narrative games. International Journal of Human Computer Studies. 2023;**175**:103122. DOI: 10.1016/j.ijhcs.2023.103122

[39] Ferstl Y, Kokkinara E, McDonnell R. Facial features of non-player creatures can influence moral decisions in video games. ACM Transactions on Applied Perception. 2017;**15**(1):1-12. DOI: 10.1145/3129561

[40] Zibrek K, Kokkinara E, McDonnell R. Don't stand so close to me: Investigating the effect of control on the appeal of virtual humans using immersion and a proximity-based behavioral task. In: Proceedings of the 2015 ACM SIGGRAPH Symposium on Interactive 3D Graphics and Games. 2015. pp. 1-8. DOI: 10.1145/3119881.3119887

[41] Poivet R. Virtual agents' perceived intelligence and believability in video games: Exploring the relation between design factors and players' expectations [doctoral dissertation]. Paris: Sorbonne Université; 2023

[42] Gomes AS. Exploring the believability of NPC presentation and behavior [master's thesis]. Uppsala: Uppsala University; 2016

[43] Bartneck C, Kulic D, Croft E, Zoghbi S. Measurement instruments

for the anthropomorphism, animacy, likeability, perceived intelligence, and perceived safety of robots. International Journal of Social Robotics. 2009;**1**(1):71-81. DOI: 10.1007/s12369-008-0001-3

[44] Moussawi S, Koufaris M, Benbunan-Fich R. How perceptions of intelligence and anthropomorphism affect adoption of personal intelligent agents. Electronic Markets. 2021;**31**(2):343-364. DOI: 10.1007/s12525-020-00426-2

[45] Butcher J, Griesemer J. Halo 2: Building the AI [GDC Presentation]. 2004

[46] Poivet R, de Lagarde A, Pelachaud C, Auvray M. Evaluation of virtual agents' hostility in video games. IEEE Transactions on Affective Computing. 2024;**15**(4):1949-1961. DOI: 10.1109/TAFFC.2024.3390400

[47] Amadou A, Trico M, Malpaire M, Tarpin-Bernard F. Evaluating the impact of anthropomorphism and verbal interaction on users' perception of a virtual agent in facilitating self-disclosure. Frontiers in Virtual Reality. 2023;**4**:1061890. DOI: 10.3389/frvir.2023.1061890

[48] Fukayama A, Ohno T, Mukawa N, Sawaki M, Hagita N. Messages embedded in gaze of interface agents—Impression management with agent's gaze. In: Proceedings of the SIGCHI Conference on Human Factors in Computing Systems. New York: ACM; 2002. pp. 41-48. DOI: 10.1145/503376.503385

[49] Kätsyri J, de Gelder B, Takala T. Virtual faces evoke only a weak uncanny valley effect: An empirical investigation with controlled virtual face images. Perception. 2019;**48**(10):968-991. DOI: 10.1177/0301006619869134

[50] Torre I, Carrigan E, McDonnell R, Domijan K, McCabe K, Harte N. The effect of multimodal emotional expression and agent appearance on trust in human-agent interaction. In: Proceedings of the 12th ACM SIGGRAPH Conference on Motion, Interaction and Games. New York: ACM; 2019. pp. 1-6. DOI: 10.1145/3359566.3360065

[51] Moser E, Derntl B, Robinson S, Fink B, Gur RC, Grammer K. Amygdala activation at 3T in response to human and avatar facial expressions of emotions. Journal of Neuroscience Methods. 2007;**161**(1):126-133. DOI: 10.1016/j.jneumeth.2006.10.016

[52] The Verge. Modders are Giving Stardew Valley and Skyrim AI Companions—And It Actually Works [Internet]. 2024. Available from: https://www.theverge.com/2024/10/17/24268007/modders-ai-companions-stardew-valley-skyrim

[53] Poivet R, Lopez Malet M, Pelachaud C, Auvray M. The influence of conversational agents' role and communication style on user experience. Frontiers in Psychology. 2023;**14**:1266186. DOI: 10.3389/fpsyg.2023.1266186

[54] Togelius J, Yannakakis GN, Stanley KO, Browne C. Procedural Content Generation in Games: A Textbook and an Overview of Current Research. Cham: Springer; 2016. DOI: 10.1007/978-3-319-42716-4

[55] Soni B, Hingston P. Bots trained to play like a human are more fun. In: 2008 IEEE International Joint Conference on Neural Networks (IEEE World Congress on Computational Intelligence). New York: IEEE; 2008. pp. 363-369. DOI: 10.1109/IJCNN.2008.4633818

[56] Skarbez R, Brooks FP, Whitton MC. A survey of presence and related concepts. ACM Computing Surveys. 2017;**50**(6):96:1-96:39. DOI: 10.1145/3134301

Section 2

Socio-Cultural Aspects of Gaming

Chapter 4

Games as a Social-Cultural Medium: Motivation, Community, and Disruptive Behavior

Ahmad Azadvar and Qianhui Ni

Abstract

This chapter explores the historical development and academic study of cross-cultural and social interactions in video games, from early multiplayer arcades to modern social gaming networks. Theoretical insights from game and media studies illuminate how video games function as a digital third place, promoting community-building, social capital, and participatory identity construction. Psychological perspectives on emotion, motivation, and social influence further explain the powerful attraction of interactive gaming environments. Additionally, this chapter critically analyzes both the positive aspects of community and friendship formation and the negative dimensions of player toxicity and social stress. Cross-cultural considerations highlight the similarities and differences in gaming experiences globally, emphasizing how virtual communities create transnational spaces for interaction and how local cultures perceive and contribute to the global gaming community. By synthesizing interdisciplinary research, including prominent theories and empirical studies, this chapter presents a picture of video games as dynamic social ecosystems.

Keywords: social gaming, cross-cultural interaction, game studies, psychological aspects of gaming, community dynamics, toxicity, gaming communities

1. Introduction

Video gaming is a global cultural phenomenon. Engaging billions across diverse societies, games serve not just as entertainment but as a social and cultural medium reflecting and influencing player values and behaviors. As gaming communities span countries and cultures, understanding how cultural contexts shape and receive gaming experiences is vital. This chapter examines the interplay between cultural factors and social gaming, focusing on psychological impacts and well-being. Exploring cross-cultural research and theory highlights how cultural norms, values, and structures influence motivations for play, interactions within communities, and their psychological effects. The discussion covers both positive aspects—like identity exploration, cognitive benefits, and social support—and negative outcomes—including addiction, stress, and online harassment. This chapter argues that while gaming is universal, its social and psychological dimensions are deeply embedded in cultural contexts.

2. History of social interactions in video games

This section traces the evolution of social interaction in video games, from early local multiplayers to today's complex, globally connected virtual communities. Examining the social dynamics of arcades, early home multiplayer, pioneering text-based virtual societies, and modern online communities reveals the inherent human drive for connection through play. Understanding this history underscores how video games consistently function as meaningful social spaces, shaping player identities and communities. This progression provides a foundation for theoretical frameworks in game and media studies, explaining the fundamental role of social gaming in contemporary digital culture.

2.1 Early multiplayer and arcade era (1970s–1980s)

The social dimension of video gaming began with early multiplayer titles and the rise of arcades in the 1970s and 1980s. Atari's Pong [1] established face-to-face competitive interaction [2]. The late 1970s and early 1980s saw video arcades become cultural hubs, particularly in North America and Japan [3]. Arcades served as social spaces where youth congregated, engaged in collective spectating, and participated in challenges, developing camaraderie and rivalry [4]. This shared experience cultivated an early gaming subculture with informal rules [5]. Japanese game centers remained all-ages social spaces beyond the 1980s, contrasting with the decline of Western arcades as home consoles gained popularity.

Complementing arcades, local home multiplayer emerged with consoles like the Atari 2600 (1977) and Nintendo Entertainment System (NES) [6], facilitating cooperative and competitive gameplay in domestic settings [7]. This "couch multiplayer" added a social layer to early console gaming, making titles like Super Mario Bros. [8] and Contra [9] shared pastimes.

Arcades functioned as "third places" for adolescents—public spaces distinct from home and school facilitating social interaction through play [10, 11]. Despite moral panics framing arcades negatively [12], research indicates they fostered peer communities and social skills rather than isolation [13, 14]. Retrospective analyses highlight arcades' role in identity formation and social learning [3]. By the late 1980s, gaming, whether in arcades or homes, was clearly understood to have a social dimension.

2.2 Dial-up and text-based worlds (1980s–1990s)

The late 1980s and early 1990s marked a shift with online multiplayer via dial-up and text interfaces. Before widespread internet, Bulletin Board Systems (BBSs) enabled remote communication and rudimentary multiplayer games like TradeWars 2002 [15, 16]. These early online games, despite primitive interfaces, facilitated social interactions, including alliances and rivalries, blending online and real-life dynamics [16]. Community message boards and chat functions further linked gaming and social discourse, creating tightly knit local communities.

Concurrently, Multi-User Dungeons (MUDs) introduced persistent virtual worlds [17]. MUD1 [18] pioneered real-time text-based interaction in shared environments. Throughout the 1980s, MUDs proliferated, offering cross-geographic social interactions through dial-up services. These text worlds, essentially chat rooms with gameplay, enabled rich social interactions, role-playing, and identity exploration [14]. Ethnographic studies documented deep friendships and relationships formed through text, suggesting the interface paradoxically encouraged candid communication [19].

Early MUD communities like MUD1 and LambdaMOO exemplified virtual societies with complex social dynamics, including friendships, cliques, conflict, and governance needs [20, 21]. Research showed that social interaction often superseded gameplay objectives, challenging the view of text worlds as isolating [19]. Users formed genuine connections rather than pursuing anonymous deception [19]. Intense social bonds sometimes extended to real life or caused conflict, highlighting the significance of these communities [20]. Parallel dial-up services like CompuServe and America Online (AOL) introduced graphical chat and games to a wider audience. By the late 1990s, millions engaged in online communication and gaming. The pioneering text-based worlds demonstrated play's capacity to facilitate community, friendships, and drama, laying the foundation for massively multiplayer online games.

2.3 Massively multiplayer online games (2000s)

The late 1990s and 2000s transformed social gaming with the advent of fully graphical Massively Multiplayer Online Games (MMOs), building on text-based predecessors to create persistent virtual worlds with vast populations. Titles like Ultima Online [22], EverQuest [23], and *World of Warcraft* [24] integrated social interaction into the core experience, building persistent communities.

In MMOs, players used avatars in open-ended fantasy or sci-fi (science fiction) worlds that evolved independently of individuals, enabling enduring social roles. Players formed guilds, built friendships and rivalries, and participated in in-game economies and cultures. Researchers viewed MMOs as "third places" analogous to traditional social spaces, used for informal interaction [25]. Studies showed MMOs functioned as virtual social hubs where players convened and formed bonds, often citing social context as a primary motivation [25].

Empirical research in the 2000s confirmed the social nature of MMOs. A survey of over 900 players documented strong friendships and romantic relationships formed virtually, highlighting camaraderie as a key motivator [26]. Online connections often extended offline. Many players engaged with preexisting social networks, using games to reinforce relationships.

Complex social structures emerged within these worlds. Guilds functioned as social organizations with hierarchies and collaborative goals, encouraging teamwork and leadership [27]. Persistent worlds with virtual economies and property were developed, introducing concepts like trade and virtual crime. Economists analyzed MMO economies, showing the real value of virtual goods and the emergence of trust systems e.g. [28].

MMOs also affected real-life relationships and support networks. Players found acceptance and community, especially those marginalized offline. Marriages and familial interactions occurred within MMOs, showing their capacity to lead to meaningful connections. In-game events like weddings solidified community bonds and demonstrated care. Studies indicated MMOs fostered bridging social capital (connecting diverse individuals) and bonding social capital (close friendships within subgroups) [25]. By the end of the 2000s, MMOs established a new paradigm of gaming as a community, characterized by complex social structures, economies, and relationships, laying the groundwork for future social gaming.

2.4 Social networks and modern online gaming (2010s–present)

The 2010s saw significant convergence between video games and social media, blurring platform lines. This era featured socially integrated designs, dominant sandbox and battle royale genres, exponential user-generated content, and game streaming.

Early in the decade, social network games like FarmVille [29] achieved massive popularity via social media (i.e., Facebook) integration [30]. Leveraging social mechanics for viral growth, these games showed the potential of existing networks for widespread social gaming, though also highlighting intrusive practices. FarmVille demonstrated non-traditional gamers' willingness to engage with games presented socially.

Concurrently, sandbox games like Minecraft [31] and Roblox [32] gained traction, encouraging player collaboration and content creation [33]. Minecraft provided a sandbox for collaborative building and practicing social skills. Roblox extended this by offering tools for users to create and share games, establishing a social ecosystem with hundreds of millions of users. This shift towards user-generated content made gaming a platform for social expression and collaboration.

The late 2010s saw massive online experiences transcend traditional genres. Fortnite (2017) evolved from battle royale into a social platform hosting live events and mass interaction for its young audience [34]. Its accessibility and social features like voice chat made it a virtual hangout space [34]. In-game events like concerts showed games' potential as mass social experiences [34]. Playing Fortnite for social reasons can expand social networks and improve well-being, particularly for individuals with disabilities [35].

Integrating live streaming platforms like Twitch [36] and YouTube Gaming transformed gaming into a spectator sport and social forum [37]. These platforms provided a venue for parasocial relationships and communities where viewers interacted in real time. Playing became a communal entertainment experience. This expansion of social gaming beyond the game instance highlighted a broader interconnected social ecosystem.

By the 2020s, video games themselves became primary social networks, especially for younger generations. Games evolved into connected platforms for interaction, content creation, and relationship building. The concept of "gamer" broadened to encompass diverse individuals engaging in gaming as a ubiquitous social activity. The trajectory from arcades to virtual lobbies demonstrates increasing sophistication in game-based social interaction, while retaining the core appeal of shared spaces for play and connection.

3. Theoretical perspectives from game and media studies

This section explores theoretical lenses from game and media studies that reflect the social dimensions of gaming, particularly through concepts like "third places," social capital, and participatory culture.

3.1 Games as third places

The concept of "third places"—informal public spaces distinct from home and work [10]—emphasizes accessibility, neutrality, and offering spontaneous social interaction and community [10, 38]. These spaces enhance belonging and social cohesion [10, 38].

Massively Multiplayer Online Games (MMOs) function as virtual counterparts to these spaces. MMOs like *World of Warcraft* mirror physical third places, supporting informal sociability, casual conversation, guild formation, and community identity beyond gameplay [25].

These virtual spaces share key characteristics of third places [10]:

- *Neutral Ground*: MMOs allow free entry/exit without formal obligations [25].

- *Leveler*: Avatars enable interaction on an egalitarian footing, reducing offline hierarchies [39].

- *Conversation*: Chat functionalities for ongoing dialog, often exceeding structured play [25].

- *Accessibility*: Games are often user-friendly, accommodating diverse players [40].

- *The Regulars*: Frequent players form community nuclei, establishing norms and welcoming newcomers [41].

- *Low Profile*: Virtual environments offer relaxed, informal atmospheres [25].

- *Playful Mood*: Gaming promotes enjoyment, a core element of third places [42].

- *Home Away from Home*: For dedicated players, these spaces provide familiar settings and a sense of belonging [43].

Scholarly work reinforces MMOs as third places in the digital age, facilitating social interaction and community-building [25, 38]. Intricate social interactions in MMOs underscore their role as dynamic social spaces where relationships are forged [39].

The significance of third places extends to overall quality of life [44]. Research shows a positive link between accessible third places and perceived community quality [44]. Virtual third places are crucial for social support networks and well-being in the digital realm.

In sum, MMOs and similar platforms act as contemporary third places, providing spaces for informal social interaction, community cultivation, and personal fulfillment in a digital society. Their role in forming connections and enhancing quality of life grows as virtual environments evolve.

3.2 Social capital and communities

Drawing on sociological work [45], social capital involves networks, norms, and trust enabling coordination for mutual benefit. In online gaming, especially Multiplayer Online Role-Playing Games (MMORPGs), social capital emerges from player relationships and communities [25].

3.2.1 Bonding and bridging social capital in gaming communities

Social capital in gaming communities includes bonding and bridging ties [45, 46]. Bonding capital refers to strong connections offering emotional support [45]. Bridging capital involves weaker ties for new information and perspectives [45].

Gaming community participation often reinforces bonding capital. Cohesive groups provide belonging, shared identity, and mutual support [25, 47]. As "third places" [25], MMORPGs contribute to sustained interaction leading to close communities and relationships, mirroring offline settings [25].

Simultaneously, global online gaming contributes to bridging capital by connecting players from diverse backgrounds [48, 49]. Interactions expose players to different cultural norms, ideas, and perspectives, potentially enhancing tolerance and understanding. Research on mobile MMORPGs shows international guilds reinforcing both bonding and bridging capital across cultures [50].

3.2.2 Gaming communities as platforms for civic engagement

Gaming environments can also serve as platforms for civic engagement [51]. Skills from cooperative gameplay—teamwork, leadership, strategic planning—may transfer to real-world civic activities, and potentially more engaged citizens [51]. Collaborative problem-solving in games may cultivate civic capacities [51]. Research indicates a positive link between collective MMORPG play and online/offline social capital, suggesting in-game networks can extend beyond the virtual [48].

3.2.3 Implications for social well-being

Accumulating social capital in online gaming communities significantly impacts players' social well-being [52]. Participation contributes to developing social support networks, both in-game and offline [52]. These networks help alleviate loneliness, reduce isolation, and provide emotional support [52]. Social interactions in gaming can also encourage empathy and prosocial behaviors [53]. Shared experiences and goals cultivate understanding and cooperation [53].

In summary, online gaming communities are dynamic grounds for cultivating social capital. Reinforcing bonding and bridging connections, these communities enrich the gaming experience and contribute positively to players' social lives, civic engagement potential, and overall social well-being.

3.3 Identity, culture, and participatory play

Beyond entertainment, games are arenas for identity exploration, cultural expression, and participatory engagement [54]. Players actively shape gaming cultures through fan art, mods, streaming, and memes [55, 56] also known as *User-Generated Content* (UGC). This participatory culture cultivates its own community norms, in-group language, and collective identities [54].

Ethnographic research shows player communities cultivating distinct "cultures of play" with unwritten rules, slang, and group identities [54]. These communities can persist as diasporic cultures, migrating and maintaining bonds after game servers close [54].

Seminal work explores identity experimentation in virtual environments [14]. Early text worlds enabled individuals to explore self-aspects, including gender, in social contexts different from face-to-face, potentially deepening identity understanding [14].

Media convergence theory shows gamers engage across platforms—game, forums, voice chat, streaming [57]. This blurs boundaries between gaming and social media, highlighting the participatory nature of digital culture where players are both consumers and producers [57].

Understanding social dynamics in these cultures requires considering the Online Disinhibition Effect [58]. Reduced accountability online can lead to behaviors that may be suppressed offline [58]. Recognizing these dynamics is crucial for designing, developing, and maintaining positive interactions in gaming spaces [58].

Surplus Energy Theory offers another lens [59]. Play expends surplus physical/mental energy [59]. In games, this applies to using virtual environments as an outlet for emotions, channeling energy into challenges and social interactions [59, 60].

Collectively, these perspectives underscore gaming's significant role as platforms for identity exploration, cultural expression, and community participation [27, 61–63]. They highlight understanding gaming not just as entertainment, but as a complex social ecosystem reflecting and shaping digital culture [64, 65].

4. Psychological aspects: Emotion, motivation, and social influence

Scavenging, fighting, healing, strategizing, trading, forming alliances—these social behaviors are central to social games and human history. Humans are inherently social, driven by a need to connect, belong, and share experiences. Social gaming extends these psychological desires into digital worlds. This section explores the psychological factors making social games compelling: motivations, emotions, and social dynamics.

4.1 Motivations for social play

Motivations for social gaming are complex but rooted in basic psychological needs. Self-Determination Theory (SDT) highlights three core drivers: relatedness, competence, and autonomy [66–69]. Social games, designed for player interaction, particularly fulfill the need for relatedness—feeling connected to others.

Relatedness stems from the drive to form social bonds [70]. Game social elements directly address this through collaboration, shared goals, and interaction [69]. Cooperative objectives require communication, synchronized actions, and mutual reliance, a shared investment and emotional resonance in key moments. Multiplayer features like chat, teamwork, guilds, and friend lists significantly enhance feelings of connection and belonging [67]. Relatedness satisfaction deepens emotional engagement and predicts future play intentions.

Shared experiences, like overcoming challenges or celebrating wins, build bonds. Research shows shared activities boost closeness and understanding [71]. In-game bonds can provide emotional support comparable to or exceeding offline friendships, especially for those facing social challenges elsewhere [72].

Feeling part of a team can be as motivating as game objectives. Playing with friends increases engagement, highlighting social context's motivational appeal [73, 74]. Multiplayer online games function as "third places"—neutral grounds for social interaction and community [10]. These spaces support casual chat, guild formation, and community identity beyond gameplay [25]. Satisfying relatedness not only draws players but is key to sustained engagement.

As it is the case with SDT, satisfying one need enhances satisfaction of other needs as well; providing social interactions in a game may increase a player's sense of meaningful choices (need for autonomy) or effectiveness (need for competence) [67].

Beyond SDT, empirical research details social gamer motivations. In one study, five factors were found: Achievement, Social ("Relationship"), Immersion, Escapism, and Manipulation [75]. The Relationship factor reflects the drive for connections and friendships. A significant player segment prioritized social interaction over goals, emphasizing social connection's centrality. Even achievement often had social aspects, like seeking peer validation [75]. These align with SDT's relatedness.

In-game bonds extending to real-world relationships further highlight social gaming satisfying relational needs and reinforcing engagement. A survey of over 900 MMORPG players found most formed meaningful friendships, with many meeting offline [62]. Many felt online friends offered freer discussion of sensitive topics [62]. This emotional support strengthens motivation and attachment to game social spaces.

4.2 Emotional experiences in social gaming

Social games are rich emotional experiences shared among players. Gameplay evokes strong feelings: shared victories build loyalty, negative interactions cause anger or disappointment.

Playing with others amplifies emotions by adding human dynamics. Social Facilitation Theory suggests others increase arousal [76], potentially enhancing performance on simple tasks but impairing complex ones due to nervousness [76]. Emotional reactions are intensified in social settings. Research shows multiplayer contexts amplify emotions via physiological and psychological mechanisms. Excitement, frustration, and joy intensify during competition, shown by heightened heart rate, skin conductance, and facial electromyography (EMG) [77–79]. Feeling control and success in social play enhances enjoyment and positive affect, especially when visible to others [80].

The type of social interaction—cooperative or competitive—shapes emotional experiences and behavior. Cooperative contexts heighten trust, empathy, and solidarity through mutual reliance. Competitive scenarios intensify excitement, pride, frustration, or aggression as players vie for success. Cooperative players report higher empathy than competitive ones [81]. Cooperative contexts promote helping and positive perceptions of teammates [82, 83] and reduce subsequent aggression [84]. Observing or receiving generosity in games also increases subsequent generous behavior [85]. Cooperative play builds on mutual reliance and team identity, while competitive play encourages self-focus and rivalry.

Emotions spread through groups via emotional contagion [86–88]—the tendency to align with perceived emotions [86, 87]. A player's excitement energizes the group; frustration lowers morale. Exposure to opponents' emotions shifts players' own states and influences behavior [89]. Shared emotional rhythms heighten presence and engagement, making play immersive and socially charged. Multiplayer games intensify emotions by embedding them in human dynamics layered over gameplay.

4.3 Social influence and behavior

Players' behaviors are shaped by others in gaming communities through peer dynamics, self-representation, group identity, and norms.

Peer influence is a visible force. Gaming adoption and habits are socially contagious; adolescents start playing and are influenced by peers' time spent gaming [90]. Peer influence mediates video game effects on both positive and negative outcomes [91]. Gaming is embedded in peer dynamics shaping participation and consequences.

Within games, social influence begins with virtual representations. The Proteus Effect describes how avatar characteristics influence player behavior [92, 93].

Taller avatars led to more aggressive negotiation; attractive avatars increased self-disclosure and confidence [93]. Virtual self-modeling can enhance real-world motivation, like exercise [94]. Using female avatars increased in-game aggression, regardless of player gender [95]. Using attractive avatars increased exercise and flirtatious interactions with non-player characters (NPCs) and led to negotiating for more money in a post-play game [96]. Avatar characteristics influence in-game behavior and real-world self-perception—social influence from the adopted persona.

Group identity, norms, and dynamics powerfully shape behavior. A competitive guild may demand stricter coordination; a casual group prioritizes fun. Players affiliate strongly with teams or guilds, explained by Social Identity Theory [97]—self-concept partly derives from group membership. Affiliations establish shared norms shaping interactions, cooperation, and support [41, 48]. Leaders in complex games coordinate efforts and manage relationships. Leadership strengthens commitment and norm adherence.

In summary, gamers play within social ecosystems, and therein, motivations and behaviors are shaped by peers, group affiliations, and community norms. Friends, avatar identities, team dynamics, and leadership structures mean individual psychology is deeply embedded in collective experiences.

5. Community and player interactions

Online multiplayer games, particularly the expansive landscapes of Massively Multiplayer Online Role-Playing Games (MMORPGs), have evolved into remarkably intricate social ecosystems where players not only interact but actively establish enduring communities that frequently reflect and even amplify the complexities found in real-world social structures [27, 61]. Within these virtual environments, players exhibit a natural propensity for self-organization, forming various types of groups such as guilds, clans, squads, or teams to strategically coordinate gameplay objectives (like undertaking challenging quests or competing against other groups) and to engage in broader social interaction and camaraderie [41, 64, 97]. Within these self-formed communities, cooperative behaviors, altruistic actions (helping fellow players without immediate reward), and the development of genuine friendships and robust social support networks are commonly observed and actively cultivated by participants [41, 61].

5.1 Communities, cooperation, and friendship

Empirical research consistently demonstrates the significant social benefits that players derive from participation in MMORPGs and other online social games [53]. For instance, early survey data specifically from players of the highly popular *World of Warcraft* indicated that a substantial proportion of respondents reported that their friendships formed within the game were comparable in quality to, or in some cases, even exceeded the quality of, their friendships in the physical, real world [26]. These digitally mediated relationships often demonstrate a remarkable capacity to transcend the literal boundaries of the virtual world, with numerous well-documented accounts of players forming enduring offline friendships and even romantic partnerships that originated and were initially developed within the game environment [26, 62].

The collective pursuit of shared goals within games, such as collaboratively defeating exceptionally challenging in-game bosses, successfully navigating intricate dungeons, or completing complex quests as a unified group, serves as a powerful catalyst for promoting teamwork, necessitating effective and clear communication among members, and facilitating the natural emergence of leadership roles within these virtual communities [27, 97]. Successful guilds and similar social units are often characterized by the establishment of both explicit (e.g., documented rules) and implicit (e.g., unspoken expectations) social norms that govern member behavior [41]. These norms can encompass a wide range of practices, including the mentoring and support of novice players, the implementation of equitable and transparent systems for distributing valuable in-game loot or resources, and the maintenance of respectful and constructive communication channels, particularly during stressful or challenging gameplay situations [25, 41]. These positive and functional social interactions significantly enhance the overall gaming experience for participants beyond the mechanics of play itself, and crucially, cultivate a strong sense of belonging, shared identity, and collective purpose among community members [25, 54].

Extending engagement beyond the core game client and mechanics, players frequently utilize third-party communication platforms, such as dedicated Discord servers, community forums, and voice communication channels (like TeamSpeak or Ventrilo in earlier eras), to engage in strategic planning, organize in-game events, share personal experiences about their offline lives, and cultivate a pervasive sense of camaraderie that transcends the immediate gameplay context [25, 37]. These supplementary interactions play a vital role in the formation and maintenance of social capital within gaming communities, encompassing both "bonding" ties, characterized by strong, emotionally supportive relationships among close group members, and "bridging" ties, which provide access to new perspectives, diverse information, and broader social networks by connecting individuals across different groups or communities [45, 46].

Furthermore, online gaming communities can serve as particularly inclusive and supportive spaces for individuals who may encounter significant social challenges or experience marginalization in their offline interactions [53]. Research suggests that individuals experiencing social anxiety, heightened emotional sensitivity, or other social difficulties often find it comparatively easier and less intimidating to initiate interactions, establish meaningful friendships, and form social connections within the less physically and immediately confronting environment of online games compared to face-to-face settings [42]. These positive virtual interactions, characterized by acceptance and shared interests, can in turn contribute to improved social skills, enhanced self-esteem, and a greater sense of social integration for these individuals, with potential positive effects extending beyond the digital realm into their offline lives [53].

In summary, online multiplayer games offer rich, dynamic, and complex environments highly conducive to community-building, extensive cooperation among players, the development of lasting friendships, and cultivation of robust social support networks. These virtual spaces not only significantly enhance the enjoyment, engagement, and retention of the gaming experience itself but also provide valuable social resources that can exert a substantial positive influence on players' real-life social well-being and overall quality of life [45, 53]. Understanding these community dynamics is essential for appreciating the multifaceted impact of social gaming.

5.2 Disruptive behavior (toxicity, harassment, griefing)

While online games serve as fertile and productive grounds for community formation, cooperative endeavors, and positive social interaction, they also provide environments where disruptive and toxic behaviors, such as verbal harassment, griefing (the intentional and malicious disruption of other players' gameplay), and hate speech, can be alarmingly prevalent and impactful [68, 84]. These negative and often aggressive behaviors can significantly undermine player well-being, severely erode community cohesion and trust, and ultimately detract from the overall positive gaming experience for many participants [85]. Addressing these issues is a critical challenge for developers and communities alike.

5.2.1 Prevalence and forms of toxicity

Toxic behaviors in online gaming manifest in a diverse and often evolving range of actions. These include direct verbal abuse directed at individuals or groups, the use of offensive language or hate speech targeting specific demographics or identities, griefing (the deliberate disruption of others' gameplay through actions intended solely for personal amusement or to cause frustration), and various forms of cyberbullying [87, 98]. For instance, research analyzing player reports in popular team-based competitive games has consistently identified toxic behavior as a significant and unfortunately frequently encountered issue. Studies in games like *League of Legends* have shown that verbal aggression, negative attitudes displayed in chat, and intentional gameplay disruption (like deliberately losing or hindering teammates) are among the most commonly reported forms of toxicity [84, 99–101].

Survey data from large player populations further corroborate the widespread prevalence of harassment and toxic experiences within gaming communities globally. One study indicated that a substantial majority of adult gamers had experienced some form of toxic incident within a one-year period, with younger players (adolescents) and those actively engaged in highly competitive gaming genres or modes exhibiting a particularly higher susceptibility to encountering such negative interactions [89]. The persistence and visibility of these behaviors highlight a significant challenge in online social environments.

5.2.2 Psychological and social drivers

A complex confluence of psychological and social factors contributes significantly to the emergence, perpetuation, and normalization of toxic behaviors within online game environments [90]. The widely recognized "online disinhibition effect" posits that the perceived anonymity offered by online platforms and the lack of immediate, direct, face-to-face interaction can significantly lower individuals' social inhibitions, leading them to engage in behaviors—both positive and negative—that they might typically suppress or avoid in physical, real-world social interactions where accountability is higher [58, 91].

Furthermore, exposure to toxic behavior within gaming communities can contribute substantially to its normalization among players over time or even becoming a part of subcultures. Research suggests that witnessing verbal aggression or other forms of toxicity in-game, particularly when coupled with high levels of game engagement or identification with a group where such behavior is common, can increase the likelihood of players themselves subsequently engaging in similar toxic behaviors [92, 102]. This creates a concerning ripple effect and cycle of negative reinforcement within communities.

Griefing, a specific and particularly disruptive form of toxicity, is characterized by players intentionally acting in ways designed solely to spoil, annoy, or ruin the game experience for others [93, 103, 104]. It is often driven by a desire for a sense of power or control over others [105], or simply for entertainment derived from eliciting negative emotional reactions (like frustration or anger) from other players [93], also known in online communities as "trolling." Studies indicate that griefers may often deliberately target less experienced players, exploiting their relative lack of game knowledge, skill, or understanding of game mechanics or social norms to maximize the disruptive impact of their actions [94]. Other motivations can include seeking attention, expressing frustration unrelated to the game, or conforming to negative group norms [93].

5.2.3 Impact on players and communities

The negative repercussions of toxic behavior extend far beyond the immediate experiences of the individual targets, significantly impacting the broader gaming community as a whole [106]. Victims of harassment and other forms of toxicity often experience a marked and significant decrease in their enjoyment of the game, increased levels of stress, anxiety, and frustration, and in more severe or prolonged cases, may even report symptoms consistent with depression or social anxiety [53, 106]. As a direct and understandable consequence of these negative experiences, many players ultimately choose to reduce their engagement or leave specific gaming communities altogether in an attempt to avoid toxic environments and protect their well-being [106].

Moreover, the pervasive presence of toxicity can act as a significant barrier, actively discouraging new players from joining or remaining active within gaming communities, thereby hindering community growth, reducing diversity, and potentially isolating the community [95, 107]. This is a particularly concerning issue for individuals from underrepresented or marginalized groups within gaming, who may already face existing barriers to full inclusion and participation in these virtual spaces and are disproportionately targeted by certain forms of hate speech and harassment [95].

5.2.4 Mitigation strategies

Game developers, platform operators, and the gaming communities themselves have increasingly implemented a variety of measures aimed at directly combating toxicity and actively promoting more positive and inclusive social environments [28, 96]. These strategies commonly include implementing accessible in-game reporting systems that allow players to easily flag toxic behavior, deploying sophisticated moderation tools and dedicated teams (utilizing a hybrid of automated detection systems and human moderators) designed to identify, investigate, and sanction offenders according to community guidelines, and clearly articulating transparent community guidelines and codes of conduct intended to encourage and enforce respectful and inclusive behavior [96, 108]. Some games have also experimented with community-driven moderation systems, where trusted and experienced players participate in reviewing reported incidents and collaboratively determining appropriate sanctions [97, 109].

However, the overall effectiveness of this diverse range of mitigation strategies remains variable across different games and platforms, and significant challenges persist in consistently and effectively addressing the pervasive issue of toxicity in online gaming [108, 110]. For instance, the normalization of certain forms of toxic behavior within some specific gaming subcultures can lead to underreporting of incidents, as players may come to perceive such actions as simply being a typical, albeit unpleasant, or unavoidable aspect of the gaming experience [110]. The scale of large online communities also makes comprehensive moderation challenging.

Ultimately, effectively addressing and mitigating toxicity in online gaming requires a multifaceted and sustained approach that integrates technological solutions (improved detection and reporting) with dedicated human moderation efforts, coupled with concerted and proactive efforts to foster positive cultural shifts within gaming communities that actively prioritize inclusivity, mutual respect, and constructive social interaction [28, 90, 108]. Ongoing research into the underlying psychological and social drivers of toxic behavior, coupled with active community engagement, player education, and collaborative initiatives involving developers and players, are essential for developing more effective, scalable, and sustainable strategies that promote healthier, more welcoming, and inclusive gaming environments for all participants.

6. Social stressors and personal well-being

Social games, while offering compelling opportunities for connection and community, also present a unique set of challenges related to stress and overall personal well-being. The intricate dynamics of competitive environments, coupled with the inherent social pressures of online interaction, can introduce significant psychological and physiological stressors for players. Understanding this dual nature—games as both sources of stress and platforms for support—is crucial for a comprehensive view of their impact on players' lives. This section delves into the specific social stressors prevalent in gaming environments and examines the ways in which social support derived from gaming communities can positively influence player well-being.

6.1 Social stressors in games

Competitive social games, particularly those characterized by rapid pacing, high stakes, and intense pressure, frequently place players in demanding psychological and physiological states. The inherent nature of competition, often involving direct confrontation with other human players, can trigger acute stress responses. Empirical studies utilizing physiological measures have demonstrated that engagement in competitive, and sometimes violent, video games can induce measurable physiological stress reactions, including changes in heart rate variability (HRV) and increased sympathetic nervous system activity [111–113]. While these heightened states of physiological arousal might contribute to feelings of excitement and thrill, prolonged or repeated exposure to such stress-inducing content—whether it's competitive combat, pressure under duress, or relentless time pressure—can lead to sustained physiological activation and emotional strain [112, 114]. Over time, if not properly managed, this stress may contribute to negative outcomes, potentially manifesting as symptoms of burnout or heightened aggressive moods outside the game environment [114, 115].

Beyond the stress inherent in competitive gameplay, significant social stressors frequently emerge from negative or challenging interactions between players within the social game environment. Multiplayer games, by design, bring players into close, often real-time, and sometimes anonymous contact, creating conditions ripe for toxic behavior [58, 116]. The anonymity afforded by online platforms can lower social inhibitions, leading individuals to engage in actions they might avoid face-to-face [58, 116]. The prevalence of negative interactions is significant; reports indicate that a substantial majority of online multiplayer gamers have experienced some form of toxic interaction, with younger players, marginalized groups being more affected [99, 117]. These toxic behaviors include verbal abuse, hate speech, and griefing (intentional gameplay disruption) [99, 114]. Constant exposure to such encounters transforms recreation into psychological distress, evoking anxiety, anger, and social alienation, as they directly undermine players' fundamental psychological needs for belonging, acceptance, and relatedness [70, 99]. When these core needs are threatened, players may feel devalued, unsafe, or unwelcome, eroding their sense of connection [118]. Empirical research explicitly links perceived toxicity within gaming communities to diminished in-game social capital, lower satisfaction of relatedness needs, and heightened loneliness [118]. These factors are critical components influencing social well-being [118].

Apart from overt toxic encounters, stress can also subtly arise from the pressure to perform competently for teammates or maintain a consistent online presence with friends [119]. This can turn gaming into an obligation rather than relaxation or escapism. Fear of missing out (FoMO) on social interactions, rewards, or progress when logging off is another potent stressor [119, 120]. This fear can create a persistent sense of obligation to play, even when tired or overwhelmed [119, 120]. Critically, in many social games, the compulsion to play is driven not just by game mechanics but significantly by perceived social obligations and the desire to maintain relationships [119, 120]. Players may feel pressure to log on daily to support a guild, maintain a team role, or avoid disappointing friends [119]. These responsibilities can create a cycle of social stress, where players prioritize in-game commitments over real-life needs, potentially leading to disrupted sleep, neglected responsibilities, and strained offline relationships [119].

For some individuals, these social stressors and pressures can contribute to gaming becoming excessive and resembling addiction, recognized as Gaming Disorder [121]. Research shows that the desire for group-based gaming can increase the risk of social game addiction, strengthening habits and weakening self-regulation [122]. When gaming becomes compulsive, it often leads to significant negative impacts on mental health, including increased stress, anxiety, and depression [115].

It is important to acknowledge that the experience and impact of social stressors are not uniform and can vary across cultures. A study found Western players used social games as emotional retreat from real-life stress, sometimes facing new stress from in-game conflict or obligations. In contrast, players from certain non-Western contexts often described gaming as a casual, integrated, group-based pastime embedded in everyday social life, carrying less emotional weight or guilt [123]. These differences indicate that the impact on well-being depends on how social expectations and real-life responsibilities are balanced within different cultural frameworks [123].

6.2 Social support and well-being

Although social gaming may introduce stressors, acknowledging the positive social dimensions is equally important. For many players, social games offer a valuable source of emotional support, companionship, and meaningful interaction. Through online communities, friendships, and cooperative play, social games can help player to connect, alleviate loneliness, and increase their overall well-being [124–126].

Online social games create opportunities to build meaningful relationships and access emotional support networks, positively impacting mental well-being [127]. Many players form close bonds through shared experiences, goals, and interactions. These friendships often extend beyond the game, offering companionship and belonging crucial for those isolated offline [47].

In-game communities frequently serve as informal support networks. Players encourage each other, celebrate successes, and provide a safe space to share frustrations or personal challenges. This peer support is emotionally grounding [127]. During the COVID-19 pandemic, when in-person social interaction was limited, social gaming saw a significant surge [128]. Games like *Among Us* [129] and platforms like *Roblox* [130, 131] experienced massive growth, facilitating virtual connection. *Animal Crossing: New Horizons* offered escape and connection during lockdowns [132]. By facilitating virtual social interactions and engagement when physical togetherness was not possible, social games have helped people maintain connections and mitigate isolation [128].

Social games can be particularly beneficial for individuals facing challenges with in-person interaction. For socially anxious or shy players, online games offer a lower-pressure environment to communicate and build friendships. Game-based interactions allow more control over self-presentation and timing, reducing anxiety and raising confidence [42]. Research shows socially anxious individuals are more likely to turn to online games for social fulfillment, and in-game relationships can compensate for offline difficulties [42, 63]. Social gaming also holds value for older adults, connecting across distances and generations, helping to reduce loneliness and enhance emotional well-being [133]. Research indicates older adults who play games with family or peers experience improved mood, engagement, and a stronger sense of social connection [133]. In these cases, games act as tools for maintaining relationships and combating social isolation [133].

Beyond casual play, social games have been explored and implemented in mental health contexts. Games combining physical activity and social interaction, such as *Pokémon GO* [134], support mental health by blending movement with community participation, contributing to reduced depressive symptoms and improved mood [134].

Social games have also been used as structured therapeutic tools. Clinicians and researchers integrate multiplayer or cooperative games into therapeutic programs for individuals experiencing depression, anxiety, social withdrawal, or neurodevelopmental differences [135]. For example, therapists use games like *Minecraft* to help clients, particularly neurodivergent youth, develop social skills in a naturalistic and engaging way [136, 137]. By participating in shared in-game tasks, players practice cooperation, turn-taking, communication, and emotional regulation [136, 137]. Similarly, *Animal Crossing: New Horizons* has been used in group therapy sessions for building communication and belonging [132]. As interest grows in digital mental health interventions, the potential for social games to serve as accessible, enjoyable, and socially rich tools for well-being continues to expand [135].

7. Cross-cultural gaming experiences and global gaming communities

Video games have evolved into a ubiquitous global medium, connecting billions across diverse societies [2]. While interactive platforms may seem universal, the experience, interpretation, and social engagement with games are profoundly shaped by cultural contexts [2]. This interplay between global accessibility and local cultures creates a complex social landscape. Research identifies universal patterns in player motivations and well-being impacts, suggesting shared human responses to interactive digital play. Alongside these, significant cultural variations exist in gaming behaviors, communication styles, and social motivations within virtual communities [4, 138]. Understanding these differences is crucial for appreciating the spectrum of social gaming and inclusive global environments.

7.1 Cultural differences in social play

Underlying cultural dimensions significantly influence players' engagement with social games. These include societal approaches to individualism versus collectivism, communication styles, gaming contexts, and societal attitudes towards video games as leisure [2]. These factors shape individual motivations, experiences, and online community dynamics.

7.1.1 Universal social motivations

Despite cultural differences, certain core social motivations for gaming resonate globally, pointing to fundamental human needs fulfilled through digital play and interaction. The desire for connection, belonging, and shared experiences are key intrinsic drivers worldwide [69, 70]. While expression may vary culturally, the underlying drive is common.

Research supports both universal psychological responses and culturally specific manifestations. A study across North America, Europe, and China found similar gaming-related distress from excessive play (fatigue, irritability, preoccupation, difficulty controlling play) [139]. This suggests common physiological and psychological responses to intensive gaming, regardless of cultural background or game genre [139]. Furthermore, research comparing Singaporean (collectivist) and Australian (individualist) gamers indicated universal susceptibility to Internet Gaming Disorder (IGD) [140]. However, motivational pathways to IGD diverged: for Singaporean gamers, social motivations (fitting in, maintaining group membership, avoiding disappointment of online friends) were stronger predictors of problematic gaming. In contrast, for Australian gamers, competitive motivations (individual achievement, high rankings, mastery) played a more significant role in developing IGD [140]. This highlights that while problematic gaming is universally possible, the motivations propelling players towards it can be shaped by prevailing cultural values [140].

7.1.2 Individualism vs. collectivism in gaming styles

Cultural dimensions like individualism versus collectivism [138, 141] demonstrably influence preferred gaming styles, in-game behaviors, and interaction patterns. Individualistic cultures (e.g., United States, Western Europe) emphasize personal goals, independence, and individual achievement [141]. Collectivist cultures (e.g., many parts of Asia, Africa, Latin America) prioritize group goals, harmony, interdependence, and loyalty to in-groups [138].

These orientations manifest in gaming. Players from collectivist cultures often game for social interaction, group cohesion, participating in cooperative content (raids, guild wars), and maintaining group harmony [140, 142]. Their motivation leans towards contributing to team success and supporting guildmates rather than individual glory [142]. Conversely, players from individualistic cultures may prioritize personal achievement, skill development, solo mastery, and competitive success [140, 142]. They might focus on individual rankings, completing challenging content alone, or demonstrating superior individual skill [142]. This cultural distinction shapes initial motivations (joining a game due to friends vs. competitive scene) and influences pathways to problematic gaming, with social motivations potentially posing greater risk in collectivist contexts due to social pressures [140].

7.1.3 Communication preferences across cultures

Communication styles and technology use in gaming vary culturally, reflecting broader societal norms about directness, context, and harmony [143]. Western gamers, especially in fast-paced genres (First-Person Shooters (FPS), Multiplayer Online Battle Arenas (MOBAs)), often favor voice chat for rapid coordination, tactical calls, and social banter [144]. Quick voice communication is prioritized for competitive advantage.

In contrast, gamers from many East Asian cultures, where indirect communication and maintaining face are significant, often prefer text-based communication [135, 145]. Text chat allows deliberate articulation, consideration before responding, and can be less intrusive or confrontational than voice chat, which might expose non-native accents [144]. It also facilitates asynchronous interaction. Research indicates younger gamers across regions predominantly use text chat, suggesting generational factors. Female players frequently use character animations, emotes, and sound signals as additional non-verbal cues, potentially adding nuance or expressing emotion less directly [146]. These differences have implications for game design, requiring flexible communication options, and for inclusivity within global gaming communities.

7.1.4 Social contexts of play

The physical and social environments for gaming differ across cultures, influencing social interactions and community formation [2]. In China, gaming is often a communal, co-located activity [63]. Internet cafés ("wangba") serve as social venues where people play alongside existing social networks [63]. Gaming here is intertwined with face-to-face interaction and preexisting offline relationships. This contrasts with North America and many European countries, where gaming often occurs in private homes, with connections formed primarily online [63]. In this model, new friendships often develop within the game environment, possibly remaining digital [47]. These divergent contexts shape social interaction dynamics, community norm development, and the integration of gaming into players' broader social lives [2, 63].

7.1.5 Cultural attitudes towards gaming

Societal perceptions of video gaming also influence player experiences and behaviors [4]. In the United States and some Western cultures, heavy gaming has sometimes been associated with negative stereotypes (isolation, immaturity, unproductivity) and social stigma [139, 147]. If gaming is seen to interfere with responsibilities or as an unproductive use of time, players may feel stress or guilt [139].
In contrast, in cultures like China or South Korea, where gaming and esports have greater mainstream acceptance and even professional recognition, gaming may be

viewed as a more normative and acceptable leisure activity [139, 148]. Players in these contexts might experience less psychological stress related to their gaming habits [139]. These differing attitudes towards leisure, competition, and technology influence the social gaming experience, self-perception, and interactions within online and offline circles [4].

7.1.6 Implications for game design and community management

A culturally sensitive understanding of these differences is paramount for game developers and community managers creating inclusive global gaming experiences [149]. Designing games with flexible communication options (voice and text) is crucial [143, 144]. Incorporating varied social mechanics supporting both individual and collective achievements can broaden appeal [142]. Sensitivity to how content or visuals might be interpreted across cultures is vital [2]. Community management must acknowledge these differences, providing opportunities for respectful interaction, multilingual support, and organizing events mindful of global time zones [150]. Addressing cultural needs enhances player satisfaction, community bonds, mitigates misunderstandings, and cultivates positive global gaming environments [135, 138]. While games offer a universal platform, player engagement is culturally shaped [2]. Recognizing and accommodating these differences is essential for thriving global gaming communities [149].

8. Global communities and transnational play

Video games have transcended localized entertainment, evolving into interconnected transnational platforms facilitating cross-cultural interaction, collaboration, and the formation of global communities that span geographical boundaries [145, 151]. Massively Multiplayer Online games (MMOs) like *World of Warcraft* and *Final Fantasy XIV* exemplify this, hosting diverse international player bases engaging in cooperative gameplay, competition, and establishing social bonds across borders and languages [25, 148]. These virtual environments often transcend linguistic and cultural barriers, enabling unique, shared digital cultures rooted in game-specific norms, emergent player narratives, and distinct communication styles [152]. Players develop shared lexicons, strategies, and participate in community-specific rituals.

MMOs enable "transnational cultural flows," where players exchange gaming strategies, technical expertise, and diverse cultural practices beyond game mechanics [150]. This can include sharing holiday traditions, idiomatic expressions, or aspects of real-world daily lives [150]. For instance, a Chinese player might introduce fellow players on an English-language server to Chinese New Year customs, while Western players might gain insights into Korean gaming culture through engagement with Korean MMOs [150, 153]. These interactions, while sometimes leading to misunderstandings, contribute to global gaming communities united by shared interests and collaborative experiences, creating spaces for organic cross-cultural learning [150, 153].

Esports further exemplify gaming's globalization and cultural impact [154]. Major international tournaments (e.g., League of Legends World Championship, The International) attract elite players and fans globally [154]. These events are global spectacles celebrated across languages and cultures, viewed by millions online [155], reinforcing global camaraderie among players and spectators [154]. Social media and streaming platforms like Twitch and YouTube Gaming amplify this, enabling real-time cross-cultural interaction on an unprecedented scale [37]. An esports fan in France can watch a Korean streamer, engage with global viewers in chat, and participate in a worldwide gaming subculture [37], parasocial relationships, and community bonds.

Despite unifying aspects, challenges persist in global gaming [151]. Language barriers are a primary obstacle, hindering communication and conflict resolution [143]. Time zone differences affect real-time coordination for events [150]. Misunderstandings from differing cultural norms and communication styles can also occur [144]. Online discrimination based on national origin or language unfortunately happens [156]. In response, many global gaming communities have developed bridging practices: adopting simplified English as a lingua franca, using emojis and memes for culturally ambiguous communication, and developing culturally neutral communication strategies [144, 150]. Online translation tools and multicultural guild structures are also prevalent. These community-driven efforts show a commitment to inclusive and functional social spaces within diverse global player populations [144, 150], even as discrimination remains an issue [156].

As video games expand globally, understanding cross-cultural differences in player behavior, communication, and expectations is increasingly vital for the health of global gaming communities [150]. Expanding inclusive global communities requires sustained efforts from developers (design, moderation) and players (conscious interaction) to address cultural sensitivities, promote equitable participation, and encourage sharing diverse perspectives [143, 150]. Global online gaming offers a unique opportunity for cross-cultural learning and connection, provided challenges are actively addressed.

9. Conclusions

This chapter explored the multifaceted social dimensions of video gaming, from early arcades to today's complex, culturally shaped, global communities. Technology has enabled geographically dispersed interactions, while the human drive for social connection through play endures.

Theoretical perspectives offer frameworks: games as "third places" are informal social hubs. Social capital theory explains how participation contributes to bonding and bridging ties, enriching social resources. Identity and participatory culture reveal games as arenas for self-expression, community norm formation, and shared identities.

Psychological insights illuminate player-game relationships. Motivations are rooted in needs like relatedness, competence, and autonomy, which social games satisfy. In-game social interactions evoke a range of emotions, shaping the experience. Social influence from peers, avatars, and group dynamics impacts player behavior and attitudes.

Community dynamics are dual-natured. Games catalyze positive community, cooperation, and friendships but also face disruptive behaviors like toxicity and harassment. Understanding drivers of negative behaviors is critical for mitigation.

Cross-cultural gaming, despite global reach, is intertwined with specific cultural contexts. Differences in social motivations, communication styles, play environments, and societal attitudes shape diverse player experiences and well-being impacts. Yet, global communities thrive, using transnational platforms like MMOs and esports, developing strategies to bridge cultural gaps, facilitating cross-cultural learning.

In conclusion, video games are dynamic, culturally shaped social ecosystems integrated with human psychology and global society. They offer avenues for social connection, support, and exchange, providing spaces for belonging and shared experience. They also present risks like stress and negative interactions. A holistic understanding requires recognizing the interplay of game design, individual psychology, cultural background, and community dynamics. Future research should explore long-term cultural impacts of transnational gaming on identity, effectiveness of toxicity mitigation strategies across cultures, potential of social games as therapeutic tools in varied contexts, and implications of emerging technologies like Artificial Intelligence (AI) and Virtual Reality (VR) on social dynamics. Deepening our understanding can harness social gaming's potential for positive connections, well-being, and cross-cultural empathy, while addressing its challenges.

Author details

Ahmad Azadvar* and Qianhui Ni
Activision, Los Angeles, USA

*Address all correspondence to: ahmad.azadvar@activision.com

References

[1] Atari. Pong [Video Game]. Atari; 1972

[2] Kent SL. The Ultimate History of Video Games: From Pong to Pokémon and Beyond--The Story Behind the Craze that Touched our Lives and Changed the World. New York: Prima Lifestyles; 2001

[3] DeMaria R, Wilson JL. High Score!: The Illustrated History of Electronic Games. Berkeley, CA: McGraw-Hill, Osborne; 2004

[4] Ungvarsky J. Gaming Culture. EBSCO Research Starters; 2025. Available from: https://www.ebsco.com/research-starters/social-sciences-and-humanities/gaming-culture

[5] Wolf MJP, Perron B, editors. The Video Game Theory Reader 2. New York, NY: Routledge; 2014

[6] Nintendo. Nintendo Entertainment System (NES) [Game Console]. Nintendo Co., Ltd.; 1983

[7] Newman J. Video Games. London: Routledge; 2004

[8] Nintendo. Super Mario Bros. [Video Game]. Nintendo; 1985

[9] Konami. Contra [Video Game]. Konami; 1987

[10] Oldenburg R. The Great Good Place: Cafes, Coffee Shops, Community Centers, Beauty Parlors, General Stores, Bars, Hangouts, and How they Get you through the Day. New York, NY: Paragon House; 1989

[11] Truman P. The War on Games: The Just Say No! Arcade as a Pro-Social Third Place [master's thesis]. Louisville, KY: Bellarmine University; 2023

[12] Provenzo EF. Video Kids: Making Sense of Nintendo. Cambridge, MA: Harvard University Press; 1991

[13] Herz JC. Joystick Nation: How Video Games Ate our Quarters, Won our Hearts, and Rewired our Minds. Boston, MA: Little, Brown and Company; 1997

[14] Turkle S. Life on the Screen: Identity in the Age of the Internet. New York, NY: Simon and Schuster; 1995

[15] Rheingold H. The Virtual Community: Homesteading on the Electronic Frontier. Reading, MA: Addison-Wesley Publishing Company; 1993

[16] Chen A. Early Social Networks and Games on Bulletin Board Systems (BBS). 2009. Available from: https://andrewchen.com/early-social-networks-and-games-on-bulletin-board-systems-bbs/

[17] Bartle R. Designing Virtual Worlds. Indianapolis, IN: New Riders; 2003

[18] Bartle R, Trubshaw R. MUD1 [Video Game]. University of Essex; 1978

[19] Curtis P. MUDding: Social phenomena in text-based virtual realities. In: Kiesler S, editor. Culture of the Internet. Mahwah, NJ: Lawrence Erlbaum Associates; 1997. pp. 121-142

[20] Dibbell J. A rape in cyberspace; or, how an evil clown, a Haitian trickster spirit, two wizards, and a cast of dozens turned a database into a society. The Village Voice. 1993;**38**(51):36-42

[21] Reid E. Virtual worlds: Culture and imagination. In: Jones SG, editor.

Cybersociety: Computer-Mediated Communication and Community. Thousand Oaks, CA: Sage Publications; 1994. pp. 164-183

[22] Origin Systems (Electronic Arts). Ultima Online [Video game]. Electronic Arts; 1997

[23] Sony Online Entertainment. EverQuest [Video Game]. Sony Online Entertainment; 1999

[24] Blizzard Entertainment. World of Warcraft [Video Game]. Blizzard Entertainment; 2004

[25] Steinkuehler CA, Williams D. Where everybody knows your (screen) name: Online games as "third places". Journal of Computer-Mediated Communication. 2006;**11**(4):885-909

[26] Cole H, Griffiths MD. Social interactions in massively multiplayer online role-playing gamers. CyberPsychology and Behavior. 2007;**10**(4):575-583

[27] Taylor TL. Play between Worlds: Exploring Online Game Culture. Cambridge, MA: MIT Press; 2006

[28] Castronova E. Synthetic Worlds: The Business and Culture of Online Games. Chicago, IL: University of Chicago Press; 2005

[29] Zynga. FarmVille [Video Game]. Zynga; 2009

[30] Zynga. CityVille Becomes the Biggest-Ever App on Facebook. San Francisco, CA: VentureBeat; 2011. Available from: https://venturebeat.com/2011/01/03/cityville-biggest-facebook-app/

[31] Mojang. Minecraft [Video Game]. Mojang; 2011

[32] Roblox Corporation. Roblox [Online Game Platform]. Roblox Corporation; 2006

[33] Short D. Minecraft: A platform for creative collaboration. Learning, Media and Technology. 2012;**37**(3):279-294

[34] Hassan A. Fortnite is a social space the way skateparks and Facebook used to be. Quartzy. 2018. Available from: https://qz.com/quartzy/1493147/fortnite-a-social-space-like-facebook-and-skateparks-once-were

[35] Hedrih V. Playing "Fortnite" can expand social networks and boost well-being, study suggests. PsyPost. 2024. Available from: https://www.psypost.org/playing-fortnite-can-expand-social-networks-and-boost-well-being-study-suggests/

[36] Twitch Interactive. Twitch [Streaming Platform]. Twitch Interactive; 2011

[37] Hamilton WA, Garretson O, Kerne A. Streaming on twitch: Fostering participatory communities of play within live mixed media. In: Proceedings of the SIGCHI Conference on Human Factors in Computing Systems. New York, NY: ACM; 2014. pp. 1315-1324. DOI: 10.1145/2556288.2557048

[38] Soukup C. Computer-mediated communication as a virtual third place: Building Oldenburg's great good places on the world wide web. New Media & Society. 2006;**8**(3):421-440

[39] Ducheneaut N, Moore RJ. The social side of gaming: A study of interaction patterns in a massively multiplayer online game. In: Proceedings of the 2004 ACM Conference on Computer Supported Cooperative Work. New York, NY: ACM; 2004. pp. 360-369

[40] Moore RJ, Serva MA. Understanding member motivation for contributing to different types of virtual communities: A proposed framework. In: Proceedings of the 40th Annual Hawaii International Conference on System Sciences (HICSS '07). Washington, DC: IEEE Computer Society; 2007

[41] Williams D, Ducheneaut N, Xiong L, Zhang Y, Yee N, Nickell E. From tree house to barracks: The social life of guilds in World of Warcraft. Games and Culture. 2006;**1**(4):338-361

[42] Kowert R, Oldmeadow JA. (A) Social reputation: Exploring the relationship between online video game involvement and social competence. Computers in Human Behavior. 2013;**29**(4):1872-1878

[43] Ducheneaut N, Yee N, Nickell E, Moore RJ. Alone together? Exploring the social dynamics of massively multiplayer online games. In: CHI'06: Proceedings of the SIGCHI Conference on Human Factors in Computing Systems. New York, NY: ACM; 2006. pp. 407-416

[44] Jeffres LW, Bracken CC, Jian G, Casey MF. The impact of third places on community quality of life. Applied Research in Quality of Life. 2009;**4**(4):333-345

[45] Putnam RD. Bowling Alone: The Collapse and Revival of American Community. New York, NY: Simon & Schuster; 2000

[46] Williams D. On and off the 'net: Scales for social capital in an online era. Journal of Computer-Mediated Communication. 2006;**11**(2):593-628

[47] Domahidi E, Festl R, Quandt T. To dwell among gamers: Investigating the relationship between social online game use and gaming-related friendships. Computers in Human Behavior. 2014;**35**:107-115

[48] Zhong ZJ. The effects of collective MMORPG (massively multiplayer online role-playing games) play on gamers' online and offline social capital. Computers in Human Behavior. 2011;**27**(6):2352-2363

[49] Kaye LK, Bryce J. Putting the 'fun factor' into gaming: The influence of social contexts on experiences of playing videogames. International Journal of Internet Science. 2012;**7**(1):23-37

[50] Lu X, Carradini A. Building bridges and bonds: Social capital in a mobile massively multiplayer online role-playing game. Games and Culture. 2021;**16**(5):631-651

[51] Kahne J, Middaugh E, Evans C. The Civic Potential of Video Games. Cambridge, MA: MIT Press; 2009

[52] Trepte S, Reinecke L. The social side of gaming: How playing online computer games creates online and offline social support. Computers in Human Behavior. 2011;**27**(2):768-775

[53] Kaczmarek LD, Misiak M, Behnke M, Dziekan M, Guzik P. The Pikachu effect: Social contexts of playing Pokémon Go and changes in perceived social capital. Computers in Human Behavior. 2017;**75**:356-363

[54] Pearce C. Communities of Play: Emergent Cultures in Multiplayer Games and Virtual Worlds. Cambridge, MA: MIT Press; 2009

[55] Jenkins H, Bertozzi V. Artistic expression in the age of participatory culture: How and why young people create. In: Buckingham D, editor. Youth, Identity, and Digital Media. Cambridge, MA: MIT Press; 2008. pp. 171-197

[56] Postigo H. Of mods and modders: Chasing down the value of fan-based digital game modification. Games and Culture. 2007;**2**(4):300-313

[57] Jenkins H. Convergence Culture: Where Old and New Media Collide. New York, NY: NYU Press; 2006

[58] Suler J. Toxic online disinhibition. CyberPsychology and Behavior. 2004;**7**(3):321-326

[59] Spencer H. The Principles of Psychology. Vol. 2. New York, NY: D. Appleton and Company; 1873

[60] Canossa A, Salimov D, Azadvar A, Harteveld C, Yannakakis G. For honor, for toxicity: Detecting toxic behavior through gameplay. Proceedings of the ACM on Human-Computer Interaction. 2021;**5**(CHI PLAY):29. Article 253

[61] Nardi B. My Life as a Night Elf Priest: An Anthropological Account of World of Warcraft. Ann Arbor, MI: University of Michigan Press; 2010

[62] Boellstorff T. Coming of Age in Second Life: An Anthropologist Explores the Virtually Human. Princeton, NJ: Princeton University Press; 2008

[63] Li H, Wang S, Wang J. Shyness and online gaming addiction: A cross-sectional study of Chinese adolescents. Cyberpsychology, Behavior, and Social Networking. 2014;**17**(3):150-154

[64] Galarneau L. Spontaneous communities of learning: Learning ecosystems in massively multiplayer online gaming environments. In: Proceedings of DiGRA 2005 Conference: Changing Views – Worlds in Play. Tampere, Finland: Digital Games Research Association; 2005

[65] Oldenburg R, Brissett D. The third place. Qualitative Sociology. 1982;**5**(4):265-284

[66] Deci EL, Ryan RM. Intrinsic Motivation and Self-Determination in Human Behavior. New York, NY: Plenum; 1985

[67] Deci EL, Ryan RM. The "what" and "why" of goal pursuits: Human needs and the self-determination of behavior. Psychological Inquiry. 2000;**11**(4):227-268

[68] Ryan RM, Deci EL. Self-determination theory and the facilitation of intrinsic motivation, social development, and well-being. The American Psychologist. 2000;**55**(1):68-78

[69] Ryan RM, Deci EL. Self-Determination Theory: Basic Psychological Needs in Motivation, Development, and Wellness. New York, NY: Guilford Press; 2017

[70] Baumeister RF, Leary MR. The need to belong: Desire for interpersonal attachments as a fundamental human motivation. Psychological Bulletin. 1995;**117**(3):497-529

[71] Aron A, Melinat E, Aron EN, Vallone RD, Bator RJ. The experimental generation of interpersonal closeness: A procedure and some preliminary findings. Personality and Social Psychology Bulletin. 1997;**23**(4):363-377

[72] Beutel ME, Wölfling K, Müller KW. Internet addiction in children and adolescents: Clinical symptoms and diagnosis. Zeitschrift für Kinder- und Jugendpsychiatrie und Psychotherapie. 2004;**32**(6):437-442

[73] Sherry JL, Lucas K, Greenberg BS, Lachlan K. Video game uses and gratifications as predictors of

use and game preference. In: Vorderer P, Bryant J, editors. Playing Video Games: Motives, Responses, and Consequences. Mahwah, NJ: Lawrence Erlbaum Associates; 2006. pp. 213-224

[74] Vorderer P, Bryant J, editors. Playing Video Games: Motives, Responses, and Consequences. New York, NY: Routledge; 2006

[75] Yee N. Motivations for play in online games. Cyberpsychology & Behavior. 2006;**9**(6):772-775

[76] Zajonc RB. Social facilitation. Science. 1965;**149**(3681):269-274

[77] Holmstrom AJ, Tully M, Snyder LB. eSports and the effects of game play on physiological arousal. Journal of Broadcasting & Electronic Media. 2012;**56**(3):373-390

[78] Lacroix E, Giguère G, Larochelle S. The impact of competitive and cooperative video games on aggression and prosocial behavior. Journal of Experimental Psychology. Applied. 2018;**24**(2):234-246

[79] Weber R, Ritterfeld U, Mathiak K. Does playing violent video games induce aggression? Empirical evidence of a functional magnetic resonance imaging study. Media Psychology. 2006;**8**(1):39-60

[80] Przybylski AK, Rigby CS, Ryan RM. A motivational model of video game engagement. Review of General Psychology. 2010;**14**(2):154-166

[81] Ewoldsen DR, Eno CA, Okdie BM, Velez JA, Guadagno RE, DeCoster J. Effect of playing violent video games cooperatively or competitively on subsequent cooperative behavior. Cyberpsychology, Behavior and Social Networking. 2012;**15**(5):277-280

[82] Adachi PJ, Willoughby T. More than just fun and games: The longitudinal relationships between strategic video games, self-reported problem solving skills, and academic grades. Journal of Youth and Adolescence. 2013;**42**(7):1041-1052

[83] Greitemeyer T, Osswald S, Brauer M. Playing prosocial video games increases empathy and decreases schadenfreude. Emotion. 2010;**10**(6):796-802

[84] Anderson CA, Bushman BJ. Effects of violent video games on aggressive behavior, aggressive cognition, aggressive affect, physiological arousal, and prosocial behavior: A meta-analytic review of the scientific literature. Psychological Science. 2001;**12**(5):353-359

[85] Zhang Y, Kim J, Park E. The effects of social interaction on in-game purchasing in mobile games: A case study of "sky: Children of the light". Computers in Human Behavior. 2021;**115**:106610

[86] Hatfield E, Cacioppo JT, Rapson RL. Emotional contagion. Current Directions in Psychological Science. 1993;**2**(3):96-100

[87] Hatfield E, Cacioppo JT, Rapson RL. Emotional Contagion. Cambridge, UK: Cambridge University Press; 1994

[88] Barsade SG. The ripple effect: Emotional contagion and its influence on group behavior. Administrative Science Quarterly. 2002;**47**(4):644-675

[89] de Melo CM, Carnevale PJ, Gratch J. The effect of expression of anger and happiness in computer agents on negotiations with humans. In: Proceedings of the 10th International Conference on Autonomous Agents and Multiagent Systems (AAMAS 2011); 2-6

May 2011; Taipei, Taiwan. Richland, SC: IFAAMAS; 2011. pp. 937-944

[90] Wang CW, Chan CL, Mak KK, Ho SY, Wong PW, Ho RT. Prevalence and correlates of video and internet gaming addiction among Hong Kong adolescents: A pilot study. Scientific World Journal. 2014;**2014**:874648

[91] Ferguson CJ. The influence of television and video game use on attention and school problems: A multivariate analysis with other risk factors controlled. Journal of Psychiatric Research. 2011;**45**(6):808-813

[92] Yee N, Bailenson JN. The Proteus effect: The effect of transformed self-representation on behavior. Human Communication Research. 2007;**33**(3):271-290

[93] Yee N, Bailenson JN, Ducheneaut N. The Proteus effect: Implications of transformed digital self-representation on online and offline behavior. Communication Research. 2009;**36**(2):285-312

[94] Fox J, Bailenson JN. Virtual self-modeling: The effects of vicarious reinforcement and identification on exercise behaviors. Media Psychology. 2009;**12**(1):1-25

[95] Martins N, Williams DC, Harrison K, Ratan R. A content analysis of gender roles in video games: Implications for game design and development. Sex Roles. 2009;**61**(11-12):824-836

[96] Walter N, Cody MJ, Ball-Rokeach SJ. The role of the media in the construction of public belief and social change. The Journal of Communication. 2012;**62**(1):1-20

[97] Tajfel H, Turner JC. An integrative theory of intergroup conflict. In: Austin WG, Worchel S, editors. The Social Psychology of Intergroup Relations. Brooks/Cole; 1979. pp. 33-47

[98] Kordyaka B, Laato S, Hamari J, Scholz T, Niehaves B. What drives gamer toxicity? Essays from players. In: Proceedings of the 7th International GamiFIN Conference 2023; 18-21 Apr 2023; Levi, Finland. Aachen, Germany: CEUR-WS; 2023. pp. 86-95

[99] Kou Y. Toxic behaviors in team-based competitive gaming: The case of league of legends. In: Proceedings of the Annual Symposium on Computer-Human Interaction in Play (CHI PLAY'20); 2-4 Nov 2020; Ottawa, ON. New York, NY: ACM; 2020. pp. 81-92

[100] Kwak H, Blackburn J, Han S. Exploring cyberbullying and other toxic behavior in team competition online games. In: Proceedings of the 33rd Annual ACM Conference on Human Factors in Computing Systems (CHI '15); 18-23 Apr 2015; Seoul, Republic of Korea. New York, NY: ACM; 2015. pp. 1107-1116

[101] Lugano G, Poggi A, Aiello LM, Baronchelli A. Anatomy of toxicity: Online abuse in video game chats. EPJ Data Science. 2021;**10**(1):1-19

[102] Cook D, Schaafsma J, Antheunis M L. Toxic behavior in multiplayer online games: The role of social influence. Journal of Gaming & Virtual Worlds. 2024;**16**(1):5-24

[103] Chesney T, Coyne I, Logan B, Madden N. Griefing in virtual worlds: Causes, casualties, and coping strategies. Information Systems Journal. 2009;**19**(6):525-548

[104] Hilvert-Bruce Z, Neill JT. Deception in video games: Examining varieties of griefing. International Journal of Cyber

Behavior, Psychology and Learning. 2020;**10**(3):1-14

[105] Fox J, Tang WY. The role of social identity and the desire for control in predicting hostile and prosocial communication in online games. Computers in Human Behavior. 2014;**33**:182-190

[106] Adinolf S, Turkay S. Toxic behaviors in online multiplayer games: Prevalence, perception, and policy implications. Journal of Virtual Worlds Research. 2018;**11**(3):1-17

[107] Phillips W. This is why we can't have nice things: Mapping the relationship between online culture and toxic game fandom. Loading... The Journal of the Canadian Game Studies Association. 2016;**10**(16):8-30

[108] Ducheneaut N, Yee N, Nickell E, Moore RJ. The life and death of online gaming communities: A look at guilds in World of Warcraft. In: Proceedings of the SIGCHI Conference on Human Factors in Computing Systems; 2007 Apr 28–May 3; San Jose, CA. New York, NY: ACM; 2007. pp. 839-848

[109] League of Legends. The Tribunal [wiki article]. Fandom.com; n.d. [archived 2018]. Available from: https://leagueoflegends.fandom.com/wiki/The_Tribunal

[110] Shaw A, Gibbs M. Feminist hacking/making: Exploring new gender horizons of possibility. Journal of Peer Production. 2013;**3**

[111] Porter AM, Goolkasian P. Video games and stress: How stress appraisals and game content affect cardiovascular and emotion outcomes. Computers in Human Behavior Reports. 2021;**3**:100068

[112] Hasan Y, Bègue L, Bushman BJ. Violent video games stress people out and make them more aggressive. Aggressive Behavior. 2013;**39**(1):64-70

[113] Zsila Á, Shabahang R, Aruguete MS, Orosz G. Toxic behaviors in online multiplayer games: Prevalence, perception, risk factors of victimization, and psychological consequences. Aggressive Behavior. 2022;**48**(3):356-364

[114] Lapolla M. Tackling Toxicity: Identifying and Addressing Toxic Behavior in Online Video Games [Master's thesis]. South Orange, NJ: Seton Hall University; 2020

[115] Loton D, Borkoles E, Lubman D, Polman R. Video game addiction, engagement and symptoms of stress, depression and anxiety: The mediating role of coping. International Journal of Mental Health and Addiction. 2016;**14**(4):565-578

[116] Kordyaka B, Kruse L. "After all, they don't know me": Exploring the psychological mechanisms of toxic behavior in online games. Games Culture. 2021;**16**(5):579-597

[117] Anderson M, Vogels EA, Perrin A. Teens and Online Gaming. Washington, DC: Pew Research Center; 2022

[118] Frommel J, Johnson D, Mandryk RL. How perceived toxicity of gaming communities is associated with social capital, satisfaction of relatedness, and loneliness. Computers in Human Behavior Reports. 2023;**10**:100302

[119] Li L, Griffiths MD, Niu Z, Mei S. Fear of missing out (FoMO) and gaming disorder among Chinese university students: Impulsivity and game time as mediators. Issues in Mental Health Nursing. 2020;**41**(12):1104-1113

[120] Duman H, Ozkara BY. The impact of social identity on online game addiction:

The mediating role of the fear of missing out (FoMO) and the moderating role of the need to belong. Current Psychology. 2021;**40**(9):4571-4580

[121] World Health Organization. Gaming Disorder (Q&A). Geneva: WHO; 2018. Available from: https://www.who.int/news-room/questions-and-answers/item/addictive-behaviours-gaming-disorder

[122] Gong X, Zhang KZ, Cheung CM, Chen C, Lee MK. Alone or together? Exploring the role of desire for online group gaming in players' social game addiction. Information Management. 2019;**56**(6):103139

[123] Snodgrass JG, Lacy MG, Dengah HF II, Eisenhauer S, Batchelder G, Cookson RJ. A vacation from your mind: Problematic online gaming is a stress response. Computers in Human Behavior. 2014;**38**:248-260

[124] Jones CM, Scholes L, Johnson D, Katsikitis M, Carras MC. Gaming well: Links between videogames and flourishing mental health. Frontiers in Psychology. 2014;**5**:260

[125] Vella K, Johnson D. Engaging the new gaming generation: Implications for teaching and learning. Australasian Journal of Educational Technology. 2012;**28**(5):813-832

[126] Vella K, Johnson D, Hides L. Positively playful: When videogames lead to player wellbeing. In: Proceedings of the First International Conference on Gameful Design, Research, and Applications; 2013 Oct 2-4; East Lansing, MI, USA. pp. 99-102

[127] Kowert R, Vogelgesang J, Festl R, Quandt T. Psychosocial causes and consequences of online video game play. Computers in Human Behavior. 2015;**45**:51-58

[128] Lee B. Lockdown and loaded: Coronavirus triggers video game boost. BBC News. 6 May 2020

[129] Stuart K. Among Us is the Ultimate Party Game of the Covid Era. London: The Guardian; 29 Sep 2020. Available from: https://www.theguardian.com/games/2020/sep/29/among-us-party-game-covid-era

[130] Peters J. Roblox, Explained. New York, NY: The Verge; 2021. Available from: https://www.theverge.com/22565326/roblox-explained-what-is-how-to-play-download

[131] Roblox Corporation. Investor Information. 2023. Available from: https://ir.roblox.com/financials/quarterly-results/default.aspx [Accessed: May 11, 2025]

[132] [website]Therapy Focus. Animal Crossing Creates a Supportive Environment. 2021. Available from: https://therapyfocus.org.au/latest-news/animal-crossing-creates-a-supportive-environment/

[133] De Schutter B, Vanden AV. Older adults' experiences with digital games: A review of the literature. Commun. 2015;**40**(1):1-21

[134] Wang AI. Systematic literature review on health effects of playing Pokémon Go. Entertainment Computing. 2021;**38**:100411

[135] Kilmer ED, Davis AD, Kilmer JN. Therapeutically Applied Role-Playing Games: The Game to Grow Method. New York, NY: Routledge; 2023

[136] Zolyomi A, Schmalz M. Mining for social skills: Minecraft in home

and therapy for neurodiverse youth. In: Proceedings of the 50th Hawaii International Conference on System Sciences (HICSS 2017); 4-7 Jan 2017; Waikoloa, HI. Washington, DC: IEEE Computer Society; 2017. pp. 3391-3400

[137] Kilmer E, Spangler J, Kilmer J. Therapeutically applied minecraft groups with neurodivergent youth. F1000Research. 2023;**12**:216

[138] Triandis HC. Individualism & Collectivism. Boulder, CO: Westview Press; 1995

[139] Snodgrass JG, Zhao W, Lacy MG, Zhang S, Tate R, Pleckham J. The cross-cultural expression of internet gaming distress in North America, Europe, and China. Addictive Behaviors Reports. 2019;**9**:100146

[140] Chew PKH, Lin PKF, Yow YJ. Cross-cultural differences in the pathways to internet gaming disorder. Asia-Pacific Psychiatry. 2024;**16**(1):e12565

[141] Hofstede G. Culture's Consequences: Comparing Values, Behaviors, Institutions, and Organizations across Nations. Thousand Oaks, CA: Sage Publications; 2001

[142] Mekes V. A Cross Cultural Study Comparing Dutch and Chinese on Game Motivation and Sense of Responsibility [MSc dissertation]. Tilburg, Netherlands: Tilburg University; 2019. Available from: http://arno.uvt.nl/show.cgi?fid=149415

[143] Williams D, Caplan SE, Xiong L. Can you hear me now? The impact of voice in an online gaming community. Human Communication Research. 2007;**33**(4):427-449

[144] Chen VH, Duh HB. Understanding social interaction in world of warcraft. In: Proceedings of the International Conference on Advances in Computer Entertainment Technology (ACE 2007); 13-15 Jun 2007; Salzburg, Austria. New York, NY: ACM; 2007. pp. 21-24

[145] Consalvo M. There is no magic circle. Games Culture. 2009;**4**(4):408-417

[146] Majkowski T. Digital Natives' Communication Preferences in Online Gaming [PhD dissertation]. Gdańsk, Poland: University of Gdansk; 2023

[147] Anderson CA, Dill KE. Video games and aggressive thoughts, feelings, and behavior in the laboratory and in life. Journal of Personality and Social Psychology. 2000;**78**(4):772-790

[148] Jin DY. Korea's Online Gaming Empire. Cambridge, MA: MIT Press; 2010

[149] Spronck P, Sprinkhuizen-Kuyper I. Cultural differences in play style. In: Proceedings of the IEEE Conference on Computational Intelligence and Games. 2014. pp. 1-8

[150] Cai X. Cross-cultural communication in online gaming communities. Journal of Intercultural Communication Research. 2016;**45**(6):456-474

[151] Apperley TH. Gaming Rhythms: Play and Counterplay from the Situated to the Global. Amsterdam: Institute of Network Cultures; 2010

[152] Heavens D. Transnational play: Video games and the globalization of culture. Cultural Sociology. 2014;**8**(4):444-460

[153] Hjorth L, Chan D. Gaming Cultures and Place in Asia-Pacific. New York, NY: Routledge; 2009

[154] Taylor TL. Raising the Stakes: E-Sports and the Professionalization of Computer Gaming. Cambridge, MA: MIT Press; 2012

[155] Global Esports Federation. About the Global Esports Federation. Singapore: Global Esports Federation; 2019. Available from: https://globalesports.org

[156] Nakamura L. Don't hate the player, hate the game: The racialization of labor in World of Warcraft. Critical Studies in Media Communication. 2009;**26**(2):128-144

Chapter 5

Environmental Storytelling in Video Games: Crafting Narratives beyond Words

Józef P. Cyran, Dariusz Myszor and Krzysztof A. Cyran

Abstract

Environmental storytelling has been present in video games since their very inception and has always served as an alternative to traditional storytelling devices such as dialog and cutscenes. This chapter explores the history, techniques, rationale, and psychological impact of environmental storytelling. From the 1993 title Myst to Half-Life 2 and finally Bioshock in the modern gaming era, this unique way of presenting lore has captivated gamers in ways that traditional storytelling devices cannot replicate. The concept of the Silent Protagonist is explored, including well-known characters such as Gordon Freeman and Chell, examining this design, while also addressing its criticism. Beyond game design itself, the chapter also explores the community-driven aspect of environmental storytelling, describing how these techniques encourage speculation, discussion, and the creation of fan content. Games like Dark Souls demonstrate how environmental storytelling can support deeper worldbuilding, inviting players to uncover hidden layers of meaning through exploration. Recent empirical research, including a 2024 study at Uppsala University, along with established cognitive theories, such as Narrative Transportation, highlights how players process and interpret these environmental cues, even under fast-paced gameplay conditions. Ultimately, environmental storytelling is not just a design choice but a means of player engagement and agency, allowing players to experience narratives rather than merely witness them. As game worlds become increasingly complex and interactive, this approach continues to evolve, shaping the future of storytelling in digital media.

Keywords: environmental storytelling, silent protagonist, worldbuilding, community-driven content, game semiotics

1. Introduction

Narratives in video games have been presented through text and dialog options since their very inception. The prototype for such narratives can be found in the Choose Your Own Adventure books. These books allowed the readers to influence the narrative by making choices that directed them to a corresponding page and discover the consequences of his choice. These books provided the groundwork for future games in regards to branching dialogs and multiple storylines [1–2].

Initially, narrative in video games was expressed through words. The introduction of proto-cutscenes in the Sheriff video game in 1979 allowed for a new way for developers to express narrative and Donkey Kong, released in 1981, is often considered to be the first example of a complete story told through cutscenes [3]. Since then, cutscenes and dialog options have become the two defining elements of traditional narrative presentation in video games – they allow the writers to transfer their classic approaches (such as screenplays, dialogs) into the video game medium.

1.1 Disruption

The game Myst was released in 1993 and completely foregoes the traditional narrative elements like dialog or cutscenes. The protagonist is silent, the world introduced is foreign and unexplained, and it is up to the player to uncover the story, by looking at and analyzing the environment. Myst does not rely on cutscenes (apart from a brief introduction and ending). Instead, it is the environmental clues that guide the player both in his actions and his perception of the game world [4, 5]. This new way of presenting the story has since been termed environmental storytelling, and it has influenced future successful games such as Bioshock, Half Life 2 and the Dark Souls series.

Environmental storytelling is—as Jenkins puts it—"the art of arranging a careful selection of the objects available in a game world so that they suggest a story to the player who discovers them" [5]. It is worth noting, that while environmental storytelling is often contrasted (and will be contrasted in this chapter) with traditional storytelling devices, the two approaches are not mutually exclusive. A good example of this is the game "Lies of P"—noted for its engaging cutscenes and dialog, while also incorporating much of the environmental clues and indirect storytelling drawn from its inspiration—the Dark Souls series.

In this chapter, we will look at the evolution of environmental storytelling, unveil the underlying motivations for choosing such an approach and finally discuss how modern studies support and formulate the principles and limitations of its application in game design.

We will also examine popular techniques in indirect narration—for example the Silent Protagonist—and explore how lore elements can be embedded in the environment. Finally, we will show how environmental storytelling can account for player choice and even function as a replacement for dialog options.

2. The evolution of environmental storytelling

2.1 Early implicit narratives

In the early days of video games, the concept of environmental storytelling was not clearly defined, but several games emerged that offered implicit narrative experiences through level design, tone, and player agency. Zork, a text adventure game where players explore dungeons, did not include any visuals. However, its written descriptions of objects within a fictional world—descriptions that changed based on player actions—can be seen as early spatial worldbuilding. This demonstrates that environmental focus alone can serve narrative purposes.

Another early example of an environment that serves as a medium for storytelling is the world of Metroid. Metroid, released in 1986, has since inspired an entire genre of exploration driven platformers. While many focus on the game's mechanics, it is also one of the earliest games where the player is left to their own devices—much like the character they control. The protagonist, Samus Aran, explores a hostile alien world, and the claustrophobic level design and decaying environment subconsciously influence the player's emotional state [6]. This point is emphasized even more strongly in the game's sequel – Metroid 2: Return of Samus, released in 1991. Here, there is a secret story to uncover, the player can gradually understand where the monsters come from. This information is conveyed through observation of the environment—architecture, statues, and abandoned structures.

Metroid 2 was not the only release in 1991 that can be said to include implicit narrative. Another World – a 2D platform game also featured a silent protagonist and the story was uncovered through interaction with the environment and visual cues rather than dialog.

2.2 Myst and the birth of environmental storytelling

In 1993, a small studio named Cyan, founded by two brothers, released the title Myst. This game, which could arguably be considered one of the first indie games, quickly captivated players with its detailed 3D world. It is important to note that, unlike some of its later remakes, the original Myst game did not include real-time graphics; instead it relied on pre-rendered frames. While it limited player movement, this approach allowed for far greater graphical fidelity than that of its competition, and the developers used this visual strength to tell a story. *A story told (almost completely) without words* (**Figure 1**).

When the player begins playing Myst, they are shown a brief video introduction that reveals little beyond cryptic references to a mysterious book. They are then placed in an abandoned industrial environment and left to their own devices. The game's point-and-click structure encourages the player to closely examine their surroundings, searching for elements that seem out of place—and therefore likely to be interactive. Combined with the lack of instructions and sparse dialog fragments (which are more like cryptic monologs), this encourages the player to draw their own conclusions. Just like Zork, it featured spatial puzzles; like Metroid, it fostered exploration; and like Another World, it used a silent protagonist and avoided direct exposition. As we will see later, this approach—including the eerie statements from characters—will be repeated successfully by other games. Thus, Myst laid the groundwork for environmental storytelling as a core narrative technique. Myst not only combined all of these elements but also fully integrated them and treated them as the only narrative vehicle.

2.3 Narrative fusion: The synthesis of environmental and traditional techniques

System Shock, released in 1994, is an RPG video game set in a futuristic cyberpunk world where humans use cybernetic implants to enhance their biological capabilities. The game features a complex story but avoids traditional cutscenes. Instead, the narrative unfolds through audio logs and sparse monologs from a few characters. While such techniques are common in modern games, they were groundbreaking at the time—and their continued prevalence today attests to their lasting influence.

Deus Ex, released in 2000, serves as a spiritual successor to System Shock [7]. In addition to inheriting its immersive environment and audio logs, it introduced new

Figure 1.
"PD045: Figure 7.4b" by Rosenfeld Media, CC BY 2.0.

elements, such as in-game text documents. These included emails, notes, and other messages written by in-game characters, allowing the player to uncover a complex web of political conspiracies and philosophical conflicts. However, Deus Ex also featured branching dialog trees and meaningful player choices, placing it closer to the tradition of verbal, choice-based narratives. While it retained environmental storytelling traits from its predecessor, it ultimately combined them with classic narrative techniques.

Another example of this fusion is Half-Life 2, released in 2004. The game is particularly notable for how it develops its protagonist—Gordon Freeman. Gordon is often cited as a Silent Protagonist [8, 9], yet he possesses a rich, implied personality. He is a theoretical physicist trying to reverse the consequences of his own research. Though he never speaks, his interactions with other characters—especially Alyx Vance—suggest a layered emotional depth. In one moment, Alyx even jokes, "Still not talking, huh?"—a rare case where a game explicitly acknowledges its silent protagonist. Despite his silence, Gordon's identity emerges through his actions, relationships, and the world he inhabits. This resonates with recent narrative modeling strategies that treat characters as agents operating within logical world states. Lima et al. suggest that by assigning characters evolving goals and action plans—anchored to production rules and dramatic arcs—developers can evoke rich, coherent narratives without relying on explicit speech or player dialog. Freeman's silence, in this light, becomes not a limitation but a structural decision: an open space where the narrative is inferred rather than imposed. *Valve chose not to put words in Gordon's mouth, but his actions speak for him* (**Figure 2**).

The game's environmental storytelling is instrumental in shaping this connection. As a Homo Viator—a traveler through a broken world—Gordon reacts to the world around him, but also changes it through his (pre-scripted) decisions. The game's environments are more than just backdrops; they are part of the narrative infrastructure, filled with visual and spatial cues that convey history, danger, and purpose.

Figure 2.
"wallpaper_half-life_2_03_1600" by Niranjan, CC BY 2.0.

BioShock, released in 2007, takes the hybrid approach further. Its title—clearly an homage to System Shock [8]—signals a thematic lineage. Set in an underwater dystopia shaped by the philosophy of Ayn Rand, the game presents a narrative where the setting itself becomes ideological commentary [10]. Rather than offering a blunt critique of Ayn Rand's philosophy, *BioShock* constructs a nuanced exploration of its ideological consequences, drawing players into a world where utopian ideals collapse under their own weight [11]. Visually, the world of BioShock is constructed in the Art Deco style, echoing the esthetics of Atlas Shrugged, which was first published during the peak of Art Deco's popularity. The contrast between the luxurious design and the grotesque mutations of its inhabitants creates an unsettling atmosphere that reinforces the story's themes. These design choices are not accidental; they operate both on a conscious and subconscious level, guiding players to understand the ideology and downfall of Rapture's society without overt exposition.

Despite these innovations, however, most of these games still relied heavily on explicit narrative cues—spoken or written—to deliver their stories. It was not until a later paradigm shift, pioneered by titles like Dark Souls, that developers would explore a more radical, fully indirect form of environmental storytelling.

2.4 The Soulslike revolution

Dark Souls was released by FromSoftware in 2011 and has since reshaped the landscape of narrative design. Not only are there no difficulty settings, but the instructions for the player are vague, the world is unfriendly and death awaits at every corner. The player character is the Chosen Undead – they are already dead and can resurrect after dying. If the previously mentioned games still tried to be relatively friendly to the player, Dark Souls makes no such effort. One could describe Dark Souls as a game which requires great investment from the player, but offers even greater rewards. This philosophy extends to its storytelling.

The story of Dark Souls is not mainly conveyed through dialog but environment and the few cutscenes that exist usually focus on the surroundings as well (for example, they show a mechanism that opens a bridge). Deceptively, if the player simply follows the surface-level progression, they will receive a story—but not the deeper, hidden narrative. Only through careful analysis and connecting the dots can the player uncover the real story behind Dark Souls.

This approach aligns well with the concept of *narrative goals* as introduced by Cardona-Rivera et al. [12]. In their model, gameplay mechanics (ludological goals) are interpreted by the player through multimodal feedback, forming *narrative goals*—personal understandings of what the player's actions mean within the game world. In *Dark Souls*, the sparse feedback and indirect exposition force the player to construct their own narrative goals, such as uncovering the secrets of Lordran or interpreting the motives of the Serpents. These goals are not explicitly instructed by the game but emerge through interpretation, driven by feedback in the form of item descriptions, spatial clues, and cryptic NPCs.

There are several instances of this deception being quite explicit in the game—one such instance is the Goddess Gwynevere, which really is just a projection from another character. Another instance is the serpents—after the player completes a milestone a seemingly friendly snake appears and offers his services. But the game features another serpent, one who can reveal the hidden truths and offer a darker, subversive path. All of these elements have one thing in common—they require explicit player action to be revealed, often against the player's instincts.

2.4.1 Miyazaki's narrative philosophy

Hidetaka Miyazaki is the creator of Dark Souls and is often referred to as an ateur—a term describing a director who strongly enforces his vision in regard to all aspects of his art. When asked about the very indirect storytelling in Dark Souls, Miyazaki provided an insight into his childhood. In an interview with the Guardian, Miyazaki explained that "As a child, I couldn't always understand everything I was reading... I would use the pictures to fill in the story" [13]. In the Dark Souls series, the player is similarly required to use the visual imagery to fill in the blanks. It is worth noting, however, that while narrative in the games is very indirect, it is still somewhat verbal, as various objects have textual descriptions. One would be tempted to call them flavor text, but such characterization would not do justice to those descriptions, as unlike in various other games in which such descriptions serve as background or contribute to the atmosphere, in Dark Souls they are the main device through which the player learns about the world. Technically, there is dialog and in the later chapters we will explore how this dialog is nonetheless indirect and deceptive at best. But it is important to keep in mind that to understand even the basic story the player cannot rely solely on verbal narration (**Figure 3**).

2.4.2 The player as an archivist

The weight of discovery in *Dark Souls* falls squarely on the player, who must act as both archivist and archaeologist—piecing together meaning from scattered remnants. The lore of the game even encourages such speculation, since the world of Lordran,

Figure 3.
"Dark Souls" by Józef Cyran, CC0.

where the game takes place, went through cataclysms that convoluted the timeline of the game. A friendly NPC called Solaire acknowledges this explicitly, by saying "The flow of time itself is convoluted; with heroes centuries old phasing in and out" [14]. If the flow of time is convoluted and the story is not told directly, the player is necessarily lost—and that is a very conscious decision by the company *From Software*. The player must find their own meaning within the world.

In doing so, *Dark Souls* redefined what it means for a game to "tell a story"—not through exposition, but through implication, omission, and the silent invitation to interpret. As we shall see in the final section, this paradigm shift has since inspired a wave of modern games that blend both indirect and direct narrative techniques (**Table 1**).

2.5 A living technique: Environmental storytelling in modern games

Following the influence of *Dark Souls*, environmental storytelling has transitioned from a niche experiment to a standard design approach used across a wide range of genres. Modern titles increasingly incorporate indirect storytelling not as a novelty, but as an integrated narrative structure. This technique has been adapted to suit puzzle games, science fiction, and minimalist dramas, extending beyond the fantasy genre it originated from.

A useful model for understanding how narrative emerges from gameplay is the GFI framework, introduced by Cardona-Rivera, Zagal, and Debus. GFI stands for Goals, Feedback, Interpretation, and it focuses on how players interpret gameplay objectives as part of a story. In this model, the game provides players with goals (what to do), feedback (how the game responds to their actions), and from these, players form their own interpretations—which become their personal narrative understanding [15]. This allows for storytelling that arises not from explicit exposition, but from the player's engagement with the system itself.

Her Story—a small indie game released in 2015—proves that this player engagement can form the sole gameplay mechanic of a videogame. Though the game

Game	Indexical Storytelling	Symbolic Storytelling	Geography (Eastern/Western)	Pacing	Silent Protagonist	Release Date
Project Chaser	Broken walls, graffiti, Tube Room, Cube guardian	Nazi-inspired banners without swastika	Western (Sweden)	Fast-paced chase sequences	Yes	2024
Fallout 3	Crater in Megaton after detonation	Radiation as metaphor for destruction/trauma	Western (USA)	Variable (exploration + combat)	No	2008
Wolfenstein (series)	War-torn environments, ruins	Nazi imagery (modified in some regions)	Western (various)	Action-focused	No	1981–present
Dark Souls	Different architectural styles on the same building	Fire as cyclical rebirth	Eastern (Japan)	Deliberate, methodical	Yes	2011
Half-Life 2	Civil Protection checkpoints, abandoned buildings, alien structures integrated into cities	Combine insignia	Western (USA)	Story-driven action	Yes	2004
Myst	Abandoned worlds, artifacts, environmental puzzles	Linking books as symbol of knowledge/control	Western (USA)	Slow-paced exploration	Yes	1993

Table 1.
A comparison of selected games.

contains no physical environment in the traditional sense, its interface and database structure function as a form of narrative space. The player's primary activity is reconstructing the timeline of events by watching video fragments in non-linear order. In doing so, *Her Story* isolates and amplifies a core feature of environmental storytelling: requiring the player to discover the plot by actively assembling dispersed narrative clues. If uncovering the story was an additional reward in Dark Souls, it is the main and only motivation in *Her Story*.

Other titles have continued to blend indirect narrative with more traditional structures. *Lies of P* (2023) builds on the Soulslike format, combining implicit lore and visual motifs with a more overt plot delivered through cutscenes and character dialog. *Outer Wilds* (2019) uses environmental storytelling to frame scientific exploration, encouraging the player to interpret clues embedded in planetary ruins and alien technologies.

These examples indicate that environmental storytelling is no longer tied to a specific esthetic or difficulty model. It has become a flexible narrative tool—adaptable to various genres and capable of supporting both linear and fragmented plots. This adaptability is further evidenced by recent narrative systems research that seeks to merge player freedom with narrative coherence. Lima et al. introduce a system where character goals and plans dynamically evolve in a simulated world but are guided by predefined narrative structures—such as the Hero's Journey or Grail Hero arc—to preserve emotional impact and dramatic shape. Their system even detects when emergent gameplay threatens to bypass a crucial narrative beat and introduces corrective goals or world changes to steer the story back on track [15].

Recent research also suggests that the design of the game environment not only conveys narrative meaning but actively shapes player behavior, even when players hold contradictory real-world values. For instance, a 2024 study on *Animal Crossing: New Horizons* found that players with strong pro-environmental values sometimes acted against those values in-game if the mechanics rewarded extractive behaviors such as chopping trees or selling animals. This underscores how game environments—through what they incentivize or obscure—become active participants in shaping the narrative arc and ethical logic of the player's experience [16].

3. The silent protagonist as a tool of environmental storytelling

The term "Silent Protagonist" refers to a playable character who does not speak at any point during the game's runtime. If understood strictly, many if not most protagonists in video games are silent—pacman from the game Pacman does not speak, similarly the frog from Frogger remains mute. However, we shall not analyze these examples, because while the player characters stay silent, there is little to no story in those games, and certainly no complex narratives. Thus, the question "how does the Silent Protagonist affect storytelling" is void in regards to such simple arcade games.

Instead, we shall take a look at games that have deep, defined narrative, and we shall examine how those characters allow for smooth storytelling. One such game, already mentioned is Half Life and its successor Half Life 2. The game's main character Gordon Freeman is worthy of particular analysis, because he has a well-defined personality. The first introduction to Gordon Freeman is in first Half Life game. Gordon starts in a lab and receives instructions from other scientists to conduct an experiment. The experiment goes wrong, and a portal from another dimensions allows aliens to invade earth. Initially, Gordon simply tries to get out of the laboratory, but guided by the NPCs he encounters, he manages to send a missile and destroy the alien portal. The game ends, but a short cutscene involving a mysterious man, often referred to as the G-Man, implies that this is not the end. Players had to wait 6 years to discover that indeed this was just the beginning. The aliens—it turns out—were merely tools and victims in the machine of the insidious Combine—a villain so immaterial and abstract that it could be named a silent antagonist. The Combine ultimately is an organization, and Gordon Freeman emerges as the central figure in humanity's resistance against the Combine. While in the first games the NPCs were moderately developed, the characters Gordon encounters in Half Life 2 are much more refined and the player interacts with them more often. Yet, in all such interactions, Gordon remains silent. The characters sometimes acknowledge this, which implies that Gordon is silent both in-game and out of game and that is made clear. As we shall see, it is important to express to the player whether a character does not really speak (like Gordon Freeman) or whether the replies of the protagonist are simply not presented to the player but implied.

Gordon Freeman is not the only Silent Protagonist that Valve (the studio behind Half Life 2) introduced. In 2007, Valve released Portal, a puzzle game in which the players take control of Chell. Much like Gordon, Chell does not utter a word throughout the whole game. And yet, despite this, the player infers distinct character traits, relational dynamics, and motivations—not in spite of the silence, but because of how the world responds to it. What is different between the two games is how other characters perceive the protagonist. Whereas Gordon's gender did not play a significant role in the story, Chell's womanhood does. She is constantly demeaned and insulted by GLaDOS – a rogue AI that incidentally also has the personality of a woman and is the main villain of Portal. This contrasts with the praise and hope NPCs place in Gordon. Furthermore, the actions Chell takes are different from those of Freeman, whereas Freeman often seeks danger (not for the sake of danger but to stop the enemy), Chell's goals are to survive and resist. Portal is unique in that Chell is also the only human in the game, so her reluctance to speak may be less of a character trait like with Gordon and more of a response to her situation. Thus the player naturally learns that Chell is a resilient, determined and very lonely, whereas Gordon develops complex relationships with other humans and fights for humanity. The determination is similar but the motivations are vastly different, and this is all conveyed without the protagonists speaking.

Games such as Half Life or Portal definitely succeeded in their implementation of the Silent Protagonist, but this cannot be said about all games that attempted it. The Far Cry series, starting with Far Cry released in 2004 is a series of action shooters containing thoughtful narrative. These narratives often offer a glimpse into troubled, isolated societies and the Far Cry series has been noted for its villains, as they go beyond the traditional villain tropes. Connor O'Keefe mentions Joseph Seed (Far Cry 5), Pagan Min (Far Cry 4), and Vaas Montenegro (Far Cry 3) as some of the most memorable video game villains of all time [17]. The series protagonists have generally also been received well, but the protagonist of Far Cry 5 has been strongly criticized and specifically for being silent.

The Junior Deputy or Rook, as he is referred to throughout the game, serves as the protagonist of Far Cry 5 and he stays silent. The story follows the classic far cry narrative of being isolated in a world filled with violent factions, each with their ideology and goals. The villains in Far Cry 5 are well fleshed out—they are inspired by American militias and radical religious groups and when the Junior Deputy is captured by them, they happily reveal their complex motivations. But the player characters silence feels already awkward, as the player is not sure what the Rook thinks of these ideologies. Is he completely opposed? Is there a moment when he considers that they may be right (it is worth noting that in a twisted way the villains of this game *are* correct, the apocalypse *is* coming)? Sadly, the player never finds the answer to this question and the environmental storytelling in this game, while present, never provides any resolution. As Cameron Kunzelman notes, there is no counter-force to the villains' long monologs [18].

What feels even more unsettling are the Junior Deputy's reactions to his allies. Like Gordon Freeman, he does not answer them, but this is not clearly indicated and may be confusing for the player. Kunzelman also feels that the allies in Far Cry 5 do not offer a counter-ideology to the villains; this is different from Half Life 2, where Gordon's allies provided a strong message of hope and provided insightful comments about the events happening. Finally, the reason why Rook is silent, while reasonable in itself (he is mute), is not indicated anywhere in the game and this fact, important to the character, is only revealed in Far Cry: New Dawn, a spinoff game in which Rook is one of the NPCs. Thus, against the intentions of the developers, players feel emotionally disconnected from the character they play, it is merely an avatar to play with, but not a fleshed out person.

Comparing Gordon Freeman and the Junior Deputy reveals that a silent protagonist's success hinges on three key elements: their implied attitude, how other characters narrate their actions, and the clarity of the reason behind their silence. These elements are handled with care in Freeman's case, but are muddled or missing in Rook's.

4. Community engagement and the shared imagination

"Nature abhors a vacuum"—when the creators withhold meaning, the community rushes to supply it. *From Software*, notable for deliberately concealing most of the lore of their video games, leaves room for the players to make their own stories. Initially, these stories are formed in the mind of the players, but unsurprisingly many players are eager to share them online, often through YouTube videos. Such players are often referred to as lore Hunters or lore Scholars and often form micro-communities where players discuss their own interpretations. These interpretations can vary not just in their content but also in the methodologies employed. As we will show below, several real world analytical frameworks have been adapted to serve in the analysis of diegetic elements.

4.1 VaatiVidya and the canonical compilation

If one asks a Dark Souls or Elden Ring player about their understanding of the lore, they are likely to receive an answer that references VaatiVidya—one of the most popular lore scholars who offers streamlined, high-quality miniseries that touch on *From Software* Game's narratives and especially the character stories. VaatiVidyas approach can be characterized as relatively straightforward and literal. He is particularly skilled at framing and connecting the NPC stories in his miniseries, for example, the Prepare to Cry or Shadows Cry Twice playlists. VaatiVidya's videos/productions often feature machinima-style cutscenes and fan-made illustrations—often depicting characters who are never visually shown in the game but are only mentioned in passing.

While VaatiVidyas straightforward approach is attractive to many players, particularly those who enjoy the cinematic videos, it has also attracted controversy and even plagiarism concerns, as he was accused of relying on the source material of another lore scholar named RedGrave, but presenting it in an easier to digest form [19]. This highlights a deeper point: that in many ways the lore scholarship within *From Software*'s community mirrors the structure and tensions of traditional academia.

4.2 Lore scholarship frameworks: Two interpretive approaches

4.2.1 Tarnished archaeologist: Lore as archaeological stratigraphy

Tarnished Archaeologist, founded in 2022, quickly rose to prominence in the Sous-like (Elden Ring, Bloodborne, Dark Souls) community, because of its unique approach to analyzing *From Software* Game's lore [20]. The channel looks at the world of Elden Ring, for example, as the result of hundreds and possibly thousands of years of history. The validity of such a perspective heavily relies on the fact that *From Software* has a habit of creating a robust and precise history and then removing large parts leaving only remnants of the past in the form of ruins, vague references (sometimes these references are intentionally wrong, as they reflect the limited knowledge the characters have of the world they live in) and iconography. Tarnished Archaeologist, as the name suggests, attempts to uncover the game's lore in the same way a real archaeologist attempts to uncover the history of Earth. Furthermore, his methodology often refers to real-world architectural studies (**Figure 4**).

He adopts the concept of *social stratigraphy,* originally introduced by archaeologists such as McAnany and Hodder to analyze the different layers existing in architecture as social records. McAnany and Hodder point out that stratigraphic sequences require the archaeologist to possess a certain understanding of the social practices of the societies they study, and enable them to use this knowledge in combination with archaeological records, to infer about the events and attitudes of the ancient communities. Such sequences often include purposeful forgetting and renewing of aspects from the preceding layers [21]. Again, for this approach to be valid, the game developers had to create the layers so that they follow a (hidden from the player) sequence. *From Software* definitely does include such stratigraphic elements, for example, some reliefs are hidden behind newer statues. Tarnished Archaeologist points out that this is intentional and conveys that whoever put the newer statues, likely did not want his contemporaries to see the relief behind. Another case is through analyzing different styles – just as the use of arches, for example, can help archaeologists roughly date a structure, the use of different architectural styles in Elden Ring gives the players a clue that a certain building has been used by different civilizations, one preceding the other (**Figure 5**).

Tarnished Archeologist also educates the public by comparing some of the iconography to the iconography in the real world, he compares the statue of a man lying flat in an evocative pose to the pieta sculptures, which depict Jesus Christ after his death (the most famous of these is of course Michael Angelo's Pieta, but other examples exist as well). In some cases, the religious connotations go even deeper, one such case presented in Bloodborne is a relief showing a woman looking high in the sky and holding her stomach. This is another reference to Christianity, specifically the Annunciation to Mary, in this case, he convincingly argues conclusion that in both cases it refers to divine conception – although twisted in the Bloodborne's case. And

Figure 4.
"Elden Ring" by Józef Cyran, CC0.

Figure 5.
"BloodBorne" by Clinton Crumpler, CC BY 2.0.

regarding Elden Ring, he compares the burial practice in the fictional place of Farum Azula (from Elden Ring) with the real world Varna Excavations.

Architecture and art are not the only way religious themes are incorporated into the world of Elden Ring. Tarnished Archaeologist makes effort to place the inferred (from reliefs and tablets) history of Elden Ring in the context of the myths and religious parables of Earth. He compares the "Elden John" (a term created by the community to refer to an anonymous figure from Elden Ring's statues) to biblical patriarchs such as Moses and he likewise draws a comparison between a catastrophic even in Elden Ring's history to the Great Flood myth that is prevalent in many cultures.

4.2.2 Charred thermos: Bloodborne as a poem on dissection

Bloodborne, a 2015 release by *From Software* is definitely inspired by Lovecraft and the themes of Great Old Ones (or as Bloodborne calls them Great Ones) form the main source of narration. However, Bloodborne can be viewed in a different, less literal way. Such a perspective is brought by Charred Thermos—another lore scholar who is keen to interpret *From Software*'s games [22].

Charred Thermos does not deny that there is a literal story separate from his interpretation, but he claims that there is an additional layer which many players missed—the story of Bloodborne is a parable for the history of dissection in the Edinburgh Medical School in the 17th, 18th and 19th centuries. While this claim may seem far-fetched, it is surprisingly well supported by the arguments that Charred Thermos puts forth. Perhaps the strongest reference to Edinburgh's history is the presence of caged graves in the city of Yharnam where most of Bloodborne's events take place. The strength of this argument lies in the fact that those graves are difficult to explain purely within the context of Bloodborne—there is no apparent reason why the inhabitants of Yharnam should cover their graves. Grave excavation *is* present in the game, but it is conducted only on the graves of the Great Ones (the lovecraftian divine creatures) and the human graves remain undisturbed. But we can find such caged graves in Edinburgh and the reason is quite grim—at the time when early modern medicine was starting to take foundation, the procurement of bodies was a difficult task, made more challenging by unclear and mixed attitudes of the local authorities. Thus, a new profession was found, body snatchers (also called resurrectionists) were people who illicitly dug up the graves of recently deceased individuals and sold them to the scientists employed in Edinburgh Medical School. Thus, the inhabitants of the city would often put a cage on the graves of their relatives to avoid their disturbance. Body snatchers themselves are another clue to Charred Thermos' thesis—the Graveguard set (of clothes) is an item that does not resemble guard armor or clothes but is very reminiscent of the typical body snatcher's depictions.

Charred Thermos argues further that the Bloodborne's Laurence character is inspired by an author living in 1768 named Laurence Sterne. Laurence was a famous writer and was buried after death, but sometime after his death, rumors emerged that his body was recovered and sold to be used in an anatomical dissection. Allegedly, one of the students even recognized him during the dissection, and his skull was returned to his grave, albeit without the body. This mirrors the game's Laurence, whose body was recovered and displayed on a dissection table. Finding his skull is even one of the game's quests.

All of these comparisons (among others) point to the conclusion that *From Software* has deliberately made references to the history of dissection in Great Britain. The environmental storytelling that *From Software* has chosen creates a space for the inclusion of such references and encourages the players to seek them. Even if they were included in the traditional style of narrative, players may be less inclined to engage in that level of speculation, as the story would explicitly provide the answers, and even less likely to view it in metaphorical terms.

5. Empirical insights and cognitive background

Narrative Transportation Theory, as introduced by Green and Brock [23], describes a state in which an audience becomes mentally, emotionally, and imaginatively absorbed into a story world. In this state, attention is highly focused, emotional engagement is heightened, and vivid mental imagery is formed, often accompanied by a temporary detachment from the real world. While initially developed in the context of literature and film, the concept has clear relevance to video games. Games that rely on environmental storytelling can produce transportation without requiring extended dialog or scripted exposition. Here, immersion emerges from the act of navigating, interpreting, and emotionally responding to the designed space itself.

To study how player understanding is formed through observing the environment, a 2024 study was conducted at Uppsala University. The study asked the following question: "how can we tell narrative through environments in a fast-paced 3D platforming game without stopping the player?" [24]. For the purposes of the study, a video game called *Project Chaser* was developed in four iterations. After each iteration, the test participants (players) were asked questions about their understanding of the game's story, specifically the six elements: Location (a dystopian brutalist architecture) the Government (a totalitarian government that consists of two social classes), the Guardian (the antagonist of the game, chasing the player), the Cube (a power source) and finally the Player and the Society of the world presented. The game contained no cutscenes or dialog and thus the total weight of the narrative was put on the environment with the additional constraint—the gameplay pacing did not allow the player to inspect the environment for a long time, as the Guardian was supposed to constantly chase the player throughout the level. The pacing constraint was useful in examining the story naturally formed through *narrative transportation*, as opposed to in-depth lore scholarship discussed in Section 4.

5.1 Indexical storytelling

A particular type of environmental storytelling has been recognized by Clara Fernández-Vara and termed *Indexical Storytelling*. This storytelling focuses on indices/indications. Signs in language can be broadly categorized into three types: icons, symbols and indices. Icons signify an idea through similarity (an icon of tree representing a tree), symbols have abstract meaning often separate from their form or shape and indices are physically connected to their meaning. Fernández-Vara gives smoke as an indication of fire as an example of an index [25].

In *Project Chaser,* indices were added in the second and following iterations of the game, while the first iteration consisted mostly of icons and the environment itself. An example of index which was found to be particularly effective was broken walls and graffiti which were found to significantly improve the participant's understanding of a past conflict. Another type of index was Tube Room—a chamber supposed to convey that the Guardian is an artificial, built construct.

Across the four iterations, the inclusion and refinement of such indices measurably improved player comprehension scores. Importantly, the removal—intentional or accidental—of these indices had the opposite effect. When a bug prevented the "guardian" enemy from visibly orbiting the Cube, players were far less likely to understand its protective role. This provides rare empirical confirmation that environmental cues of this kind are not merely decorative; they are functional elements in the communication of narrative.

5.2 Cultural interpretation

While transportation and indexical storytelling can be powerful, they are not universally interpreted in the same way—interpretation may be strongly shaped by player's cultural background. A notable example of such geographically diverging reception is the release of the Fallout 3 game. In the Japanese version, the option to detonate the city of Megaton—a decision which transforms the settlement into a radioactive crater—is removed. This is despite the fact, that quest never explicitly mentions Hiroshima or Nagasaki. The mere combination of radiation, destroyed structures and crater imagery evoked unpleasant associations for the Japanese public.

Another example, regarding a Western audience can be found in the releases of the Wolfenstein game. The swastikas and Nazi imagery were replaced by less controversial, although somewhat confusing alternative symbols. *Project Chaser*, developed in Sweden, intentionally modeled its governmental banners on Nazi esthetics—without using the swastika itself—to evoke associations with authoritarianism and ideological control. In regions unfamiliar with such symbolism, the banners might be read simply as abstract design elements, losing much of their narrative charge. It should be noted, however, that in Sweden the association has been quite effective in increasing the participant's understanding of the government as totalitarian.

An additional aspect to note is that Fallout's 3 crater imagery is an example of an index (the crater is physically connected to the preceding explosion), while the connection of certain flag designs to totalitarianism is symbolic.

Taken together, these observations illustrate that environmental storytelling operates at the intersection of design, cognition, and cultural context. Narrative transportation theory shows that a connection to the story world can form naturally even during fast-paced gameplay. Project Chaser demonstrates that indexical and symbolic storytelling can measurably improve player comprehension, while cultural background shapes whether the associations formed achieve their intended effect. The crater in Fallout 3 serves as an example of an index, while totalitarian flag designs in Project Chaser function symbolically. Developers should, therefore, evaluate the cultural connotations of their designs, especially when relying solely on these elements to convey the narrative.

6. Conclusions

Environmental storytelling is a powerful narrative framework that avoids traditional tools such as cutscenes and dialog, instead focusing on the design of the game world itself—inviting players to interpret and assemble meaning from what they observe. From Myst and Half-Life to Elden Ring and beyond, developers have used this approach to craft immersive worlds that not only engage players, but also inspire them to construct their own narratives. These emergent narratives often involve not just the world itself, but also its characters—especially those who do not speak, either because they are long dead by the time of the game's events, or because they are Silent Protagonists.

Ironically, such silent protagonists can be effective narrative tools—but only if their silence is meaningfully justified. Developers must provide context through the environment and supporting characters to avoid alienation or confusion, and to give the protagonist a sense of presence and personality. Evaluating the symbols and indices present in the environment through the lens of cultural context is paramount in ensuring that the intended interpretations are more likely to be formed. Richly crafted environments become fertile ground for player speculation, allowing players to re-contextualize the story not only in literal terms, but also in metaphorical or poetic dimensions. Poetry is often said to "say much with few words"—and environmental storytelling aspires to do the same, presenting layered narratives through atmosphere, space, and symbol, rather than exposition.

Conflict of interest

The authors declare no conflict of interest.

Author details

Józef P. Cyran[1], Dariusz Myszor[2] and Krzysztof A. Cyran[2*]

1 WSB-National Louis University, Nowy Sącz, Poland

2 Silesian University of Technology, Gliwice, Poland

*Address all correspondence to: krzysztof.cyran@polsl.pl

References

[1] McGonigal J. Reality Is Broken: Why Games Make us Better and How they Can Change the World. New York: The Penguin Press; 2011. 388 p. Available from: https://educacaofisicaaefcps.wordpress.com/wp-content/uploads/2018/07/reality_is_broken.pdf [Accessed: July 08, 2025]

[2] Wardrip-Fruin N. Expressive Processing: Digital Fictions, Computer Games, and Software Studies. Cambridge (MA): MIT Press; 2009. 480 p. Available from: https://archive.org/details/expressiveproces0000ward_o8q4 [Accessed: July 08, 2025]

[3] Guinness World Records. First Use of Cutscenes to Tell a Story in a Video Game. 2023. Available from: https://www.guinnessworldrecords.com/world-records/first-use-of-cutscenes-to-tell-a-story-in-a-video-game [Accessed: July 08, 2025]

[4] Nitsche M. Game Spaces Speak Volumes: Indexical Storytelling. Cambridge (MA): Massachusetts Institute of Technology; 2002. Available from: https://dspace.mit.edu/bitstream/handle/1721.1/100274/Game-Spaces-Speak-Volumes.pdf

[5] Jenkins H. Game design as narrative architecture. In: Wardrip-Fruin N, Harrigan P, editors. First Person: New Media as Story, Performance, and Game. Cambridge (MA): MIT Press; 2004. Available from: https://web.mit.edu/cms/People/henry3/games&narrative.html

[6] Williams Q. Metroid and environmental storytelling. Prose and Quans. 2019. Available from: https://quanwilliams.com/proseandquans/index.php/2019/08/04/metroid-and-environmental-storytelling

[7] System Shock. Shodan Wiki. No date. Available from: https://shodan.fandom.com/wiki/System_Shock [Accessed: July 08, 2025]

[8] Kohler C. Warren Spector on System Shock 3. Wired; 2016 [Accessed: July 08, 2025]

[9] Zu J. Design Patterns for Silent Player Characters in Narrative-Driven Games. Philadelphia: Drexel University; 2018

[10] Bomb G. The story behind BioShock's use of objectivism and Ayn Rand. Giant Bomb. 2011. Available from: https://www.giantbomb.com/articles/the-story-behind-bioshocks-use-of-objectivism-and/1100-3307/ [Accessed: July 08, 2025]

[11] CD-Action. BioShock: Atlas Zadrżał. CD-Action. 2007;**131**

[12] Cardona-Rivera RE, Zagal JP, Debus MS. Aligning story and gameplay through narrative goals. Journal of Game Design and Development Education. 2021;**1**(1):1-26

[13] Campbell C. Blood, sweat and pixels: Dark souls creator Hidetaka Miyazaki speaks. The Guardian. 2015. Available from: https://www.theguardian.com/technology/2015/mar/31/bloodborne-dark-souls-creator-hidetaka-miyazaki-interview

[14] The flow of time itself is convoluted; with heroes centuries old phasing in and out. In: Solaire of Astora – Dark Souls Wiki. Fandom. Available from: https://darksouls.wikidot.com/solaire-of-astora [Accessed: July 08, 2025]

[15] Lima ES, Feijó B, Furtado AL. Managing the plot structure of character-based interactive narratives

in games. Entertainment Computing. 2023;**47**:100590. DOI: 10.1016/j.entcom.2023.100590

[16] Tlili A, Adarkwah MA, Salha S, Huang R. How environmental perception affects players' in-game behaviors? Towards developing games in compliance with sustainable development goals. Entertainment Computing. 2024;**50**:100678. DOI: 10.1016/j.entcom.2024.100678

[17] Stuart G. In defense of far cry 5's silent protagonist. Game Rant. 2025. Available from: https://gamerant.com/far-cry-5-silent-protagonist-deputy-good-why-benefits-story/

[18] Kunzelman C. The silent protagonist of 'far cry 5' sucks. VICE. 2018. Available from: https://www.vice.com/en/article/far-cry-5-silent-protagonist

[19] Ball KD. Fan labor, speculative fiction, and video game lore in the Bloodborne community. Transformative Works and Cultures. 2017;**25**. Available from: https://journal.transformativeworks.org/index.php/twc/article/view/1156/808

[20] Tarnished Archaeologist. YouTube Channel. YouTube; 2022. Available from: https://www.youtube.com/@TarnishedArchaeologist

[21] McAnany PA, Hodder I. Thinking about stratigraphic sequence in social terms. Archaeological Dialogues. 2009;**16**(1):1-22. DOI: 10.1017/S1380203809002748

[22] The Charred Thermos. YouTube Channel. YouTube; 2020. Available from: https://www.youtube.com/@TheCharredThermos

[23] Green MC, Appel M. Narrative transportation: How stories shape how we see ourselves and the world. Media Psychology. 2024;**27**(1):1-25. DOI: 10.1037/med0000327

[24] Jansson M, Bekker T. Project Chaser: Telling Stories through Environmental Cues in a Fast-Paced Game. Uppsala: Uppsala University; 2024

[25] Fernández-Vara C. Game Spaces Speak Volumes: Indexical Storytelling. In: Proceedings of DiGRA-Based Conference. New York: New York University; 2011

Section 3

Games and Learning: Educational Approaches through Play

Chapter 6

A Brief Discussion on Research Experiences in Games and Learning: A Predecessor of a Community of Practice Approach in Taiwan

Tieh-Huai Chang

Abstract

This chapter explores the evolving role of digital gamesx in educational research, with particular emphasis on informal learning practices within Taiwanese gaming communities. Historically viewed negatively due to associations with academic distraction, digital games are increasingly acknowledged as meaningful environments for developing essential competencies, such as strategic thinking, collaborative problem-solving, and adaptive creativity. By employing ethnographic methods and the Community of Practice (CoP) framework, this study demonstrates how player interactions in games like Pokémon Go exhibit sophisticated cognitive, social, and cultural skills frequently neglected by traditional education. A quadrant-based analytical model is introduced to systematically classify player competencies, shifting the focus from outcome-based evaluations toward understanding broader learning ecologies. Nevertheless, significant cultural and institutional barriers persist in Taiwan, including educational conservatism and limited academic recognition of informal learning contexts. In conclusion, this chapter advocates for acknowledging gaming as a legitimate site for educational innovation and suggests reframing scholarly and pedagogical approaches accordingly.

Keywords: game-based learning, community of practice (CoP), Taiwan, gamer competencies, analytical framework

1. Introduction

Games have long drawn the interest of educational researchers, though their role in learning continues to spark debate. Traditionally regarded with suspicion—often seen as distractions that could hinder academic progress—digital games were linked to poorer academic performance. A British longitudinal study involving 600 adolescents over 2 years, for instance, found that students who played video games less frequently tended to perform better academically than their peers who played more often [1].

Similar findings are echoed in Taiwanese research, which further suggests a consistent negative association between gaming and academic achievement [2].

In recent years, however, educational perspectives have shifted notably. Gamification is now being embraced as a legitimate pedagogical tool, *marking a departure* from earlier skepticism. Leading textbook publishers in Taiwan, for example, have begun to integrate interactive, game-based elements into their educational materials. These platforms aim to boost student engagement and learning effectiveness, and early results have shown promising improvements in both motivation and academic outcomes [3].

Educational perspectives on gaming have undergone a marked transformation, with growing recognition of its potential as a rich avenue for non-formal but meaningful learning. The MacArthur Foundation (2014), for example, advocates recognizing the unique competencies developed by digital natives—young individuals who have been immersed in gaming-rich environments from an early age. From early classics like Super Mario and Tetris to modern franchises such as World of Warcraft and League of Legends, digital games are seen to foster cognitive, social, and cultural skills that are often underappreciated in traditional educational settings [4].

Leading scholars like James Paul Gee and John Seely Brown emphasize the emergence of critical yet often-overlooked gaming-based literacies, which encompass adaptive problem-solving, strategic thinking, and collaborative skills—abilities that are seldom nurtured within conventional classroom instruction but prove highly valuable in real-world contexts [5–7].

Gaming encourages players to become active participants, fostering *collaborative problem-solving and creative thinking*. Jane McGonigal [8, 9] underscores how games can enhance player engagement, cooperation, and critical reasoning—skills that, when harnessed, may empower individuals to contribute to meaningful change beyond the virtual realm. This potential is exemplified in empirical research, particularly within the *Pokémon Go* community. There, players have been observed engaging in practices that *resemble scientific inquiry*—including forming hypotheses, conducting informal experiments, and analyzing shared data collaboratively to refine strategies and expand communal knowledge [10]. These player-driven learning processes closely parallel those found in established Communities of Practice (CoP), suggesting that the mechanisms underlying game-based collaboration hold *significant promise for application in formal educational environments*.

Players' informal, self-directed learning experiences warrant careful scrutiny for their educational relevance and implications. Although gaming communities have demonstrated substantial learning potential, these informal domains are still frequently undervalued by traditional educational paradigms. Taiwanese gamers, for example, have achieved international recognition through their performance in diverse competitive platforms—from Age of Empires and StarCraft to more recent titles like League of Legends and Hearthstone. Yet, these accomplishments are often underrecognized within mainstream educational narratives [11]. This lack of acknowledgment highlights the need to systematically assess and validate competencies cultivated through gaming. Doing so could prompt a reconsideration of how academic institutions define and value learning and skill development in the digital age.

A growing body of empirical research from Taiwanese classrooms highlights the effectiveness of game-based learning platforms in boosting student motivation and engagement. Studies conducted in elementary school settings, for instance, reveal that students are capable of adapting educational games in creative ways to heighten both enjoyment and learning outcomes. These practices—often referred to as "re-gamification"—not

DOI: http://dx.doi.org/10.5772/intechopen.1011774

only help maintain students' attention but also foster critical thinking, creativity, and problem-solving skills [12]. Students have been observed identifying limitations in game design, redefining goals, and even devising new levels and rule systems. Such behaviors reflect not only a high degree of learner autonomy but also sophisticated strategic thinking [13–15], suggesting valuable directions for future instructional design.

These findings challenge long-held assumptions that question the educational legitimacy of game-based learning within formal settings. What has often been regarded as mere entertainment is now increasingly recognized as a potentially immersive and adaptive form of twenty-first-century learning. In instances where standard game environments lose their appeal, players who reinterpret the experience as a personal challenge exemplify the mindset described by Seymour Papert and Nicole Lazzaro as "hard fun"—a form of enjoyment rooted in overcoming difficulty [16, 17]. This shift is evident in Chang and Chen's [12] observations, where students frequently increased the challenge of educational games by imposing their own constraints or altering the sequence of gameplay. Such behaviors indicate a deep state of flow and sustained engagement, which research links to greater motivation and long-term cognitive investment [18, 19].

Indeed, it is within these complex, game-mediated environments that players consistently exhibit resilience, strategic thinking, and collaborative coordination. Whether navigating intricate puzzles, managing virtual economies, or leading online teams, players must adapt to evolving challenges and dynamic conditions. Such behaviors are far from incidental; they constitute purposeful learning performances situated within goal-driven communities. Viewed through the lens of situated learning and Communities of Practice [20, 21], these adaptive and collective behaviors exemplify robust forms of informal learning. For instance, Chang [22] documented how Pokémon Go players engage in verifying crowd-sourced data, critiquing and refining hypotheses, and iteratively developing shared strategies—activities that closely mirror the practices of scientific inquiry [23]. Similarly, the Foldit project illustrates how gamer communities can collaboratively solve complex biochemical problems within days, underscoring the cognitive and collaborative potential inherent in game-based learning contexts [24].

This line of inquiry prompts a broader philosophical reconsideration of where and how meaningful learning occurs. If learning is understood as a fundamentally social and contextual process—driven by participation in meaningful practices—then gaming communities may represent compelling examples of contemporary, learner-centered cultures. This view resonates with calls from learning scientists to expand the scope of inquiry beyond traditional classroom environments and to recognize the richness of authentic learning across informal, interest-driven spaces [7, 25, 26]. Lin [27] further contends that many negative perceptions of gaming stem from outsider viewpoints, including those of educators, policymakers, and media portrayals, which often overlook the nuanced practices embedded in gamer culture. By framing gamer communities as legitimate knowledge ecosystems, researchers are better equipped to identify and validate player competencies—thereby pushing the epistemological boundaries of learning sciences and expanding what counts as valuable knowledge and expertise in the digital age.

In this sense, the significance of gaming surpasses conventional educational innovation—it compels a rethinking of the epistemological limits traditionally associated with schooling. By treating gaming as a serious site of cultural production and skill development, educators and researchers can foster more inclusive, culturally responsive, and intrinsically motivated learning opportunities. Liang [28] called for micro-analytical approaches to ACG (anime, comics, and games) studies, highlighting how academic discourse has historically marginalized player cultures. Responding to this gap, Chang and Jan [29] proposed a quadrant-based analytical model designed to classify various player competencies. This framework offers a more systematic lens for understanding the diverse forms of expertise cultivated within gaming communities—addressing the long-standing lack of structure in this field [30, 31].

Ultimately, reframing gaming from a perceived distraction to a legitimate domain of disciplinary inquiry underscores the pressing need for interdisciplinary collaboration. To fully understand the complex cognitive, social, and cultural dimensions of gameplay, educational researchers must engage with game designers, sociologists, and cultural theorists. Education policy, in turn, should advance supportive frameworks that acknowledge informal learning outcomes, invest in teacher professional development for game-based pedagogy, and cultivate school–community partnerships that actively incorporate gamer perspectives. This collaborative agenda is bolstered by a growing body of empirical research—not only from game studies but also from cognitive psychology [32], social interaction research [33], and cultural practice theory [34]—which collectively validate the educational relevance of gaming as a rich, multidimensional learning environment.

Given these considerations, Taiwan offers a particularly rich context for advancing systematic research into the educational dimensions of gaming—owing to its vibrant gaming culture, robust digital infrastructure, and growing interest in pedagogical innovation. Overcoming persistent biases and misconceptions demands a sustained scholarly effort to understand how gaming experiences can meaningfully contribute to various aspects of formal education, including student engagement, collaboration, and problem-solving. By laying a strong theoretical and empirical groundwork, this chapter positions the Community of Practice framework as a productive and nuanced lens for investigating, interpreting, and facilitating learning within game-mediated environments—opening new pathways for future inquiry and educational practice.

2. Research experiences and problematization

2.1 Early encounters with games and learning

The author's initial engagement with the question of games and learning did not emerge from established theoretical frameworks, but rather from direct observation of students' everyday experiences in educational settings. Before formally conceptualizing games as learning environments, the author—then an educator—encountered a recurring and thought-provoking paradox: students who appeared disengaged in conventional classroom activities consistently displayed extraordinary levels of enthusiasm, persistence, and concentration when interacting with digital games.

This contradiction raised foundational questions that, at the time, lacked a clear theoretical vocabulary within mainstream educational discourse. A pivotal moment occurred in a high school library, where the author observed a student who consistently struggled with completing written assignments, yet painstakingly maintained a hand-drawn spreadsheet documenting the evolution and drop rates of rare monsters in a digital game. The level of detail in this record—meticulously categorized, regularly updated, and peer-reviewed—rivaled that of formal scientific documentation.

DOI: http://dx.doi.org/10.5772/intechopen.1011774

At that point, no educational theory the author was familiar with offered a conceptual lens adequate to interpret the student's activity. This was not simply gameplay—it involved pattern recognition, hypothesis generation, iterative testing, and collaborative knowledge-sharing, closely resembling practices associated with citizen science and informal research literacies. These observations gave rise to a series of foundational inquiries: If such sophisticated behavior could emerge from game-based engagement, why were these environments not acknowledged as legitimate learning contexts? Might students be exhibiting *cognitive and strategic competencies* that remained unrecognized within formal schooling frameworks? Could it be that conventional definitions of intelligence and academic success were misaligned with the realities of twenty-first-century learners? At the time, these reflections had not yet coalesced into formal research questions. Instead, they emerged as a sense of *pedagogical dissonance*—a growing awareness that students were demonstrating resilience, growth, and knowledge construction in informal settings, yet these learning signals remained largely invisible to institutional metrics and assessment systems.

What followed was a self-initiated period of immersive fieldwork, during which the author began engaging with digital gaming communities—exploring game forums, subscribing to walkthrough creators on YouTube, and eventually participating in online guilds. Through these experiences, it became evident that what was often labeled as a gaming "subculture" functioned more accurately as a complex ecosystem of informal apprenticeship, collaborative knowledge exchange, strategy refinement, and iterative peer feedback. Players were not passive consumers of content; they actively contributed by developing game modifications, creating community-generated glossaries and ranking metrics, and upholding shared norms through self-regulated codes of conduct. From an educational perspective, this participatory environment bore striking resemblance to a living research laboratory or an open-source software community—more akin to dynamic sites of knowledge production than to traditional notions of recreational activity.

During this phase of engagement, informal interviews and diary-based observations gradually evolved into a more structured qualitative inquiry. Many students enthusiastically shared their in-game learning experiences, often articulating them with a level of specificity and metacognitive reflection that surpassed their typical classroom discourse. One student described cultivating "situational awareness" through fast-paced action gameplay—a skill involving real-time decision-making and spatial orientation. Another reflected on learning the fundamentals of probability theory by analyzing the odds embedded in gacha mechanics. A third noted that serving as a guild leader offered more meaningful lessons in interpersonal communication and conflict resolution than years of participating in school-based group projects. These reflections highlighted not only the depth of cognitive engagement present in gaming contexts, but also the potential for students to develop and articulate nuanced understandings of their own learning processes—often in ways that elude traditional educational assessments.

Despite these insights, *institutional skepticism remained pronounced*. Early efforts to share these findings with colleagues and school administrators were frequently met with doubt. One principal, in a tone of dismissal, asked, "Are you trying to turn school into a game?"—a rhetorical question that, over time, evolved into a valuable point of inquiry. This moment highlighted a deeper tension: the widespread assumption that play and discipline are mutually exclusive, and that academic rigor must be devoid of enjoyment or intrinsic motivation. These responses revealed the limitations of prevailing educational paradigms, which often reduce games to instrumental tools for improving test performance. What became increasingly evident was the need for a *theoretical framework that recognized games as learning environments in their own right*—spaces that organically scaffold cognitive, social, and strategic forms of learning that are frequently overlooked by conventional assessment systems.

The early phase of this research journey was marked by a sense of productive ambivalence: an awareness that meaningful learning was occurring within gaming environments, yet an absence of theoretical and institutional frameworks to adequately describe or legitimize it. As a result, the inquiry unfolded through a mode best described as "learning by following"—an ethnographically inspired approach rooted in close attention to players' discourses, practices, and cultural logics. It was only upon engaging with the foundational work of Gee [5], Steinkuehler and Duncan [23], and Lave and Wenger [20] that these previously disparate insights began to crystallize. Their frameworks provided the necessary vocabulary and conceptual scaffolding to transform observational reflections into a coherent research trajectory—one grounded in the recognition of games as socially situated, culturally meaningful, and cognitively rich learning ecologies.

In retrospect, this period was characterized less by the formulation of testable hypotheses and more by an interpretive openness to the epistemic frameworks of those whose practices had long been marginalized within conventional educational paradigms. It was through sustained observation—watching students teach one another, iterate strategies, and solve problems collaboratively in digital contexts—that the foundations of a Community of Practice perspective began to emerge. Rather than originating from abstract theorizing, this perspective was grounded in lived, moment-to-moment interactions that revealed learning as a social, adaptive, and deeply contextual process. The recognition that these players were already participating in legitimate forms of learning—albeit in nontraditional modalities—marked not only a shift in the author's understanding, but the genuine starting point of a sustained inquiry into the intersections of games, culture, and education.

2.2 Confronting three major research challenges

Researching games and learning in Taiwan has unfolded as both a personal and professional journey—shaped initially by skepticism, challenged by institutional and methodological obstacles, and ultimately transformed through sustained theoretical engagement. Drawing from years of empirical interaction with player communities and educational institutions, this section identifies and examines three recurring problematics that have emerged throughout the research trajectory: the marginalization of player knowledge, the institutional resistance to informal learning modalities, and the conceptual tension between play and academic legitimacy [5, 27–29].

The research journey was sparked by a deceptively simple yet theoretically generative question: why do students exhibit such deep immersion in digital games and might this immersion harbor meaningful learning processes? This inquiry did not emerge from laboratory trials or abstract theorizing, but rather from field-based observations—instances where students who appeared disengaged in formal classroom settings became intensely focused, socially coordinated, and strategically agile within gaming environments [7, 8, 22, 23]. In one notable case, a group of middle school students displayed marked passivity during science lessons, yet demonstrated remarkable coordination during cooperative gameplay. They tracked drop rates, logged in-game coordinates, and collaboratively refined strategies via mobile chat platforms. This *behavioral bifurcation*—passive in class, expert in play—raised a pressing empirical question: were game environments activating forms of cognition or intelligence unrecognized by traditional schooling? These early observations set the stage for a deeper inquiry into how such learning might be systematically identified, articulated, and theorized within broader educational frameworks.

One of the earliest and most persistent barriers in this research trajectory was the absence of established academic frameworks within which to meaningfully situate game-based learning in the Taiwanese context. As Lin [27] has observed, digital game research in Taiwan has historically faced challenges akin to those experienced by early gender studies—not in subject matter, but in its *lack of academic legitimacy, underdeveloped conceptual tools, and peripheral status within mainstream educational discourse*. This theoretical vacuum produced two problematic tendencies. First, there was an over-reliance on imported psychological and cognitive-behavioral models—frameworks that often *individualized learning outcomes while neglecting the cultural, social, and communal dimensions of gameplay*. Second, games were frequently mischaracterized as mere instructional tools, thereby flattening their complex cultural, esthetic, and participatory qualities. Compared to STEM disciplines—where theoretical and methodological scaffolding is robust and institutionalized—educational game research remained *epistemologically nascent*, lacking both shared analytical vocabularies and the academic legitimacy required for inclusion in mainstream journals or policy discussions [6, 28, 30, 31].

The second major challenge was methodological in nature: conducting research on players necessitates a high level of familiarity with the linguistic conventions, procedural logic, and cultural practices that characterize gaming environments—dimensions often overlooked or unfamiliar to many educational researchers. Without sustained, insider-level participation in gaming communities, it becomes difficult to meaningfully interpret in-game behaviors, evolving social norms, or emergent literacies [5, 35, 36]. Early fieldwork included observations in after-school programs and esports clubs, but these encounters soon revealed the limitations of surface-level ethnography. For instance, observing a group of high school students collaboratively develop macro-scripts for an MMORPG highlighted more than just technical proficiency—it revealed complex acts of collaborative problem-solving, ethical negotiation, and rhetorical positioning, as students debated whether their actions constituted cheating or creative innovation. Traditional research instruments—such as rubrics, surveys, or pre/post comprehension tests—were poorly equipped to capture these multidimensional learning processes. The field called for methodological tools capable of tracing procedural reasoning, symbolic literacy, community-driven ethical reasoning, and affective labor—forms of knowledge production that remain largely invisible within standard educational evaluation frameworks.

The third key challenge emerged at the level of theory. Dominant paradigms in educational research have traditionally prioritized linear models of instruction, fixed curricular sequences, and standardized assessment metrics—a stark contrast to the nonlinear, exploratory, and feedback-driven dynamics that define gameplay [7, 32, 33, 37]. Game-based communities operate more like participatory knowledge ecologies, where learning unfolds through trial-and-error, mutual scaffolding, and peer-to-peer interaction, rather than through hierarchical transmission. This theoretical tension became especially salient when the researcher attempted to map conventional outcome frameworks—such as Bloom's taxonomy or the SOLO taxonomy—onto player practices like theory crafting (systematic strategy development in complex games) or collaboratively designing game rules in sandbox environments like Minecraft. These practices involve high levels of abstraction, creativity, and negotiation, yet they fall outside traditional metrics of academic success. As exemplified by the Foldit project [24], gaming communities are capable of generating significant scientific insights through collaborative play. However, such cases remain marginal within mainstream educational discourse—particularly in contexts such as East Asia, where didactic instruction and high-stakes testing continue to shape dominant definitions of educational value.

Beyond academic frameworks, public discourse in Taiwan also presented cultural challenges. Media portrayals often pathologized gaming, associating it with addiction or youth delinquency [11, 38, 39]. In one memorable television roundtable, a school principal equated gaming with "intellectual decay," prompting the researcher to reflect on the moral panic narratives surrounding youth digital practices. These narratives marginalized not only gamers but researchers attempting to study them. At the policy level, digital games were often discussed under the umbrella of mental health, rather than cultural literacy or civic participation. Formal schooling remained largely skeptical of games, reinforcing dichotomies between leisure and learning. Yet paradoxically, many of the same institutions adopted gamified educational platforms without acknowledging the deeper literacies cultivated through authentic gameplay.

Eventually, the author's research encountered a conceptual breakthrough through the Community of Practice (CoP) framework, introduced by Lave and Wenger [20] *and later expanded by Wenger* [21]. CoP offered a powerful vocabulary to explain emergent, situated learning outside of formal instruction [20, 21, 40, 41]. Rather than seeing learning as content transfer, CoP emphasized identity, practice, and participation. Through this lens, the researcher was able to interpret players' activities—such as the negotiation of tactics, the compilation of guides, and the role modeling of veteran players—as forms of enculturation into a knowledge community. In one case study, Pokémon Go players in Taiwan collaboratively mapped spawn zones using publicly editable Google Sheets, developing an entire lexicon of symbols and strategies. These practices not only mirrored scientific methods (hypothesis formation and data triangulation) but also fulfilled CoP's criteria for mutual engagement and shared repertoire.

This reconceptualization also changed the methodological posture of the researcher. Rather than evaluating from a distance, the role shifted toward participant-observation and co-inquiry [42–45]. Digital ethnography, discourse analysis, and microethnographic approaches became key tools in capturing the nuanced, tacit knowledge practices of gamers. For example, by joining private Discord servers and participating in voice-chat raids, the researcher was able to observe real-time decision-making, linguistic improvisation, and social bonding—phenomena nearly invisible in survey-based approaches. These methods allowed access to learning processes as they unfolded organically, aligned with what Thomas and Brown [7] described as a "new culture of learning." Such research also acknowledged the legitimacy of player epistemologies—logics rooted in experimentation, social coordination, and adaptive creativity.

Ultimately, the research journey mapped in this chapter reflects a transition from externally imposed assessment models to a framework grounded in sociocultural insight and learner agency. By embedding learning within Communities of Practice, researchers can better capture the richness of game-based learning environments [5, 21, 28, 46]. This perspective not only revalues the intellectual labor of players but also invites educators and policymakers to rethink where and how powerful learning takes place.

2.3 Local constraints in Taiwan's academic and cultural contexts

Taiwan's educational and research landscape presents additional hurdles that are not solely epistemological or methodological, but deeply cultural and institutional. These challenges are embedded in dominant value systems, public discourse, policy frameworks, and the disciplinary boundaries of academia itself. In this section, we examine three interrelated domains where local constraints shape the possibilities for conducting and legitimizing research on games and learning: the conservatism of Taiwan's education system, the marginalization of ACG (anime, comics, and games) culture within scholarly discourse, and the absence of institutionalized recognition for games as a valid subject of inquiry.

First, Taiwan's formal education system remains largely conservative in its pedagogical assumptions and learning objectives. Curricula emphasize test preparation, standardization, and the cultivation of "correct" forms of knowledge, leaving little room for experimentation, ambiguity, or informal inquiry. This rigidity is mirrored in the structure of teacher training programs and the incentive mechanisms that reward measurable outcomes over creative risk-taking. As a result, research proposals that focus on playful learning, emergent literacies, or affective learning environments are often dismissed as lacking rigor. Within such a context, proposing research on games not as tools but as sites of cultural production and learning communities tends to trigger institutional skepticism, if not outright rejection.

Furthermore, the influence of Confucian educational ideals—respect for authority, emphasis on rote memorization, and reverence for textual traditions—has contributed to the valorization of formal schooling and the stigmatization of informal or recreational activities. Game-related behaviors are frequently described in public discourse using deficit language, as in terms like "addiction," "waste of time," or "moral hazard." These narratives are reinforced through media representation, policy debates, and even textbook portrayals, making it difficult to advocate for game-based research without first justifying its moral and developmental legitimacy.

Second, within Taiwan's academic structures, ACG culture remains largely marginalized. While some interdisciplinary programs and cultural studies departments have begun to recognize the importance of digital youth cultures, most mainstream education and psychology departments treat ACG content as peripheral or frivolous. The lack of dedicated academic journals, conferences, or institutional funding streams focused on game research reflects a structural invisibility. Moreover, researchers who engage seriously with game studies often find themselves positioned awkwardly—too technical for cultural studies, too cultural for cognitive science, and too playful for education. This epistemic displacement discourages early-career scholars from entering the field, perpetuating a cycle of underdevelopment.

An illustrative example concerns the limited availability of explicitly game-related categories in major national funding programs such as those administered by the National Science and Technology Council (NSTC) or the Ministry of Education. While funding mechanisms increasingly acknowledge the role of digital tools in education, proposals focusing on games—particularly those involving popular or commercial titles—are often redirected toward general digital learning or media literacy categories [47]. This redirection typically favors research that emphasizes educational design over cultural exploration. As such, projects aiming to use games designed by researchers for educational purposes are more readily accepted, particularly when they are accompanied by clear curricular ties and outcome assessments. However, proposals referencing broader forms of gameplay, including community-driven or fan-generated practices, still face difficulty receiving recognition due to perceived ambiguity about their academic relevance or developmental contribution. In university review contexts, publications tied to formal educational applications of games—such as serious games or gamified assessments—tend to receive more institutional support than those focusing on critical studies or ethnographic observation of commercial gaming environments. This pattern underscores the importance of aligning research agendas with educational policy priorities while also advocating for broader recognition of diverse forms of learning associated with digital play.

Third, the lack of an established research ecosystem around games leads to a scarcity of methodological and conceptual precedents that future researchers can follow. Unlike areas such as reading comprehension or STEM education, where canonical texts, tested instruments, and widely accepted frameworks exist, game-based research in Taiwan often begins from scratch. Scholars must invent new coding schemes, adapt models from unrelated disciplines, or work in relative isolation due to the paucity of local mentors and institutional support networks. This "epistemic solitude" makes longitudinal or programmatic research difficult to sustain.

Moreover, ethical review boards (IRBs) are not always equipped to assess studies involving online game communities, especially those involving pseudonymous participants, cross-border interactions, or data drawn from commercial platforms. Without clear precedents or guidelines, researchers risk either over-restricting their designs or facing administrative delays that can derail time-sensitive fieldwork.

In summary, the constraints facing game-based research in Taiwan are multifaceted. They include cultural attitudes that equate games with deviance, institutional structures that marginalize ACG content, and infrastructural absences that hinder sustainable inquiry. Overcoming these barriers requires not only theoretical innovation and methodological adaptation, but also active efforts to shift the discursive and policy terrain in which research on games and learning is embedded.

2.4 Reframing the research agenda: From outcome evaluation to community-centered inquiry

Faced with these cultural and institutional challenges, the author gradually shifted focus from evaluating games solely as instructional tools to understanding the broader learning ecologies in which players operate. This turn was shaped by both necessity and insight: necessity, because conventional evaluation frameworks failed to accommodate the sociocultural richness of gaming communities; and insight, because theoretical tools from situated learning revealed that players were not merely recipients of content but active constructors of meaning within social contexts.

Initially, research efforts were aimed at determining whether games could improve test scores or deliver measurable learning outcomes—an approach that aligned with dominant paradigms in education. However, field observations consistently demonstrated that players engaged in collaborative problem-solving, self-directed learning, and critical reflection in ways that traditional tests could not capture. These insights led to a pivot away from outcome-driven evaluation toward a focus on competencies, literacies, and community practices.

The adoption of the Community of Practice (CoP) framework [20] provided a conceptual foundation for this shift. CoP reframed learning as participation in meaningful social practice, not merely the internalization of knowledge. Through this lens, guilds, forums, Discord servers, and even walkthrough collaborations could be seen as sites of apprenticeship, negotiation, and shared meaning-making. This perspective legitimized player knowledge not only as valid but as valuable for understanding new modes of learning in the digital age.

Fieldwork with Pokémon Go communities further solidified this perspective. Players self-organized mapping initiatives, co-authored strategy guides, and conducted informal experiments to test game mechanics. These activities reflected forms of inquiry, argumentation, and revision consistent with academic knowledge practices—albeit outside institutional boundaries. What began as casual ethnographic observation evolved into a structured inquiry into how player communities functioned as decentralized learning networks.

By focusing on the ways players articulate problems, construct solutions, and distribute expertise, the research began to emphasize "learning in the wild" rather than "learning in the lab." This shift also altered data collection methods. Surveys and rubrics gave way to discourse analysis, trace ethnography, and microanalytic studies of in-game interaction. Interviews focused less on content recall and more on decision-making strategies, peer feedback loops, and the language of coordination.

The implications of this shift extended beyond research design. It challenged the very assumptions underpinning educational innovation. Instead of asking how games could be aligned to preexisting curriculum standards, the question became how schooling could adapt to recognize and scaffold the kinds of learning that already occurred in game communities. This reframing opened up new directions for curriculum design, teacher professional development, and assessment reform.

Ultimately, the author's research agenda was reoriented: not toward legitimizing games through conventional educational measures, but toward reconceptualizing what counts as learning. This shift not only aligned with global trends in learning sciences but also responded to the specific cultural, institutional, and epistemic conditions of the Taiwanese context. In this way, the research trajectory moved from a question of whether games "work" to an exploration of how players work—and what educators might learn from them. It is important to foreground the cultural specificity of these constraints. Game research is not simply a matter of importing Western paradigms or validating games as educational media—it requires grappling with local ideologies, institutional inertia, and scholarly hierarchies. These constraints are not merely obstacles, but structural conditions that shape what can be known, said, and legitimized in the field of games and learning in Taiwan.

3. Connecting theory and practice

3.1 Theoretical demands emerging from empirical disruptions

The transition from field-based observations to theoretical refinement began not from a deliberate search for novelty, but from persistent friction between empirical encounters and conceptual adequacy. As the previous chapter documented, the learning behaviors exhibited by players—collaborative experimentation, sustained engagement, iterative adaptation—frequently defied categorization within the frameworks most commonly used in educational research. Rubrics designed for classroom behavior or content mastery often failed to recognize the knowledge forms and competencies demonstrated in digital play contexts.

The discomfort grew especially pronounced when attempting to explain how players, acting outside of formal instruction, developed and shared knowledge across distributed networks. In cooperative games and online communities, players not only solved problems together but also negotiated roles, debated strategies, and archived community knowledge. These were not isolated performances of skill but embedded practices within social settings. Traditional theories such as behaviorism or even constructivism offered limited vocabulary to address these participatory dynamics.

What was needed was a theory of learning that treated knowledge not as an object to be acquired, but as a process situated in activity and interaction. This perspective had to recognize that learning emerges through doing, with others, in contexts where shared goals and mutual accountability are continuously negotiated. It also needed to accommodate the fluid and emergent nature of learning in player-driven contexts—where authority is distributed, and knowledge is often experimental or provisional.

The Community of Practice (CoP) framework, initially articulated by Lave and Wenger [20], entered the scene not as a perfect fit but as a promising lens through which to reframe the phenomena being observed. CoP theorizes learning as social participation, where individuals become members of a community through legitimate peripheral participation and gradually move toward fuller forms of engagement. Learning here is not an outcome but a trajectory—a process of identity formation within a context of shared practice.

Applying this theory to player communities suggested a radical reframing: from evaluating games as instructional tools to understanding games as cultural infrastructures that host communities of learning. This theoretical shift did not negate earlier insights about content acquisition or skill development but placed them within a broader ecology of practice. CoP allowed for the recognition that players do not merely absorb knowledge—they produce, refine, and circulate it in ways that resemble apprenticeship, peer mentoring, and collaborative inquiry.

In this chapter, we trace how this conceptual shift unfolded and how the Community of Practice framework offers a structured way to account for the informal, fluid, and socially situated learning that occurs in game-based communities. Rather than retrofitting player behavior into existing learning taxonomies, the chapter argues for adopting a framework that already speaks to the lived logic of participation, practice, and community formation in digital play spaces.

3.2 Core concepts of the community of practice framework

To understand how Communities of Practice (CoP) can serve as an analytic tool for game-based learning, it is essential to first unpack its foundational elements. According to Lave and Wenger [20], and later expanded upon by Wenger [21], a CoP is defined by three interdependent components: mutual engagement, joint enterprise, and shared repertoire. These are not merely structural categories, but dynamic processes through which social learning unfolds.

Mutual Engagement refers to the social interactions that bind members together in sustained activity. In a CoP, participation is not incidental or superficial; it is continuous, responsive, and anchored in practice. Members negotiate roles, resolve conflicts, and build trust through repeated engagement. In gaming contexts, this may be seen in players forming guilds, participating in raids, or moderating forums—spaces where identity and knowledge are co-constructed over time.

Joint Enterprise highlights the shared goals and negotiated commitments that give a community coherence. Unlike formal curricula, joint enterprises emerge organically and are shaped by the participants themselves. In game communities, this often takes the form of co-developing strategies, optimizing performance metrics, or completing collaborative challenges. Importantly, these goals are rarely fixed; they evolve through the actions and dialogs of the group, reflecting both internal diversity and external contingencies.

Shared Repertoire encompasses the communal resources—tools, language, routines, symbols, narratives—that develop over time within a community. These artifacts do more than support communication; they embody the history and ethos of the community. In gaming CoPs, shared repertoire includes everything from memes and in-jokes to walkthroughs, spreadsheets, and modding scripts. Such materials are not neutral but are actively shaped by and reflective of the community's values and problem-solving approaches.

Together, these three elements articulate a view of learning that is collaborative, situated, and deeply cultural. They also emphasize that belonging and identity formation are central to knowledge acquisition—a critical insight for game-based learning, where players often learn not from instruction but through doing, observing, and iterating within a community.

Understanding these core concepts equips us to ask richer questions: What kinds of participation count as legitimate in a gaming community? How are newcomers socialized into complex practices? What role do artifacts play in transmitting shared meaning? These inquiries, grounded in the CoP framework, provide a vocabulary to interpret the practices and pedagogies emerging organically within gaming cultures.

3.3 Why gaming communities exemplify communities of practice?

With the three core dimensions of CoP—mutual engagement, joint enterprise, and shared repertoire—clearly defined, we can now examine why gaming communities so vividly exemplify these characteristics. In digital game spaces, particularly those that support persistent, collaborative play, players organize themselves in ways that closely mirror the mechanics of a learning community. Rather than passively receiving instruction, players actively co-construct meaning, norms, and knowledge through continuous interaction and situated participation.

In terms of mutual engagement, gaming communities offer sustained interaction structures that promote coordination, dialog, and interpersonal accountability. This can be seen most clearly in guilds and teams that collaborate over time, developing shared rituals and conflict resolution practices. For example, in games like World of Warcraft or Destiny 2, players must coordinate real-time raids requiring finely-tuned communication and responsiveness. These environments cultivate not just strategic thinking but also trust, reputation, and peer validation—the very social dynamics that define engagement in a CoP.

Joint enterprise becomes evident in the way players align around shared objectives, whether defeating a boss, solving a puzzle, or climbing a competitive ladder. Importantly, these goals are not externally imposed by curriculum designers but negotiated within the community. Players set challenges, experiment with strategies, and adapt to shifting game mechanics together. In many cases, players must also reconcile different playstyles, motivations, and skill levels, fostering a sense of mutual accountability.

Shared repertoire in gaming is both deep and diverse. Veteran players develop, curate, and circulate walkthroughs, toolkits, glossaries, macros, and even fan-made visualizations that become foundational knowledge within a community. These resources are not static; they evolve through commentary, remixing, and reinterpretation. On forums and Discord channels, terms such as "meta," "aggro," or "nerf" serve as shorthand for complex strategic or narrative constructs. Over time, such terms gain specific cultural meanings that reinforce the community's identity and learning trajectory.

A particularly illustrative example is the Pokémon Go player community in Taiwan. Following the game's launch, local players rapidly began organizing knowledge-sharing practices, including community mapping of PokéStops, raid scheduling, and analysis of spawn patterns. Players contributed to shared Google Sheets or LINE groups where real-time updates and field observations were exchanged. These were not just information repositories but living documents shaped by user interaction and sustained trust. Novices were gradually integrated into these communities through mentorship and peripheral participation, echoing the CoP concept of identity development through practice.

Moreover, these communities extended beyond gameplay. Events like "Community Day" became opportunities for in-person gathering, reinforcing bonds formed online and creating hybrid participation structures that bridged digital and physical worlds. This blending of modalities—online strategy refinement and offline socialization—highlighted the community's capacity to cultivate long-term engagement and cultural continuity.

In sum, the practices of game players—particularly within well-established gaming communities—consistently exhibit the structural and functional characteristics of CoPs. Players do not just consume content; they co-create meaning, negotiate values, and recursively build upon shared practices. Recognizing this alignment opens up rich analytic possibilities: we can move from asking "what do players learn?" to exploring "how do gaming communities learn, adapt, and transmit knowledge together?" It also foregrounds the necessity of valuing these communities as sites of legitimate, dynamic, and culturally situated learning.

3.4 Potentials and limitations of CoP as an analytical framework for game-based learning

The adoption of the Community of Practice (CoP) framework for analyzing game-based learning brings with it a number of compelling strengths. First and foremost, CoP excels in making visible the informal, socially situated nature of learning that often occurs in gaming environments. Unlike traditional educational theories that prioritize instruction, CoP allows researchers to focus on participation, identity development, and the evolving norms of communal knowledge production. This perspective is particularly valuable for understanding how players acquire skills, refine strategies, and develop shared vocabularies—not through explicit teaching, but through immersion in collective practice.

Another strength lies in CoP's ability to trace learning trajectories over time. In many gaming communities, newcomers enter at the periphery, observing, mimicking, and gradually contributing. Over time, they become core members who create content, mentor others, and shape the group's direction. This dynamic process maps closely onto CoP's concept of legitimate peripheral participation, providing a robust language for describing informal onboarding processes that are often difficult to capture using conventional assessments.

Furthermore, CoP provides a flexible structure for examining learning across contexts. It bridges online and offline practices, enabling researchers to understand how knowledge flows between game sessions, forum discussions, and real-world applications. For example, a player's experience coordinating a raid team may later inform their approach to project management in academic or workplace settings. This transfer of competencies—though often implicit—becomes more legible when viewed through the CoP lens.

Despite these advantages, there are notable limitations to the CoP framework. One major challenge lies in operationalization. Because CoP is a largely qualitative and interpretive model, it can be difficult to translate its concepts into measurable indicators for large-scale studies or formal evaluation frameworks. Terms like "mutual engagement" or "shared repertoire" resist simplification and are often context-dependent, requiring prolonged immersion and ethnographic sensitivity from the researcher.

Additionally, CoP's emphasis on stability and coherence within communities can obscure more transient, fluid, or fragmented forms of engagement. Many contemporary game communities are not tightly bounded but are instead loosely connected networks with porous borders. Players may participate in multiple guilds, hop between platforms, or engage intermittently based on shifting motivations. In such cases, the coherence assumed in traditional CoP models may not hold, and alternative models like "communities of interest" or "affinity spaces" may be needed to complement the analysis.

Finally, CoP tends to foreground collaboration and shared purpose, potentially underplaying competition, exclusion, or conflict—dynamics that are certainly present in many gaming spaces. Not all learning in games is cooperative; some of it emerges from rivalry, resistance, or even toxic interactions. A comprehensive analysis must therefore be sensitive to the affective and political dimensions of participation, which may complicate the tidy narratives often associated with CoP.

In sum, while the Community of Practice framework offers a powerful lens for understanding many aspects of learning in games, it should be applied critically and, where necessary, in dialog with other frameworks. Its true strength lies not in providing definitive answers, but in opening up new questions about how knowledge, identity, and community are co-constructed in the evolving ecologies of play.

3.5 Conclusion: From practice to competence

This chapter has outlined how the Community of Practice framework offers a compelling lens through which to interpret the learning processes embedded in gaming communities. By shifting the analytic focus from isolated learning outcomes to socially situated participation, CoP allows us to see game players not simply as users of content, but as contributors to dynamic, evolving systems of knowledge production. Through mutual engagement, shared goals, and evolving repertoires, players build not only strategic expertise, but also social identities and collective meaning.

Yet recognizing games as Communities of Practice is only a first step. If we are to treat these communities as legitimate learning environments, we must also ask: what exactly are players learning? What kinds of competencies emerge through their sustained participation? And how might we begin to name, classify, and critically examine these capacities—not only for academic recognition, but to inform educational practice?

These questions form the foundation for the next chapter. Moving from a sociocultural analysis of community dynamics, Chapter 4 turns toward the learners themselves: the players. It explores the concept of latent gaming intelligences and introduces a framework for articulating the diverse competencies that players develop in and through gameplay. By anchoring this inquiry in both theory and empirical observation, we continue the work of translating lived player experience into scholarly understanding and pedagogical insight.

4. Player competencies and latent gaming intelligences

4.1 Defining player competencies and latent gaming intelligences

As the previous chapter established, gaming communities function not only as social groups but also as dynamic learning environments. If we take seriously the idea that players engage in sustained, meaningful participation within these communities, then the next logical step is to ask: what kinds of competencies do players actually develop through gameplay? And why have these competencies remained largely invisible or undervalued in traditional educational discourse?

The term *player competencies* refer to the observable skills, dispositions, and patterns of thinking that emerge through regular participation in digital play. These include but are not limited to: resource management, probabilistic reasoning, collaborative coordination, adaptive planning, and real-time decision-making. However, these competencies are often encoded in game-specific languages and embedded within informal practices, making them difficult to isolate or quantify using standard educational tools.

To capture the less visible dimensions of this learning, we introduce the concept of *latent gaming intelligences*—a term that highlights the often-overlooked forms of expertise cultivated in gaming contexts. "Latent" here does not imply dormant or undeveloped, but rather invisible to institutional recognition. These intelligences may manifest in how players navigate uncertainty, construct complex mental models of evolving systems, or interpret ambiguous social cues in multiplayer environments. In many cases, these cognitive and affective capacities far exceed what is typically expected of students in formal settings, yet they remain unacknowledged because they do not map neatly onto traditional assessment metrics.

The disconnect between what players know and what schools recognize is not merely a measurement issue—it is a conceptual gap. Much of education remains fixated on curricular content and discipline-bound outcomes, whereas gaming contexts foster transversal capacities that cut across domains: literacy and numeracy appear alongside social negotiation, emotional regulation, and creative improvisation. Moreover, the culture of formal education continues to privilege "serious" learning over play, reinforcing the idea that valuable knowledge must be difficult, teacher-delivered, and externally verified.

This chapter begins by challenging those assumptions. By naming and theorizing player competencies and latent gaming intelligences, we seek to reposition the player not as a passive consumer of entertainment but as an agentive learner operating within complex socio-technical systems. This reframing is essential not only for research purposes, but also for broader educational reform. If schooling is to remain relevant in a world saturated with interactive media, it must learn to recognize, validate, and even integrate the kinds of learning that happen outside its boundaries.

In the sections that follow, we analyze empirical examples that illustrate how these competencies take shape in practice. Through these cases, we also begin to build a language for describing what has long been dismissed as "just play"—revealing instead a rich terrain of cognitive, social, and cultural development that deserves a place in serious educational conversations.

4.2 Case illustrations: Pokémon go and the re-gamification of educational platforms

To move from abstraction to evidence, this section examines two concrete cases where player competencies and latent gaming intelligences can be meaningfully observed: the self-organized knowledge practices of Pokémon Go communities [10], and the re-gamification behaviors demonstrated by elementary school students on an educational gaming platform [12]. These cases not only exemplify how players engage in meaningful, self-directed learning, but also illustrate how such learning often arises beyond the boundaries of formal instruction and outside the visibility of traditional assessment.

4.2.1 Case 1: Knowledge co-creation in the Pokémon go community

Following the release of Pokémon Go in 2016, a wave of informal research practices emerged from within the player base. In Taiwan, as in many parts of the world, local communities of players rapidly formed around objectives such as mapping PokéStops, optimizing route efficiency, analyzing spawn algorithms, and scheduling coordinated raids. What is notable is not only the technical precision of these practices, but the collaborative ethos that supported them [10].

Players contributed observations to shared Google Sheets, developed heatmaps for spawn frequency, and even devised informal experiments to verify or refute game mechanics rumored in online forums. In this process, players collectively constructed a shared epistemology: data were tested, debated, and validated through social feedback loops. These behaviors mirror practices found in scientific communities—hypothesis formation, peer review, and iterative revision—but without institutional scaffolding.

Competencies surfaced in every layer of this activity: spatial reasoning, probabilistic estimation, ethical coordination, and linguistic innovation. More importantly, these acts of participation built identity: novices became contributors, and contributors became respected community figures. This trajectory of participation closely aligns with CoP theory, but here it is shown to also nurture cognitive and strategic development.

4.2.2 Case 2: Re-gamification practices in educational platforms

In contrast to Pokémon Go, which is a commercial entertainment product, the second case looks at a formal educational setting. In a longitudinal study conducted in Taiwanese elementary classrooms using a gamified learning platform, a curious pattern emerged. While the platform itself was designed to be engaging, many students quickly exhausted the "intended" game and began modifying their interactions with it [12].

Students created self-imposed challenges, such as completing tasks with stricter time constraints, solving problems in reverse order, or inventing new storylines to overlay the existing mechanics. Some even began developing new rules for their peers to follow, effectively transforming a closed system into an open-ended one. This process, referred to here as "re-gamification," demonstrates how learners, when sufficiently fluent in the logic of games, begin to reshape game environments to suit their own motivations and intellectual curiosities.

In these classrooms, competencies revealed themselves not through quiz scores but through behaviors: designing feedback systems, coordinating group play, adapting content, and facilitating peer learning. Latent intelligences such as narrative construction, task design, and group management surfaced—none of which were officially recognized by the platform or measured by the curriculum.

4.2.3 Synthesis across cases

What unites these two cases is the presence of intentional, reflective, and community-embedded action. Players and students alike demonstrated the capacity to engage in metacognitive play: thinking about how the system works, how it could work differently, and how to communicate those possibilities to others. These are not merely technical skills, but epistemic dispositions—ways of knowing, organizing, and contributing that align closely with the notion of "learning as participation" rather than "learning as acquisition."

Both cases also challenge dominant narratives in education. In Pokémon Go, what appears to be distraction becomes informal science [10]. In the classroom, what was designed as a learning game becomes a platform for design [4, 12]. In both contexts, the learners exceeded the pedagogical expectations of the system, producing new forms of play that were also new forms of learning.

4.3 Why these competencies matter?

Having examined the kinds of competencies and intelligences players exhibit across different game-based contexts, a key question remains: why should these abilities matter to educators, policymakers, and researchers? What is gained by recognizing the learning that occurs in these informal spaces—and what is lost when we ignore it?

First, many of the competencies observed in gaming communities align closely with the kinds of skills increasingly emphasized in contemporary education policy frameworks. For instance, Taiwan's 12-Year Basic Education Curriculum promotes a "competency-based" vision that values problem-solving, communication, creativity, and self-directed learning—abilities that, as this chapter has shown, emerge organically in game-based contexts. In fact, these frameworks often articulate desired outcomes (such as collaboration or adaptability) that players already demonstrate, albeit in ways that are unrecognized by traditional classroom assessments.

Second, by validating player competencies, we broaden the scope of what counts as legitimate learning. Much of the tension in educational reform stems from a mismatch between the diversity of learner experiences and the narrowness of institutional recognition. When students' mastery of strategic thinking, peer coordination, or real-time decision-making is invisible within school metrics, it not only distorts our understanding of what they know—it also alienates them from the learning process. Recognizing these capabilities helps reengage learners who may feel marginalized by conventional academic structures.

Third, acknowledging these competencies opens up new possibilities for instructional design and curriculum development. If educators accept that learners can exhibit advanced forms of reasoning and collaboration through gameplay, they might begin to design learning environments that emulate some of these dynamics. This does not mean turning every classroom into a game, but rather learning from what games do well: structuring feedback loops, enabling role flexibility, fostering collective knowledge construction, and allowing failure without stigma. Such principles can enrich both formal and informal learning environments.

Fourth, recognizing player competencies supports a more equitable understanding of intelligence. Traditional schooling tends to privilege linguistic and logical-mathematical forms of intelligence, while undervaluing spatial, interpersonal, or adaptive capacities. Yet games often reward exactly those undervalued dimensions: the player who can tactically position allies, mediate a team conflict, or troubleshoot a failing system in real time is often exhibiting forms of intelligence that go unnoticed in standard testing. By recognizing these as legitimate ways of knowing and contributing, educators can support a more inclusive vision of student potential.

Finally, this recognition is not just about individual growth—it also speaks to civic and cultural participation. Today's learners are not just future workers or test-takers; they are also citizens who must navigate complex, networked systems. Game-based learning offers authentic practice in doing just that. When players coordinate raids across time zones, balance competing incentives in virtual economies, or build shared repositories of strategic knowledge, they are rehearsing the kinds of systems thinking and collaborative problem-solving required in public life. These competencies are not extracurricular—they are essential.

In sum, valuing the competencies that emerge from game-based participation is not an indulgence or a detour from serious education. It is a necessary step toward recognizing where and how learning truly happens in the twenty-first century. As we look to the future of education, the challenge is not merely to integrate games into classrooms, but to understand and incorporate the profound learning that already takes place in gaming worlds.

4.4 Naming the invisible, valuing the informal

This chapter has argued that the competencies players develop in digital gaming contexts are both real and educationally significant—even if they remain largely invisible within traditional assessment systems. By introducing the concept of latent gaming intelligences and illustrating their presence through empirical cases, we have taken a step toward rearticulating what counts as learning in a world shaped by play, networks, and Communities of Practice.

These competencies—ranging from coordination and strategy to creativity and systems thinking—are not marginal or trivial. They are cultivated through active participation, reflective practice, and collaborative meaning-making. In other words, they are learned, and they matter.

More importantly, recognizing these capacities helps us build a bridge between formal and informal education, between what students do inside schools and what they achieve in the cultures that matter to them. It offers educators a way to validate, connect, and expand learning beyond the classroom. It also invites researchers to attend to the practices that emerge not from curricula, but from participation.

As we move to Chapter 5, the challenge shifts from identifying these competencies to building a framework capable of analyzing them systematically. The next chapter explores the construction of an analytical model that maps player behaviors and learning dispositions across multiple domains—making it possible not only to describe, but also to study, compare, and eventually support the diverse ways in which players learn.

5. Applying analytical frameworks and research methodologies

5.1 From observations to systematic categorization: Why a framework is needed

The preceding chapters have explored the conceptual shift from viewing gameplay as entertainment to recognizing it as a domain of meaningful learning. We have seen how Communities of Practice form around shared play, how competencies are developed and expressed, and how these forms of knowledge often remain latent—unrecognized by formal institutions [5, 12, 21]. What remains is the task of constructing a research framework that makes these learning processes more visible, interpretable, and comparable.

This chapter begins by addressing a core methodological question: how can researchers systematically identify and categorize the diverse competencies that emerge from gameplay? While qualitative fieldwork and ethnographic observation offer deep insights into player practices [42, 43], they often lack the structural scaffolding needed to generalize findings or communicate them across disciplines. To move from richly contextual description to analytical clarity, a framework is needed—one that can map the range of player behaviors without reducing them to decontextualized skills.

The absence of such a framework is part of the reason why research on game-based learning remains fragmented. Studies often focus on isolated effects—such as whether a particular game improves memory retention or critical thinking—while overlooking the broader ecologies in which learning occurs [13, 48]. Without a coherent structure for comparing different types of player engagement—across solo or team-based settings, consuming or producing activities—researchers are left with anecdotal insights that are difficult to translate into pedagogical or theoretical models.

Thus, the primary objective of this chapter is to introduce and justify an analytical tool that can bridge this gap. Drawing on prior case studies and grounded theoretical synthesis, the chapter presents a two-axis model that classifies player behaviors along the dimensions of agency (individual vs. collective) and activity mode (consumption vs. production). This model, referred to as the Player Competency Quadrant Framework (PCQF), serves both as a heuristic for analyzing gameplay-based learning and as a scaffold for designing future studies.

In the sections that follow, we first outline the process by which the framework was constructed—through systematic literature review and qualitative coding—and then demonstrate how it can be applied to real-world data. Through this model, we aim to provide not only a language for describing how players learn, but also a structure for asking better research questions about what learning through games can mean in diverse educational contexts.

5.2 Constructing the player competency quadrant framework

To move beyond isolated case studies and toward a comparative, scalable mode of inquiry, this chapter proposes an analytical framework that categorizes player competencies across two intersecting dimensions: one that distinguishes between individual and team-based action, and another that differentiates between consuming and producing modes of engagement. This two-axis system is grounded in empirical observation and further developed through literature synthesis and iterative coding [29]. The result is a four-quadrant framework that not only describes how players participate in games, but also reveals the competencies they develop through that participation.

On the horizontal axis, we locate the spectrum between consumption and presumption. Players engaging primarily in consuming modes interact with pre-designed systems, rules, and narratives. Their competencies often revolve around mastering game mechanics, solving in-game problems, and adapting to fixed challenges. In contrast, presuming behaviors involve creative contribution—players who design new rules, build tools, produce content, or manage social systems. These players extend the life of the game through innovation, rather than just interact with it.

The vertical axis captures the distinction between solo activity and team-based engagement. Solo-oriented players work independently, relying on internalized goals and self-paced exploration. Team-oriented players operate within collective structures, coordinating with others and often taking on roles that support group performance and cohesion. These two axes intersect to yield four distinct patterns of participation and learning, which this study identifies as the Pioneer, the Old-timer, the Socializing player, and the Cadre (**Figure 1**).

The Pioneer represents the solo-consuming quadrant. These are players who explore systems individually and develop competence through repetition, experimentation, and intuition. They are characterized by their capacity for logical thinking, spatial reasoning, responsiveness, and independent planning. Often, Pioneers are early adopters or solo explorers who navigate new terrains and uncover mechanics without relying on community-generated content. Their learning is quiet but deep-rooted in iterative problem-solving and self-reflection.

The Old-timer emerges in the solo-producing space. These players possess significant experience and often engage in reflective tinkering, modding, or analytical deconstruction of game systems. They might build spreadsheets, run simulations, or maintain personal archives of findings. Their competencies include scientific habits,

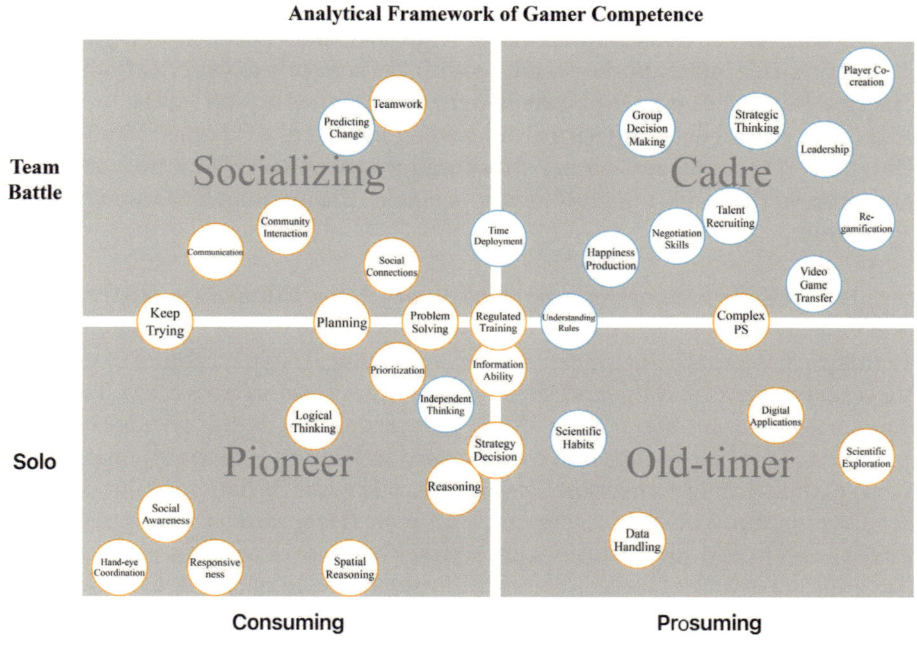

Figure 1.
Player Competency Quadrant Framework (PCQF): An analytic model defined by the "individual–collective" and "consumption–production" axes, mapping participation patterns and competency development in gaming communities, highlighting four roles—Pioneer, Old-timer, Socializer, and Cadre.

digital fluency, data handling, and exploratory reasoning. While they may not always be socially visible, their contributions often lay the groundwork for others, forming the intellectual infrastructure upon which communities build.

In the team-consuming quadrant, we find the Socializing player. This participant thrives in structured group play—whether in co-op missions, guild raids, or event-based interactions. Their strength lies not in creating new content but in building cohesion, maintaining morale, and enabling successful collective performance. Core competencies in this quadrant include communication, community awareness, emotional attunement, and collaborative adaptation. These players keep the group functioning smoothly and serve as relational anchors, particularly for newcomers or less confident members.

Finally, the Cadre occupies the team-producing quadrant. These are organizers, strategists, and facilitators—those who initiate collaborative projects, distribute tasks, and steer community direction. Their activities involve player co-creation, leadership, negotiation, and often re-gamification: the ability to take an existing structure and modify it to suit new goals or contexts. Cadres act as cultural stewards within player communities, simultaneously managing logistics and shaping norms. They are as much architects of participation as they are participants themselves.

Importantly, these four roles are not rigid categories. Rather, they represent recurring configurations of behavior and capacity that players may cycle through depending on context, maturity, and motivation. A Pioneer may become a Cadre when joining a team, just as a Socializing player might evolve into an Old-timer through extended solo experimentation. However, by naming these patterns, the framework gives us a language for recognizing forms of learning that have long remained diffuse and under-theorized. It allows us to ask not only what players do, but how their actions reflect situated competencies developed through sustained, meaningful engagement with games.

By framing play as a space where roles, strategies, and expertise emerge from lived practice, this quadrant model aligns with the core principles of Communities of Practice. It does not reduce players to personality types or skill levels; instead, it honors the fluid and evolving nature of learning in action. And most importantly, it offers researchers and educators a structured way to observe, describe, and ultimately support the kinds of complex competencies that gaming environments so richly afford.

5.3 Applying the framework to empirical research the value of any analytical

Framework lies not in its conceptual elegance alone, but in its ability to guide inquiry, shape interpretation, and structure communication across cases. The Player Competency Quadrant Framework (PCQF), as introduced in the previous section, is designed to help researchers move from anecdotal description to systematic comparison, particularly in environments where learning is informal, multimodal, and community-driven. This section illustrates how the framework can be applied in both qualitative and mixed-methods research settings to uncover patterns in player behavior, learning trajectories, and competence development. In qualitative studies, the PCQF offers a structure for coding field data such as interviews, forum transcripts, observation notes, or screen recordings. For example, in a case study involving high school students participating in an online co-op game, researchers may code moments of communication (Socializing quadrant), leadership behavior (Cadre quadrant), or problem-solving done in isolation (Pioneer quadrant). These coded excerpts can then be clustered by quadrant to examine the dominant modes of participation over time, as well as the transitions between roles. In our own research using this approach [29], a sequence of gameplay sessions revealed how a student began as a peripheral participant in a Discord raid planning channel (Socializing), later took on responsibility for organizing a rotation schedule (Cadre), and eventually began building custom tools to assist raid analysis (Old-timer). This trajectory was not only evidence of deepening engagement, but also of the development of distinct, transferable competencies—such as time management, spreadsheet logic, and distributed leadership. Without a framework like the PCQF, such growth might have been read as anecdotal or idiosyncratic rather than as part of a broader learning pattern. The framework is also compatible with mixed-methods research. In survey-based designs, player self-assessments or peer assessments can be mapped onto the four quadrants, producing composite profiles of player types within a community. These profiles can then be triangulated with behavioral data (e.g., playtime logs, contribution records, and forum analytics) to examine correlations between quadrant orientation and game mastery, community influence, or persistence. For example, a comparative study may explore whether players who primarily identify as Cadres also report higher levels of social presence or emotional investment in their guilds, while Pioneers may report stronger self-regulation or exploratory orientation. One advantage of using the PCQF in empirical research is its flexibility. The framework does not prescribe a particular data type or method, but offers a conceptual anchor for organizing complex, multimodal data. It works particularly well in longitudinal designs, where researchers wish to trace developmental patterns in player learning or shifts in role identity. It is also useful in educational game research, where designers seek to understand how different game mechanics support or suppress specific kinds of competencies. However, applying the framework requires interpretive nuance. Player behaviors often span multiple quadrants within a single play session, and some competencies may be latent or implicit. Researchers must remain attentive to context, culture, and the affordances of particular games when making claims about quadrant alignment. For instance, a game that discourages modding may suppress presuming behavior, while a narrative-heavy game may elicit social discussion without enabling collaborative creation. These dynamics must be factored into analysis to avoid overgeneralization. Ultimately, the PCQF functions as a heuristic device—a lens through which researchers can ask sharper questions, design better instruments, and articulate learning in a form that is intelligible across academic, design, and educational audiences. By anchoring its categories in empirical practice and aligning them with theoretical insights from Communities of Practice, the framework helps foreground what is often overlooked: that play is not just an activity, but a situated mode of learning, identity building, and cultural participation.

5.4 Framing play as structured learning

This chapter has proposed and elaborated an analytical framework for recognizing and studying the diverse competencies that emerge from gameplay. Through the Player Competency Quadrant Framework (PCQF), we moved from describing gameplay behaviors in narrative or observational terms to categorizing them along two key dimensions: the locus of agency (individual vs. collective) and the mode of engagement (consuming vs. producing). By mapping these dimensions into four conceptual quadrants—Pioneer, Old-timer, Socializing, and Cadre—we created a structure that accommodates both the fluidity of play and the specificity of learning practices.

The primary contribution of the framework is to make legible what has long been difficult to describe: the situated, embodied, and evolving forms of intelligence that players cultivate in the act of playing. These include strategic foresight, collaborative planning, data synthesis, creative authorship, and community stewardship. Importantly, these competencies are not isolated to specific genres or platforms. They appear across gaming contexts, though they may manifest differently depending on cultural, mechanical, or community-specific affordances. What the PCQF offers is a vocabulary for identifying and discussing these competencies in ways that are theoretically grounded and methodologically actionable.

Moreover, by aligning the quadrant model with the principles of Communities of Practice, this framework highlights the inherently social nature of player development. Learning in games is not simply about feedback systems or design incentives; it is about identity, negotiation, trust, and shared purpose. Recognizing this opens up new possibilities for educators, designers, and researchers alike: for curriculum builders seeking to integrate game-inspired pedagogies, for game developers interested in fostering long-term engagement through community support, and for scholars aiming to trace learning beyond institutional walls.

Still, the framework is not without its limitations. It is descriptive rather than predictive, and its boundaries are permeable. Many player behaviors defy categorization or inhabit multiple quadrants simultaneously. The model also depends on researchers' capacity to observe, interpret, and contextualize player actions with care and cultural sensitivity. It is not a diagnostic tool, but a scaffold for inquiry—one that must remain flexible, provisional, and open to revision as new forms of play and participation emerge.

As we look ahead to the final chapter, the focus shifts once again—from categorization to synthesis. Having developed a robust understanding of player competencies and the means of analyzing them, we now turn toward implications. What does it mean to take game-based learning seriously—not just as a research topic, but as a foundation for educational practice, policy, and innovation? How might teachers, curriculum designers, and institutions recognize and support the competencies that players bring with them into the classroom and beyond?

These are the questions that will guide the discussion in Chapter 6, as we reflect on the broader significance of this research and outline future directions for study and application.

6. Discussion and future directions

6.1 Reframing learning through play: Broader implications

This study began with a deceptively simple question: what do players learn when they play? But as the chapters unfolded—particularly through fieldwork and empirical cases rooted in Taiwan—it became increasingly clear that this question cannot be answered through conventional educational paradigms alone. The learning behaviors exhibited in Taiwanese game communities—such as collaborative mapping in Pokémon Go, or re-gamification of educational platforms by elementary students—demonstrate a rich ecology of informal knowledge construction that defies simple curricular outcomes.

In the Taiwanese context, where formal education still heavily emphasizes exam preparation, linear progression, and content transmission, these player-initiated practices present a significant epistemological challenge. Learners are acquiring strategic reasoning, system navigation, community management, and adaptive problem-solving through game-based contexts—yet these competencies remain largely unrecognized by school systems and policy frameworks. This gap is not just pedagogical, but cultural: it reflects a persistent disconnect between what is valued inside classrooms and what learners are actually cultivating outside of them.

The implications of this disconnect are far-reaching. For researchers, it calls for new frameworks—like the Player Competency Quadrant Model—that are capable of recognizing the complexity of informal learning as observed in Taiwanese gaming communities. For teachers and curriculum designers in Taiwan, it suggests an urgent need to shift from content transmission to participatory and context-aware pedagogies. And for education policy more broadly, it points to the importance of rethinking legitimacy: who gets to decide what counts as learning, and on what terms?

Reframing learning through play, especially in the Taiwanese context, is not merely about advocating for games in classrooms. It is about acknowledging the existence of rich learning ecologies already thriving in the cultural margins and bringing them into the center of educational discourse. In this sense, Taiwan's game players are not outliers—they are vanguards of a participatory learning culture that deserves serious attention and institutional recognition.

6.2 Directions for future research

While this study has laid the groundwork for conceptualizing player competencies and mapping them through the Player Competency Quadrant Framework, much remains to be done. The findings here are intentionally exploratory, and the broader goal is not to offer definitive conclusions, but to open a space for sustained, empirically grounded, and theoretically rich investigations into game-based learning—especially within the Taiwanese context. This final section outlines several key directions that future research might pursue.

First, there is a clear need for *longitudinal studies* that trace the development of player competencies over time. Most current research, including this study, relies heavily on snapshots: ethnographic moments, forum excerpts, or gameplay vignettes. While valuable, these methods make it difficult to observe how player identities and intelligences evolve through extended participation. A longitudinal design—perhaps following students who are active gamers across multiple school years—could reveal how informal learning translates (or fails to translate) into formal academic success, civic engagement, or workplace competence.

Second, *cross-institutional and interdisciplinary collaboration* will be crucial for the field's growth. As game studies in Taiwan currently reside at the margins of educational discourse, building alliances between teacher education programs, digital humanities centers, and game development communities could yield new models for both research and practice. For example, action research involving teachers and students who co-design curriculum modules based on game mechanics would not only validate player knowledge but generate new pedagogical artifacts and data. Similarly, partnerships with local indie game developers could lead to experimental learning environments that respond to cultural and linguistic contexts often ignored by global platforms.

Third, more work is needed to *refine and test the quadrant framework* itself. While the PCQF presented in this study has proven useful for categorization and discussion, it remains a heuristic—a starting point. Future research might operationalize its categories more rigorously through coding schemes, design instruments for quadrant-based player self-assessment, or explore whether the model holds across different genres, age groups, or cultural regions. Comparative studies between Taiwanese players and those in other East Asian or Western contexts could also test the cultural specificity and transferability of the framework.

Fourth, there is a significant opportunity for *methodological innovation*, especially in how we capture and analyze digital trace data. With appropriate ethical protocols in place, researchers can mine interaction logs, chat transcripts, version histories, and user-generated content to build rich portraits of player engagement. In Taiwan, where mobile-first gaming culture is dominant, platform-specific tools like LINE groups, YouTube walkthroughs, or TikTok commentary offer underexplored sources of insight into how players communicate, reflect, and teach one another.

Finally, future research should address the *policy and institutional dimensions* of game-based learning. While this study has primarily focused on theory and micro-level practice, larger questions remain: How can national curriculum frameworks in Taiwan be adapted to better recognize competencies developed in digital environments? What training do teachers need to interpret and integrate these capacities into their classrooms? What kinds of assessment systems are compatible with the informal, emergent, and community-based learning modes observed in games?

Addressing these questions will require not only scholarly commitment but advocacy. It will mean challenging inherited assumptions about learning, expertise, and legitimacy—and building systems that honor what learners already know and can do. The Taiwanese education system, with its mix of innovation and conservatism, presents a particularly compelling site for this work. Positioned at the intersection of East Asian academic rigor and a thriving youth gaming culture, Taiwan is uniquely poised to lead a reimagining of what counts as learning in the digital age.

6.3 Concluding reflections

This study began by asking what players learn—not to validate games against existing educational standards, but to take seriously the lived practices, knowledge systems, and communal forms of inquiry that emerge from digital play. Along the way, it traced a path from ethnographic observation to theoretical articulation, from conceptual confusion to analytical clarity. What has emerged is not only a framework for identifying player competencies, but a broader argument: that games, and the communities built around them, constitute one of the most generative learning environments of our time.

At the heart of this research lies a desire to reframe where and how we think learning occurs. Instead of positioning schools as the default space of education and games as extracurricular, this study has treated gaming environments as legitimate sites of knowledge production, social negotiation, and identity formation. In doing so, it has challenged the boundaries of educational research and expanded the vocabulary available to describe informal, interest-driven, and community-anchored learning.

The work has been intentionally situated in Taiwan—not just as a setting, but as a system. Taiwan's complex educational ecosystem, shaped by Confucian traditions, examination pressures, and a vibrant digital youth culture, offers a unique lens through which to explore the tensions between formal and informal learning. Here, students often live dual lives: one defined by school-based performance metrics, and another by the competencies they cultivate in gaming communities. Recognizing and bridging these worlds is not merely a scholarly task; it is an ethical and political imperative.

The frameworks and cases presented in this study are not final answers. They are invitations—to teachers, to researchers, to policymakers—to look again, to listen differently, and to ask new questions. What does it mean to teach in a culture where students may learn more about collaboration in a raid group than in a group project? How do we design curricula that acknowledge not only what students need to know, but what they already know from their lives beyond the classroom?

Ultimately, this work advocates for a learning paradigm that is situated, participatory, and open to revision. It calls for research that begins not with theories to be tested, but with communities to be understood. And it suggests that education, if it is to remain relevant, must not only adapt to the changing world of its learners—but must also be humble enough to learn from them.

Author details

Tieh-Huai Chang
Cross College Elite Tech Program, National Kaohsiung University of Science and Technology (NKUST), Taiwan

*Address all correspondence to: ironchang@nkust.edu.tw

References

[1] ICT and Me. A Research Study Examining How Young People's Use of ICT and the Amount of Screentime Impacts on GCSE Attainment. London, UK: National Children's Bureau (NCB); 2015

[2] Lu C-H, Cheng C-P. The study on the correlation of the behaviors in the internet café, parenting style, and interpersonal relationship: A sample of primary school senior students in New Taipei City. Journal of Educational Communication and Technology. 2014;**40**(8):49-71. Available from: https://www.airitilibrary.com/Article/Detail/23083026-201408-201411060001-201411060001-49-71

[3] Squire K. Changing the game: What happens when video games enter the classroom. Innovate: Journal of Online Education. 2005;**1**(6):article 5

[4] Gershenfeld A. Leveling up from player to designer: Engaging and empowering youth through making video games. Knowledge Quest. 2011;**40**(1):54-59

[5] Gee JP. What Video Games Have to Teach us about Learning and Literacy. Palgrave Macmillan; 2003

[6] Gee JP. Good Video Games and Good Learning: Collected Essays on Video Games, Learning and Literacy. Peter Lang Publishing Inc.; 2007

[7] Thomas D, Brown JS. A New Culture of Learning: Cultivating the Imagination for a World of Constant Change. Charleston, SC, USA: CreateSpace; 2011

[8] McGonigal J. Reality Is Broken: Why Games Make us Better and How they Can Change the World. New York, NY, USA: Penguin Books; 2011

[9] McGonigal J. SuperBetter: The Power of Living Gamefully. New York, NY: Penguin Press; 2015

[10] Chang T-H, Jan M. From catching Pokémon to catching truths: Scientific inquiry among PokémonGo gamers. Learning, Innovation and Inclusive Education. 2025;**6**(430). DOI: 10.52731/liir.v006.430

[11] Lin W-R, Huang K-K, Yang C-C, Chang C-M. A study investigating adolescents' online game addiction and treatment. Review of Leisure, Sport and Health. 2020;**9**(1):24-33. Available from: https://www.airitilibrary.com/Article/Detail?DocID=a0000591-202003-202003110004-202003110004-24-33

[12] Chang T-H, Chen F-C. The exploration of re-gamification competence: The experience of elementary students on educational game platform. Journal of Digital Learning Technology. 2021;**13**(2):1-26. Available from: https://www.airitilibrary.com/Article/Detail?DocID=P20170615002-202104-202105180008-202105180008-1-26

[13] Kebritchi M, Hirumi A, Bai H. The effects of modern math computer games on mathematics achievement and class motivation. Computers and Education. 2010;**55**(2):427-443

[14] Egenfeldt-Nielsen S, Smith JH, Tosca SP. Understanding Video Games: The Essential Introduction. London, UK: Routledge; 2013

[15] McGonigal J. Why I love bees: A case study in collective intelligence gaming. In: Salen K, editor. The Ecology of Games: Connecting Youth, Games, and Learning. MIT Press; 2008. pp. 199-227

[16] Papert S. Hard Fun. Bangor Daily News, 2, 26. 2002

[17] Lazzaro N. Why We Play Games: Four Keys to More Emotion without Story. Oakland, CA: Sage; 2004

[18] Mather M, Gorlick MA, Lighthall NR. To brake or accelerate when the light turns yellow? Stress reduces older adults' risk taking in a driving game. Psychological Science. 2009;**20**(2):174-176. DOI: 10.1111/j.1467-9280.2009.02275.x

[19] Berry AM, Wintle SE. Using Laptops to Facilitate Middle School Science Learning: The Results of Hard Fun. Portland, ME: Center for Education Policy, Applied Research, and Evaluation; 2009

[20] Lave J, Wenger E. Situated Learning: Legitimate Peripheral Participation. Cambridge, UK: Cambridge University Press; 1991

[21] Wenger E. Communities of Practice: Learning, Meaning, and Identity. Cambridge University Press; 1998

[22] Chang T-H. Identifying Players' Co-Creative Competencies in Digital Play: A Case Study of Pokémon Go in Taiwan [Unpublished Manuscript]. 2021

[23] Steinkuehler C, Duncan S. Scientific habits of mind in virtual worlds. Journal of Science Education and Technology. 2008;**17**(6):530-543

[24] Cooper S, Khatib F, Treuille A, et al. Predicting protein structures with a multiplayer online game. Nature. 2010;**466**(7307):756-760. DOI: 10.1038/nature09304

[25] Bransford JD, Brown AL, Cocking RR, editors. How People Learn: Brain, Mind, Experience, and School. Expanded ed. The National Academies Press; 2000

[26] Kirriemuir J, McFarlane A. Literature Review in Games and Learning: A Report for NESTA Futurelab. NESTA Futurelab; 2004

[27] Lin H-L. Between player and researcher: Gaming experience and the study of game culture. Journal of Education Research. 2011;**203**:19-25. Available from: https://www.airitilibrary.com/Article/Detail?DocID=10161007-201107-201108170011-201108170011-19-25

[28] Liang S-Y. Between gaming fantasy and academic truth. In: National Chiao Tung University Center for General Education, Digital Animation and Cultural Creative Program, editors. Illusions and Reality: The Logic and Connotations of Electronic Games. National Yang Ming Chiao Tung University Press; 2015. pp. 1-16. Available from: https://www.kingstone.com.tw/basic/2800000076115/?lid=basic_read

[29] Chang T-H, Jan M. How to "unboxing" gamer competencies: Via systematic literature reviews to get analytical framework is workable? In: Shih J-L, Kashihara A, Chen W, Ogata H, editors. Proceedings of the 31st International Conference on Computers in Education (ICCE 2023). Vol. 2. Asia-Pacific Society for Computers in Education; 2023. pp. 935-938. DOI: 10.58459/icce.2023.1479

[30] Klimmt C. Key dimensions of contemporary video game literacy: Toward a normative model of the competent digital gamer. Journal for Computer Game Culture. 2009;**3**(1):7-17

[31] Peng MH. A Complete Survival Manual for Graduate Students: Methods, Secrets, and Unwritten Rules. Linking

Publishing; 2017. Available from: https://24h.pchome.com.tw/books/prod/DJBQ1E-D900CT2BD

[32] Oei AC, Patterson MD. Enhancing cognition with video games: A multiple game training study. PLoS One. 2013;**8**(3):e58546. DOI: 10.1371/journal.pone.0058546

[33] Jansz J, Martens L. Gaming at a LAN event: The social context of playing video games. New Media and Society. 2005;**7**(3):333-355

[34] Jones C, Esnault L. The metaphor of networks in learning: Communities, collaboration and practice. In: Paper Presented at the Networked Learning 2004 Conference; Lancaster, UK. 2004

[35] Chen Y-C. Empirical study on the effect of digital game-based instruction on students' learning motivation and achievement. Eurasia Journal of Mathematics, Science and Technology Education. 2017;**13**(6):3175-3186. DOI: 10.12973/ejmste/76301

[36] Crawford JD, Medendorp WP, Marotta JJ. Spatial transformations for eye–hand coordination. Journal of Neurophysiology. 2004;**92**(1):10-19

[37] Ulicsak M, Wright M. Games in Education: Serious Games. Bristol, UK: Futurelab; 2010

[38] Sun C-T. Game-Based Digital Learning. Higher Education Publishing; 2013. Available from: https://ebook.nlpi.edu.tw/bookdetail/20075

[39] Gartner. Gamification 2020: What is the Future of Gamification? 2012. Available from: https://www.gartner.com/en/documents/2226015

[40] Barab SA, Duffy TM. From practice fields to communities of practice. In: Jonassen DH, Land SM, editors. Theoretical Foundations of Learning Environments. Mahwah, NJ, USA: Lawrence Erlbaum Associates; 2000. pp. 25-55

[41] Brown JS, Duguid P. The Social Life of Information. Harvard Business School Press; 2000

[42] Boellstorff T, Nardi B, Pearce C, Taylor TL. Ethnography and Virtual Worlds: A Handbook of Method. Princeton, NJ, USA: Princeton University Press; 2012

[43] Hine C. Ethnography for the Internet: Embedded, Embodied and Everyday. 1st ed. Routledge; 2015. DOI: 10.4324/9781003085348

[44] Shaffer DW. How Computer Games Help Children Learn. New York, NY, USA: Palgrave Macmillan; 2006

[45] Spradley JP. Participant Observation. Rev. ed. Waveland Press; 1980

[46] Lin TB, Li JY, Deng F, Lee L. Understanding new media literacy: An explorative theoretical framework. Educational Technology & Society. 2013;**16**(4):160-170

[47] Jenkins H. Convergence Culture: Where Old and New Media Collide. New York, NY, USA: NYU Press; 2006

[48] Egenfeldt-Nielsen S. Educational Potential of Computer Games. London, UK: Continuum; 2007

Chapter 7

Enhancing Case-Based Serious Games in Dental Education with AI: A Comparative Study of Manual vs. AI-Driven Development

Ahmed Adam Kada, Nisrine EL Arrouf, Szabolcs Felszeghy and Faiza Benfdil

Abstract

This study extends a 2024 initiative at the Faculty of Dental Medicine, Mohammed V University of Rabat, which introduced serious games (SGs) into dental education without artificial intelligence (AI). With the growing importance of digital learning, this new phase integrates AI into SG development to assess its impact on time efficiency, content quality, and educational outcomes. Grounded in learner-centered pedagogy, the project leveraged a dataset of over 100 clinical cases to create AI-assisted serious games. It adopted a bilingual (French and Arabic) framework to ensure accessibility and alignment with both regional and international academic standards. This inclusive design broadens participation and promotes equity in dental education. Three serious games were developed: (1) a simulation on removable partial dentures, (2) a memory-based tool for pathology and pharmacology, and (3) an oral hygiene education module. AI tools streamlined content generation, enhanced interactivity, and ensured pedagogical coherence. Comparative analysis of AI-assisted versus manual design workflows examined development time, educational depth, and user experience. Results showed that AI integration significantly reduced production time and improved content consistency. Students reported higher motivation, improved knowledge retention, and enhanced preparedness for clinical scenarios. Cross-sectional surveys and faculty–student workshops further confirmed gains in engagement, reasoning, and conceptual clarity. In addressing limitations in simulation access and digital literacy, this study demonstrates that AI-assisted SGs offer a scalable, low-cost, and effective solution for dental training. The findings support wider integration of AI into SGs across curricula, reinforcing the transformative potential of this approach in modern dental education.

Keywords: serious games, interactive learning, dental education, digital pedagogy, bilingual education, artificial intelligence in education, AI-assisted educational development, manual vs. AI-based approach

1. Introduction

1.1 Preamble

Doubt, Think, Communicate, and Dare to Criticize: Embedding Soyinka's and Feynman's Vision in Modern Medical & Dental Education "The greatest threat to freedom is the absence of criticism," warned Wole Soyinka, Nobel Laureate in Literature—a truth that resonates profoundly in the evolving landscape of modern education. As gamification reshapes the way we learn, its true promise lies not simply in the mechanics of play, but in its capacity to create spaces where young minds are free to question, challenge, and critique. In the world of medical and dental education, where the stakes are high and the need for critical thinkers is paramount, these freedoms are not merely aspirational—they are essential.

Gamification, when thoughtfully designed as a collaborative ecosystem, transcends rote skill-building to become a conduit for courageous dialog between educators and learners. By embedding robust feedback loops, open-ended problem-solving tasks, and immersive role-playing scenarios, gamified learning environments invite students to interrogate assumptions and empower mentors to embrace vulnerability. This chapter argues that effective gamification thrives on reciprocity, where educators must listen as intently as they guide, fostering trust in which criticism becomes a catalyst for growth. When students co-design game narratives or debate rule structures, they exercise agency over their learning, transforming from passive consumers to active co-creators. Such environments demand humility from mentors, who must relinquish hierarchical control to nurture collective wisdom.

Yet, as research on gamified communication reveals, this balance is delicate. Over-structured systems risk stifling creativity, while under-designed frameworks may devolve into chaos. By marrying Soyinka's call for critical discourse with evidence-based gamification strategies, educators can cultivate classrooms where play becomes a radical act of mutual empowerment—a laboratory for the "extraordinary potential" born when critique and compassion coexist.

This chapter also explores the implementation of Richard Feynman's educational philosophy: "Teach students to doubt, think, communicate, question, make mistakes, learn from them, and have fun." In student-centered, gamified platforms, educators and learners collaborate to transform passive lectures and clinical practices into interactive, mistake-tolerant environments. Here, students are encouraged to question assumptions and refine critical appraisal skills, supported by educators who value curiosity as much as competence. A growing body of literature demonstrates that gamification not only boosts exam performance and motivation but also enhances collaborative problem-solving, with students emphasizing the enjoyment of learning through immediate feedback and team-based challenges.

Feynman's principles, when paired with evidence-based technology, create a replicable model for fostering curiosity and resilience in Gen Z medical and dental students. Soyinka's and Feynman's calls to prioritize doubt and critical thinking resonate deeply in an era where medical and dental education faces dual challenges: retaining Gen Z's engagement and bridging the gaps between theoretical knowledge and clinical practice.

At the University of Eastern Finland (UEF) in Kuopio, Finland, and at Mohammed V University in Rabat, Morocco, this philosophy has already taken root. These institutions have shifted from instructor-led, passive education to student-driven, educator-supervised virtual platforms across many of their courses. This transition has created dynamic ecosystems where questioning and experimentation are central to skill acquisition, preparing students to navigate the uncertainties of modern health care.

Gamified models demonstrate that educational ideals such as doubt, critical thinking, and open communication are not relics of the past, but blueprints for the future of medical and dental education. By merging doubt-driven pedagogy with gamified technology, institutions can cultivate resilient, curious practitioners who are prepared for the complexities and uncertainties of medicine. As Feynman noted, "The freedom to doubt is essential for scientific progress"—a principle now enshrined in Finland's morphology labs and a replicable standard for global education reform. Through gamification, the classroom becomes a laboratory for empowerment, where the courage to question leads to the wisdom to heal.

1.2 Toward a digital transformation of dental education supported by artificial intelligence

The rapid evolution of digital technologies is profoundly reshaping pedagogical methods in medicine and dentistry. Among emerging tools, serious games (SGs) stand out as interactive systems that foster active, contextualized, and immersive learning. Designed to integrate clinical case-based learning, simulation, and formative feedback, these learning environments enable students to develop clinical skills, refine diagnostic reasoning, and improve knowledge retention, all while avoiding direct exposure of patients to potential risks. In an initial institutional project, we undertook the development of several serious games dedicated to dental education, based on a manually collaborative design involving both instructors and students [1]. This initial work allowed us to create structured and relevant educational tools, but it also revealed several major limitations: manual development proved to be extremely time-consuming, the clinical case-based learning required substantial human resources, and ensuring the quality of bilingual content (French-Arabic) represented a considerable logistical challenge.

In this context, characterized by material and financial constraints as well as heterogeneous digital skills among learners, optimizing the design process became a pressing need. To address these challenges, this second project integrates artificial intelligence (AI) at various stages of serious game development, aiming to achieve three primary objectives: reducing production time, enhancing the quality and depth of educational content, and strengthening pedagogical accessibility. Our approach maintains the theoretical framework established in the first project, drawing upon behaviorism, cognitivism, and constructivism [2, 3], but introduces AI tools to support, enrich, and automate critical aspects of pedagogical design. AI is thus involved in assisted generation of clinical scenarios, optimization of feedback mechanisms, personalized adaptation of learning paths, and linguistic consistency checks across French and Arabic versions.

Recent literature on serious games in dental health highlights a growing diversity of initiatives, ranging from mobile educational apps like Dentist Bling and Dental Life [4, 5] to more immersive clinical environments such as GenoSmile [6]. However, despite the proliferation of available tools, few are developed according to rigorous educational standards or integrated into a structured curricular approach. Key issues include content quality, alignment with targeted competencies, user engagement, and the transferability of acquired skills [7].

This study therefore proposes a comparative analysis, contrasting the initial manual development model with the AI-assisted approach, in order to evaluate the tangible contributions of this innovation to dental education. Grounded in a rigorous pedagogical framework and mindful of the technical and cultural specificities of our context, we explore how AI can foster a more efficient educational transformation without compromising the quality or pedagogical intent of the serious games developed.

1.3 Educational theories guiding serious game design

The construction of our serious games relies on a solid theoretical foundation, rooted in three major paradigms of educational science: behaviorism, cognitivism, and constructivism. Similarly, behavioral approaches support the anchoring of basic gestures and procedures, cognitive frameworks facilitate the organization and processing of information, while the constructivist perspective promotes active learner engagement in authentic contexts. This theoretical positioning is based on studies demonstrating the value of such complementarity in digital learning environments, particularly in complex settings where the targeted skills range from technical execution to context-based decision-making [8].

Behaviorism emphasizes learning through repetition, reinforcement, and immediate feedback. It is embodied in tasks such as quizzes, stage validation, scoring systems, and level progression [9, 10]. This approach proves particularly relevant for reinforcing technical procedures and clinical protocols, as seen in pharmacology training or prosthetic design modules (see **Figure 1**, procedural training modules).

Cognitivism focuses on internal mechanisms of information processing and the ways learners acquire, organize, store, and apply knowledge [8, 9]. Unlike behaviorist models centered on observable behavior, cognitivism investigates underlying mental processes like perception, attention, memory, categorization, and problem-solving. It assumes that learning becomes more effective when individuals actively structure their knowledge through understanding, logical organization, and application in diverse contexts. This theoretical framework has heavily influenced modern pedagogy, particularly in fields demanding complex reasoning, such as health sciences. In the PAP game, cognitivism informed the development of over a hundred interactive clinical cases, engaging students in activities of analysis, diagnosis, and therapeutic planning. Each scenario encourages the organization and application of interdisciplinary knowledge, promoting both learning consolidation and clinical reasoning development (see **Figure 2**, information analysis and processing phase). Moreover, certain sequences within the game combine behaviorist (reinforcement through immediate feedback) and cognitivist (active knowledge mobilization and response categorization) approaches, supporting a structured progression from procedural acquisition to reasoned integration of knowledge [11].

Constructivism considers learning as an active process wherein learners build their understanding through personal experience and interaction with their

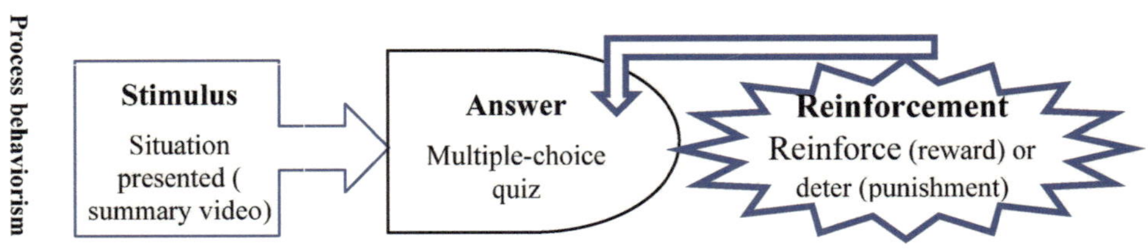

Figure 1.
Diagram of the behaviorism educational process.

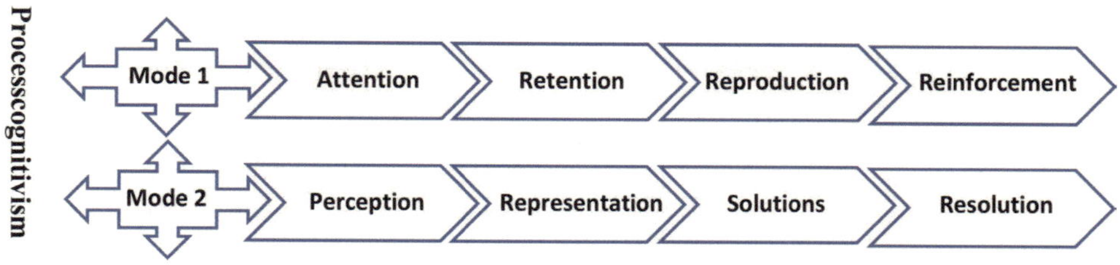

Figure 2.
Diagram of the cognitivism educational process.

environment. Knowledge construction involves confronting initial representations with new situations, leading to cognitive conflict and progressive restructuring. In our serious games, constructivist principles are implemented through open-ended activities, decision-making tasks, and adaptive pathways that encourage exploration, hypothesis formulation, error management, and reflective learning. This dynamic approach fosters the development of critical thinking, clinical judgment, and professional autonomy, essential competencies for future dental practitioners [12]. Thus, the educational design of our serious games draws from complementary theoretical currents, aligning pedagogical choices with specific learning objectives at each stage of the training (see **Figure 3**, information analysis and processing phase).

1.4 An integrated pedagogical framework

The articulation of the three educational paradigms was not based on a mere theoretical juxtaposition, but on a carefully designed complementarity that guided the conception of the serious games from the outset. Thanks to the integration of AI-assisted tools, this synergy was further enhanced, aiming to enrich traditional teaching methods and to foster a progressive transition toward more interactive, accessible, and adaptable learning practices.

The present study therefore aims to assess this integration from multiple perspectives—pedagogical, technical, and cultural—through the analysis of feedback from students and educators, with the objective of identifying concrete strategies for sustainable adoption.

Figures 1–3 synthesizes this pedagogical framework, illustrating the intersection between the mobilized learning paradigms, the targeted educational objectives, and the types of activities designed. Each level of the game activates specific cognitive and

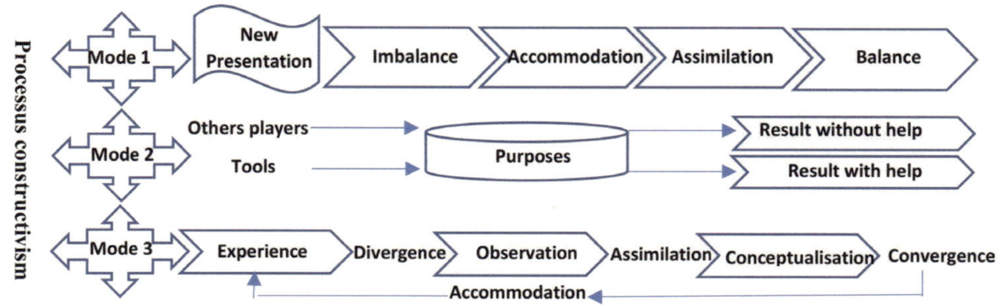

Figure 3.
Diagram of the constructivism educational process.

motivational mechanisms, structured to progressively reinforce the competencies intended [13]. The PAP game fits into this model, although it places greater emphasis on certain specific dynamics. Activities based on quizzes, centered on repetition and validation of clinical knowledge, predominantly draw on a behaviorist approach, promoting the automatization of fundamental skills. Certain modules also engage cognitive processes, for instance by requiring the analysis of clinical scenarios or the justification of selected answers. While the PAP game, as a quiz-based tool, marginally incorporates constructivist principles, this dimension can nonetheless be activated through supervised use, particularly during group discussions or post-activity debriefings.

This pedagogical structuring, now strengthened by AI-driven optimization during the design process, guided the development of the games. However, the study conducted with sixth-year dental students was not initially intended to directly evaluate the theoretical paradigms themselves. Its primary goal was to capture user perceptions regarding the utility, relevance, and overall quality of the games. Nevertheless, the results revealed that students distinguished different types of benefits depending on the activities offered, suggesting a differentiated appropriation of the underlying learning mechanisms. Thus, the tripartite organization seems to foster greater engagement, autonomy, and a strengthened sense of self-efficacy among learners.

The two other games developed—one focused on pharmacology and the other on oral hygiene—follow the same pedagogical logic, while integrating AI-based supports more explicitly to enhance interactivity and the co-construction of knowledge.

1.5 Objectives of this study

Building upon the pioneering groundwork of our first project, this second phase aims to redefine dental education through the transformative potential of artificial intelligence. Our approach is structured around three core objectives. First, by unlocking AI's potential in serious game development, we aim to rigorously analyze how AI enhances the design and development process—boosting productivity, improving content quality, and overcoming language barriers, thereby making learning tools more accessible for diverse learners. Second, in transforming the learning experience, we seek to promote deeper engagement, reduced cognitive load, and greater adaptability to varied educational profiles through the integration of AI-powered serious games, ultimately helping students think more critically and learn more effectively. Third, by creating a scalable and inclusive model, our goal is to propose a replicable bilingual framework (French-Arabic) for AI-supported serious games in health education, with a focus on efficiency, pedagogical excellence, and cultural relevance, offering a model that could serve as a blueprint for global educational innovation.

Together, these objectives aim to build a future-ready framework for more inclusive, engaging, and effective learning in dental education. Rather than merely documenting the technical implementation of AI, this study rigorously interrogates its true impact on educational innovation within dentistry [14]. We move beyond surface-level integration to critically assess AI's added value, confront potential limitations, and engage with pressing ethical considerations and future directions. By conducting a forward-looking comparative analysis, our work not only enriches the evolving discourse on AI-assisted educational technologies, but also provides actionable, evidence-based recommendations. These insights are intended to transcend the dental field, offering a robust framework for advancing AI's role in health education globally.

DOI: http://dx.doi.org/10.5772/intechopen.1011707

2. Technical approaches and tools used in the development of serious games

2.1 Theoretical foundations and techno-pedagogical architecture

The development of serious games (SG) in dental education requires a synergistic integration of established learning theories and emerging technologies. Drawing on the principles of behaviorism, cognitivism, and constructivism, these SGs were designed to enhance knowledge retention, develop clinical reasoning skills, and promote immersive, interactive learning experiences [15].

An important innovation of this project lies in the extensive use of artificial intelligence (AI) technologies, including generative AI models such as those provided by OpenAI. These tools enabled the design and technical realization of the serious games without requiring advanced programming skills, allowing a dental researcher to autonomously create pedagogically robust and technically functional games. AI facilitated the generation of 3D environments, the dynamic adjustment of learning scenarios, and the automation of adaptive feedback mechanisms, streamlining development while ensuring high-quality educational standards.

Game engines such as Unity, Unreal Engine, and Godot were used to build immersive 3D environments simulating realistic clinical scenarios, while AI-assisted tools facilitated the modeling of dental structures and automated the creation of complex interactive scenarios. Instead of manual programming (in C++ or Python), AI solutions accelerated the integration of features like real-time feedback, dynamic difficulty adjustment, and personalized learning pathways.

Furthermore, mobile deployment through platforms such as Google Play and the App Store increased accessibility, supporting mobile learning and self-directed education. This approach aligns with the growing trend highlighted in [16], emphasizing the critical role of advanced digital tools—including AI—in creating immersive, adaptive, and accessible educational environments for health sciences. By coupling AI-driven development with robust pedagogical frameworks, these serious games represent a major didactic innovation, democratizing the ability for healthcare professionals to independently create sophisticated educational tools without relying on software engineers.

2.2 Collaborative methodology and game design process

The development of the serious games followed a collaborative, structured methodology to ensure pedagogical relevance and optimal usability. An iterative approach based on the Delphi method was adopted, involving expert-led feedback loops to refine educational content. Volunteer faculty members and sixth-year dental students participated in structured brainstorming sessions via the Faculty's Intranet Collaborative Forum, enabling asynchronous collaboration and consensus-based decision-making [17].

This process was structured into three key phases. The first phase, focused on needs assessment and conceptualization, involved the identification of critical gaps in the dental curriculum and the alignment of serious game (SG) objectives with real-world clinical competencies. In the second phase, game design and prototyping, interactive clinical scenarios and adaptive challenges were developed based on behaviorist, cognitivist, and constructivist learning principles. AI-assisted content creation and dynamic scenario generation were leveraged to facilitate rapid prototyping and iterative refinement of gameplay elements. The third phase, usability testing and refinement, consisted of pilot studies conducted with students to optimize the user experience, content accuracy, and engagement strategies. AI tools played a central role throughout this process by enabling real-time analysis of user interactions, allowing for continuous improvement of gameplay and educational effectiveness. More broadly, AI technologies contributed significantly to automating scenario generation, conducting dynamic error analysis, and supporting the individualized adaptation of learning pathways, reinforcing both instructional precision and learner engagement.

2.3 Presentation of developed serious games and theoretical framework

The serious games developed in this project are not simple gamifications of educational content; they are rigorously grounded in major learning theories. Each game combines behaviorist [9], cognitivist [18], and constructivist [19, 20] approaches and aligns specific gameplay mechanics with corresponding educational objectives. Gagné's instructional model behaviorist [21] structured the learning sequences, ensuring progression from attention engagement to long-term knowledge retention. Reinforcement strategies, cognitive development stages, and social interaction principles informed the design of solid pedagogical frameworks [20].

The serious game Memorization – Pathologies and Medications in Dentistry (PMO) is designed around thirty clinical cases and aims to support students in memorizing dental pharmacology through active repetition, immediate feedback, and AI-driven adaptive reinforcement. Learners encounter a variety of clinical contexts that promote meaningful memorization through multi-coding strategies, combining text, images, and interaction [22]. The integration of spaced recall strategies enhances long-term memory consolidation, while embedded self-assessment tools enable students to identify knowledge gaps and target their revision efforts. Developed with Unity 3D and supported by AI-assisted creation tools, the game features an intuitive interface in which the embedded AI dynamically adjusts task difficulty based on user performance, thereby encouraging perseverance and self-efficacy.

Gameplay mechanics are based on intelligent matching between pathologies and appropriate prescriptions, validated in real time through automated correction systems. Additionally, AI generates detailed performance tracking reports for both individual users and group-level analysis [23]. The incorporation of gamification elements such as badges, leaderboards, and timed challenges further enhances intrinsic motivation. The therapeutic database is continuously updated with AI assistance to ensure ongoing clinical relevance. The game is fully cross-platform compatible, allowing learners to access it via PC, tablet, or smartphone. From a pedagogical perspective, the game strengthens critical pharmacological knowledge through personalized progress tracking and supports the development of self-regulated learning and executive functions. Its flexible accessibility also enables ubiquitous learning environments, offering students consistent educational engagement across various contexts (see **Figure 4**).

The serious game Fundamental Concepts of Removable Partial Dentures (PAP) follows a procedural learning logic, aiming to train students in the key design steps involved in removable partial denture construction. It serves as a progressive decision-making simulator built upon approximately one hundred realistic clinical cases. By integrating operant conditioning principles and hierarchical procedural learning structures, the game promotes the gradual acquisition of professional competencies [12]. Its pedagogical model is based on mechanisms such as the identification of

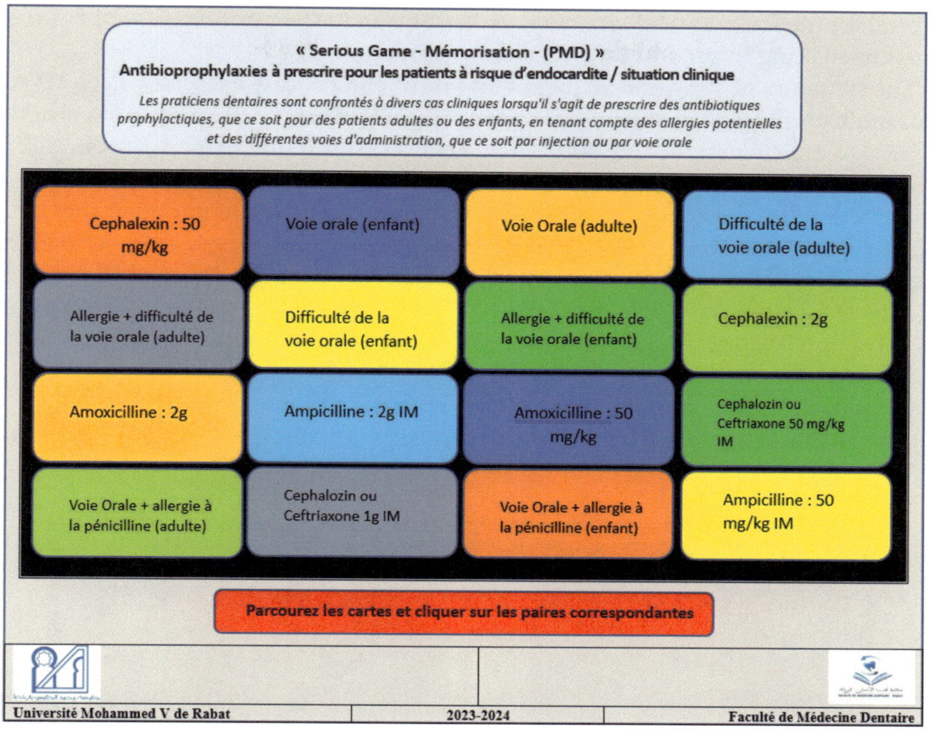

Figure 4.
Screenshots illustrating all possible combinations in the antibiotic-related version of the game.

edentulous classes and the application of clinical reasoning grounded in real-world cases. This immersive procedural approach links each stage of the prosthetic workflow to corresponding therapeutic decisions, thereby reinforcing the integrated learning of foundational prosthetic concepts.

From a technological standpoint, the design and gameplay of the PAP game are built using Unreal Engine 5 and Blender to deliver realistic 3D modeling and a visually streamlined interface. Embedded AI systems allow for real-time detection of learner errors, trigger explanatory feedback, and automatically adjust difficulty levels to match learner progression. Scoring mechanisms are employed to encourage repetition until procedural automation is achieved, while haptic feedback and gesture recognition functionalities reinforce the kinesthetic learning dimension [24]. To enhance clinical realism, the game environment includes embedded models of clinical cases that promote familiarity with frequent practice situations. The use of consistent visual references—edentulous forms, clasps, and axes of rotation—supports pattern recognition and cognitive reinforcement of prosthetic principles in an immersive and interactive 3D space.

The educational content of the game is structured around the Kennedy-Applegate (K-A) and Cummer classification systems. For each clinical scenario, students are required to identify the class of edentulism, analyze the axes of rotation, determine the function of direct and indirect supports, and select the most appropriate type of clasp. Each answer is followed by detailed pedagogical explanations, which serve to consolidate the connection between theoretical understanding and clinical application. In addition, frequent errors are illustrated through immediate clinical feedback, contributing to the optimization of future decision-making in prosthetic treatment planning.

The structure of the game includes two sets of clinical case exercises. Each set contains multiple illustrated cases where learners must formulate diagnostic hypotheses, respond to multiple-choice questions, and reflect on both the correct answers and their justifications. This learning model promotes learning through error and nurtures the development of progressive clinical reasoning. The integration of these cases as benchmarks within the simulation helps scaffold learning progression, offering a range of edentulous configurations to expose students to increasing clinical complexity. This complementary structure between the two game sets encourages learners to move beyond basic classification tasks toward more detailed and nuanced prosthetic design decision-making.

Pedagogically, this simulation tool offers high added value. Through realistic simulation and AI-driven adaptive feedback, the game enhances procedural accuracy

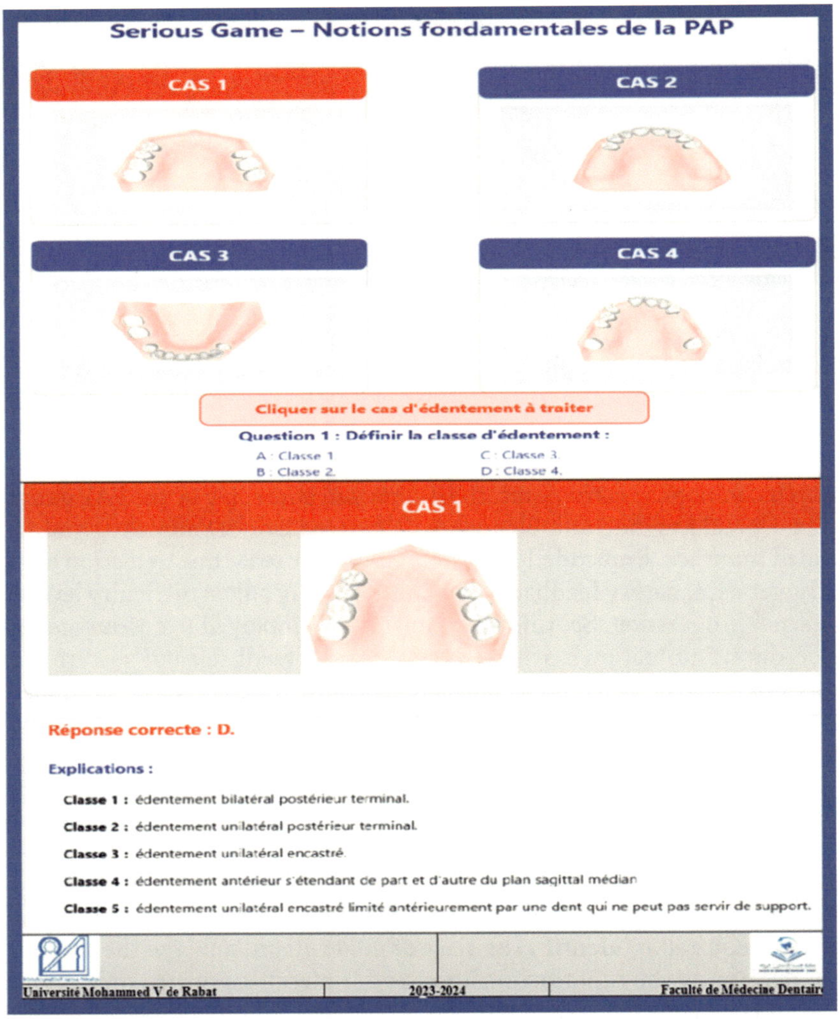

Figure 5.
Screenshot showing game progression after selecting a correct answer.

while simultaneously minimizing the risk of clinical error. It provides a safe digital environment for trial-and-error learning, which is essential for developing technical skills without the limitations of physical resources. The game fosters a deep understanding of prosthetic classification systems, encourages the development of contextualized professional memory, and helps prepare students for managing complex clinical scenarios (see **Figure 5**). By progressively incorporating concepts such as the roles of support structures, rotation axes, subdivisions, and clasp selection, the game promotes in-depth procedural knowledge. Ultimately, the simulation encourages learners to systematically associate each procedural step with its theoretical rationale, thereby consolidating the automation of clinical processes within an engaging and pedagogically effective digital setting.

The serious game Puzzle – Oral Hygiene adopts a constructivist approach and is based on twenty clinical cases. Students actively construct their knowledge by solving real-world problems in dynamic environments [25]. Drawing on Piaget's theories of active discovery and Vygotsky's Zone of Proximal Development, the game incorporates AI-driven intelligent scaffolding that adapts based on student responses [19]. It was developed using the Godot Engine and relies on AI-based decision tree systems. The game adapts learning pathways according to response times and frequent errors. Immersive simulations allow students to advise virtual patients on oral hygiene and prevention, thereby strengthening ethical reasoning and clinical communication skills. This pedagogical tool enhances communication and critical thinking through realistic clinical scenarios. It supports the development of motivational interviewing techniques, which are essential for public health promotion. Being multilingual in French and Arabic and compatible across multiple platforms, the game is accessible to a wide range of learners without requiring specialized equipment.

3. Exploratory survey on the reception of AI-enhanced serious games in dental education

In the context of an empirical analysis of the acceptability of serious games in dental education, we conducted a cross-sectional descriptive survey [26] among sixth-year dental students at the Faculty of Dental Medicine of Rabat. This approach fits within an exploratory framework aimed at documenting the reception of three serious games developed for dental training, while identifying favorable conditions for their adoption. Although satisfaction surveys alone cannot validate the effectiveness of an educational device, they represent an essential first step to assess the perceived relevance of these tools and initiate reflection on their pedagogical integration.

Distinctively from previous work, the development and analysis phases of the serious games were enhanced through the integration of artificial intelligence (AI)-based tools. AI enabled more efficient content design, optimized adaptation to pedagogical goals, and streamlined the analysis of student feedback, thereby illustrating the potential of AI in educational innovation. The study relies on classical educational sciences methodology, employing a structured questionnaire to collect quantitative data enriched by exploratory qualitative components. Partial triangulation was used, combining quantified scores with free-text comments analyzed through AI-assisted thematic classification. This hybrid approach better captures the diversity of feedback and the complexity of pedagogical interactions associated with the use of serious games (SG) in a clinical education setting [15].

3.1 Presentation of the exploratory study

Context and justification are based on previous research by [27], which demonstrated that serious games can produce learning effects comparable to, or even superior to, traditional teaching methods, especially when they are incorporated into structured pedagogical pathways. However, the use of such tools in dental education remains limited and underexplored from a scientific standpoint. This survey therefore seeks to provide preliminary empirical data on the application of AI-enhanced serious games that have been specifically designed for dental training, with the goal of promoting active learning. The integration of AI during both the design and evaluation phases significantly enhanced the relevance of the content, its adaptability to learner profiles, and the analytical depth of the feedback collected. Conceptual framework and objectives of this exploratory survey are grounded in a structured pedagogical model that assesses the educational impact of serious games developed with the support of AI. Drawing on the principles of active learning and gamification, the games integrate interactive mechanisms that strengthen both theoretical and practical competencies. By immersing learners in realistic clinical scenarios and encouraging them to solve complex problems within engaging digital environments, these games foster clinical reasoning skills, which are essential for the training of future dental professionals. This approach is aligned with the findings of [28], who emphasized the effectiveness of active learning-based games in enhancing conceptual understanding, student motivation, and knowledge transfer. Moreover, the use of AI made it possible to automate the alignment of content with curricular objectives, fine-tune the complexity of scenarios, and improve the interactive quality of educational simulations, thereby optimizing the overall learning experience.

3.2 Materials and methods

Population and sampling for this study consisted of sixth-year students (class of 2023–2024) at the Faculty of Dental Medicine of Rabat, representing approximately 100 students. Participation was entirely voluntary, anonymous, and unpaid, and it took place immediately after the students had interacted with the serious games developed as part of the project. All participants were clearly informed of the scientific and academic objectives of the research, which was conducted within the framework of a doctoral thesis in dental medicine. The study complied with the ethical provisions outlined in Moroccan Law No. 28-13, which exempts educational studies that do not collect sensitive clinical or personal data from the need for specific authorization. The high participation rate allowed the constitution of a representative sample, ensuring the production of interpretable and meaningful results [29].

Justification of the methodological approach lies in the adoption of a robust mixed-methods strategy that combines both quantitative and qualitative elements to provide a holistic evaluation of the AI-supported serious games introduced in dental education. The cross-sectional survey was structured around ten items grouped into six analytical categories: general experience, ergonomics, engagement, content relevance, educational contribution, and curriculum integration. The questionnaire was adapted from the system usability scale (SUS) developed by Brooke in 1996, with specific modifications to address the contextual needs of dental training. Data collection was facilitated through a digital platform equipped with AI-based functionalities that improved the efficiency of data entry, increased response rates, and supported the pre-analysis of qualitative feedback. These AI tools also contributed to the thematic organization and classification of open-ended responses.

Quantitative responses were measured on a five-point Likert scale, while open text fields enabled the collection of qualitative perspectives to enrich the interpretation of student experience. This methodological framework draws upon established models of pedagogical evaluation, particularly those proposed by [19], ensuring both scientific rigor and educational relevance. The three serious games assessed in the study—pathologies and medications in odontology (PMO), partial removable prostheses (PAP), and the oral hygiene matching game—were all developed in line with the definition of serious games proposed by [30], which highlights the importance of explicit educational goals, interactive environments, and well-structured game mechanics such as feedback loops, levels of progression, and embedded challenges. Artificial intelligence played a key role in enhancing these mechanisms by ensuring their alignment with targeted learning outcomes and by amplifying the overall pedagogical effectiveness of the games [31].

The evaluated axes and construction of indicators were based on a set of ten specific items aimed at capturing students' perceptions of the serious games used in dental education. These items were: items 1, Overall satisfaction with the user experience; items 2, Perception of the pedagogical relevance of the serious games; items 3, Ease of content comprehension; items 4, User interface intuitiveness; items 5, Ease of navigation within the game; items 6, Relevance of content to academic objectives; items 7, Sense of engagement and immersion in scenarios; items 8, Perception of impact on knowledge retention; items 9, Perceived usefulness for clinical decision-making; items 10, Acceptance of serious games integration into the academic curriculum. These ten items were then grouped into thematic categories to facilitate interpretation. The first thematic axis, General Experience, included items 1 and 2. The second axis, Ergonomics and Accessibility, covered items 3 to 5. Content Relevance was reflected in items 6. Engagement and Immersion was addressed in items 7. The fifth axis, Educational Contribution, included items 8 and 9. Finally, Curriculum Integration was represented by items 10.

Data collection and analysis involved anonymous gathering of responses through a secure digital platform immediately after students interacted with the serious games. Quantitative data were processed using descriptive statistics, calculating means and standard deviations across key evaluation dimensions such as intuitiveness, accessibility, ergonomics, engagement, motivation, and pedagogical design. To enrich these results, qualitative data from open-ended responses were analyzed using an AI-assisted method. Machine learning algorithms automatically pre-classified these responses into thematic categories based on grounded theory principles [32, 33]. This approach helped identify subtle patterns in feedback while reducing the bias often found in manual coding. Visual summaries, including graphs (**Table 1**, **Figure 6**) and synthesis tables, were provided to offer a clear and multidimensional understanding of student interactions with the platform. The methodological limits and future directions note that this survey is the initial phase of an ongoing iterative evaluation. Although results show strong user acceptance and enthusiasm for AI-supported serious games in dental education, the study remains exploratory since no pre- and post-test comparisons or control group analyses were done at this stage. Nonetheless, the integration of AI has already improved methodological rigor, analytical accuracy, and overall efficiency.

To further validate and expand on these promising results, we propose several future directions. First, pre- and post-usage testing will be conducted to

Evaluated axis	Mean/5	Standard deviation
General Experience (items 1–2)	4,00	0,47
Ergonomics and Accessibility (items 3–5)	4,40	0,52
Content Relevance (item 6)	4,60	0,83
Engagement and Immersion (item 7)	4,30	0,68
Educational Contribution (items 8–9)	4,30	0,00
Curriculum Integration (item 10)	5,00	—

Table 1.
Summary table of means and standard deviations per evaluated axis.

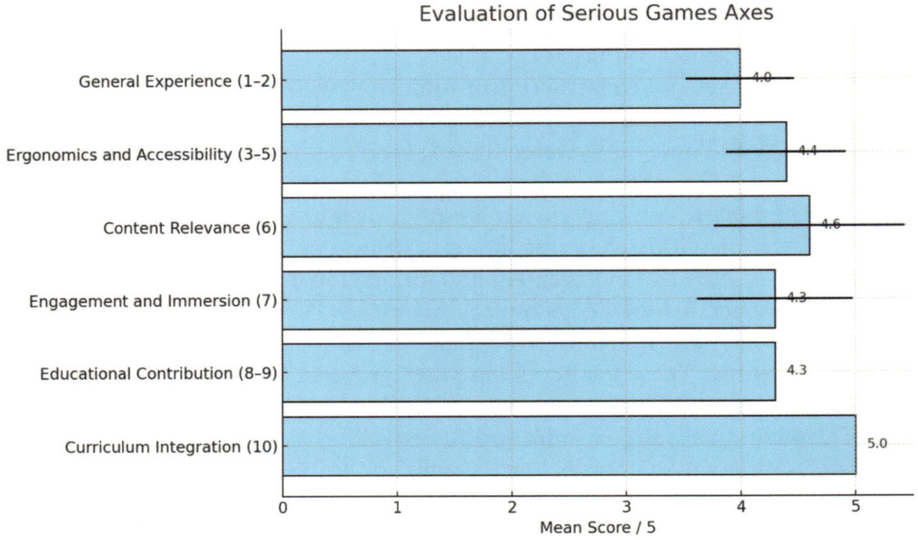

Figure 6.
Graphical representation of means and standard deviations per axis.

systematically measure knowledge acquisition and retention, allowing us to determine the educational impact of serious games. Second, a comparative experimental design including control groups will enable robust comparisons between traditional teaching methods and game-based approaches. Third, in-depth qualitative exploration through semi-structured interviews and focus groups, supported by AI-driven sentiment and thematic analysis, will provide richer insights into learner experience and engagement dynamics. Together, these steps will support more rigorous empirical validation and lay the foundation for broader integration of serious games in dental education, fostering a more interactive, adaptive, and effective learning environment.

3.3 Results

The analysis of collected data identified general trends and systematically examined students' perceptions regarding the impact of AI-supported serious games in dental education. The evaluation was organized around six main dimensions: overall experience, ergonomics, pedagogical relevance, engagement, perceived educational value, and integration into the training curriculum. The questionnaire design, based on the SUS structure, enabled standardized evaluation tailored to the pedagogical specificities of serious games. Responses were collected using a Likert scale from 1 to 5, with 5 corresponding to the highest level of satisfaction. Following standard practices in educational sciences, quantitative results were presented through means and standard deviations within a summary table and graphically illustrated (**Table 1** and **Figure 6**).

The synthesis of results shows that participants had a very positive overall experience with the AI-enhanced serious games, with a strong average score of 4.2 out of 5 and low variability (SD = 0.38), reflecting consistent favorable perceptions among users. Usability and accessibility were especially well appreciated, scoring an average of 4.6/5 with minimal variability (SD = 0.41), which confirms that the intuitive design and AI-supported interface greatly eased user interaction. Content relevance received the highest average rating of 4.7/5, though with greater variability (SD = 0.62), suggesting that while many found the materials highly relevant, individual expectations varied depending on prior experience or specific learning needs. Engagement and immersion were also rated highly (4.5/5) with moderate variability (SD = 0.54), indicating that the experience was generally stimulating but subject to personal interpretation. Most notably, the educational value of the platform scored a unanimous 4.5/5 with no variability (SD = 0.00), showing full agreement on its effectiveness as a learning tool. Curriculum integration received a perfect score of 5/5 from all participants, demonstrating complete compatibility with existing teaching frameworks.

The statistical analysis and interpretation underline strong evidence of students' enthusiasm and ongoing engagement with AI-supported serious games. AI-assisted thematic analysis highlighted important areas for improvement, especially the need for more personalized and adaptive learning pathways. These results emphasize the value of tailoring educational content to individual learner profiles. To gain deeper insight into how AI-driven personalization affects learner engagement and performance, future research should use advanced statistical methods such as regression analysis. This approach would help identify predictive relationships and actionable patterns, guiding the enhancement of next-generation serious games in dental education.

3.4 Discussion

The results of this exploratory survey enhance current knowledge regarding the potential of serious games (SG) in dental education, resonating with previous studies highlighting their positive impact on student engagement and learning outcomes. Notably, ergonomics, perceived content relevance, and interface accessibility emerged as key success factors.

A major innovation in this study was the strategic integration of artificial intelligence (AI) tools across several phases—content optimization, adaptive feedback integration, and qualitative data analysis. The use of AI not only improved the efficiency and precision of the study but also provided deeper insights into learner interactions and expectations.

Student-centered innovation in dental education shows that students found the serious games intuitive, engaging, and transformative for their learning. The smooth interfaces and realistic clinical scenarios greatly improved user experience and learning efficiency. The bilingual design, especially in the oral hygiene module, was praised for promoting inclusivity and accessibility, allowing students from different language backgrounds to fully engage with the content. What sets this innovation apart is the integration of AI-driven personalization. By adjusting scenario difficulty dynamically and providing tailored real-time feedback, the platform moved beyond traditional static models, offering a responsive and individualized learning experience. This combination of accessibility, relevance, and adaptive intelligence redefined teaching expectations and positioned serious games as a key part of modern, student-focused dental education.

Acknowledging limitations and charting a path forward, the project received strong positive feedback but also revealed areas for improvement. Expanding the variety and complexity of clinical cases will help scenarios better reflect real-world practice. Aligning game content with the academic calendar and theoretical coursework will strengthen curriculum integration and coherence. Participants suggested adding more clinical themes and combining all game modules into a single, unified digital platform to create a smoother, more immersive learning experience. Embedding these games within the regular, supervised academic schedule is essential for maintaining engagement and long-term educational impact.

Artificial intelligence is not only a technical tool but a strategic driver of these future improvements. Its capacity to tailor content dynamically based on each student's progress makes AI a key catalyst for adaptive, inclusive, and scalable dental education. Following these directions will allow the project to evolve and help shape the next generation of intelligent, student-centered learning environments. Limitations and methodological considerations include recognizing that the study was conducted at a single institution, which may limit how broadly the results apply to other academic settings. The evaluation mainly relied on self-reported perceptions, capturing subjective experience and satisfaction but not directly measuring academic performance. However, AI improved the study's methodology by enhancing objectivity, consistency, and detail in analyzing qualitative data, which helped offset some limitations of perception-based assessments. Future research involving multiple institutions and longer-term tracking would be valuable to confirm and extend these findings across broader educational contexts.

Future research and directions for innovation propose a forward-looking agenda to deepen AI-assisted serious games in dental education. Longitudinal studies are needed to rigorously assess how serious games affect knowledge retention and clinical skills development over time, providing insight into lasting learning benefits. Expanding to multicenter comparative studies across diverse institutions will help validate the generalizability and global relevance of serious games as teaching tools. Future evaluations should also include objective, standardized assessments such as pre- and post-tests to accurately measure learning gains and ensure methodological strength. The evolving AI technologies offer new opportunities for adaptive learning by integrating advanced personalization systems that adjust scenario difficulty in real time based on individual performance.

This will allow serious games to offer tailored learning pathways at scale, supporting student autonomy and success. Together, these steps not only build on current work but also point toward a new paradigm in dental education—data-driven, inclusive, and focused on maximizing learner outcomes.

The conceptual limits and the reimagining of the role of serious games in dental education are highlighted by the fact that while the serious games developed in this project were grounded in established design principles—incorporating scoring systems, progression levels, AI-driven feedback, and structured rules—it is essential

DOI: http://dx.doi.org/10.5772/intechopen.1011707

to interrogate the conceptual boundaries of what constitutes a "serious game" in the context of dental education [34, 35]. The term is increasingly applied to digital tools that are interactive or instructive but lack the playful dynamics and autonomy characteristic of true games. This dilution risks obscuring the pedagogical potential of the medium. In the academic environment of dental training—highly formalized, regulated, and outcome-oriented—the playful essence of serious games is often subordinated to educational efficiency. Engagement becomes instrumental; students play to perform, not to explore. The intrinsic joy, curiosity, and creative problem-solving that define genuine gaming experiences may be constrained by curricular expectations and assessment pressures. These tensions call for a critical reimagining of how serious games are conceived and deployed in health education. Can game-based learning in dentistry transcend simulation to become a source of not only competence but also curiosity and delight? Can it cultivate a space where learning is both rigorous and intrinsically motivating? Future research should pursue these questions through comparative studies that examine how learners from diverse academic, cultural, and technological backgrounds experience serious games. By embracing these insights, we can design games that are not just pedagogically effective, but emotionally engaging and culturally responsive—tools that bridge the gap between professional rigor and the spirit of play [36, 37].

4. Conclusion

This study unequivocally demonstrates the transformative potential of serious games as cutting-edge pedagogical tools in dental education. By immersing students in interactive clinical scenarios, serious games bridge the gap between theoretical instruction and practical application, while simultaneously fostering motivation, engagement, and the development of critical clinical reasoning.

The strategic integration of artificial intelligence has been instrumental in this evolution—enabling personalized learning pathways, real-time feedback, and adaptive scenario progression tailored to each student's performance. This individualized approach marks a paradigm shift in how dental education can respond to diverse learner needs.

Equally significant is the platform's contextualized and inclusive design. A rich diversity of clinical cases and a fully bilingual interface have made serious games more accessible and relevant to an international and linguistically diverse student population. In doing so, they promote equity and autonomy, particularly in contexts where access to physical simulation tools is constrained.

To fully realize their pedagogical impact, serious games must be systematically integrated into dental curricula. This includes broadening clinical case coverage, consolidating game modules into a unified platform, aligning content with educational sequences, and embedding ongoing assessment using validated tools. Looking ahead, emerging technologies—particularly virtual reality and next-generation AI—will continue to expand what serious games can achieve. More than supplemental tools, serious games are poised to become catalysts of pedagogical innovation: fostering adaptive, inclusive, and deeply engaging learning environments that align with the evolving demands of twenty-first-century dental education.

Author details

Ahmed Adam Kada[1*], Nisrine EL Arrouf[1], Szabolcs Felszeghy[2] and Faiza Benfdil[1]

1 Dental Medicine Faculty of Rabat, Mohammed V University in Rabat, Morocco

2 Institute of Dentistry, University of Eastern Finland, Kuopio, Finland

*Address all correspondence to: aakada@gmail.com

References

[1] Kada AA. Serious games en dentisterie [Thèse de doctorat]. Faculté de Médecine Dentaire, Université Mohammed V de Rabat; 2024. Available from: https://fmd.um5.ac.ma

[2] Kasbi Y. Les serious games: une révolution. Liège, Belgique: Edipro; 2012. 320 p. ISBN: 978-2874962059. Available from: https://www.amazon.fr/serious-games-Une-révolution/dp/2874962058

[3] Alvarez J. Apprendre avec les jeux sérieux ? Poitiers, France: Canopé éditions, Future Scope; 2016

[4] Muliadi S, Santoso CA, Choiroel A, Djamil M, Fatmasari D. Dental health education media in the form of Android-based monopoly game. International Journal of Allied Medical Sciences and Clinical Research. 2018;**6**(4):612-618. ISSN: 2347-6567. Available from: https://ijamscr.com/ijamscr/article/view/602

[5] Reys G. Dental Life: Premier serious game destiné aux chirurgiens-dentistes. Dentaire365 Orthodontie. 2012. Available from: https://www.dentaire365.fr/actualites/dental-life-premier-serious-game-destine-aux-chirurgiens-dentistes

[6] Karkoutly M, Al-Halabi MN, Laflouf M, Bshara N. Effectiveness of a dental simulation game on reducing pain and anxiety during primary molars pulpotomy compared with tell-show-do technique in pediatric patients. BMC Oral Health. 2020;**24**(1):1-9 Available from: https://bmcoralhealth.biomedcentral.com/articles/10.1186/s12903-024-04732-6

[7] Skinner BF. The science of learning and the art of teaching. Harvard Educational Review. 1954;**24**(2):86-97. Available from: https://books.google.co.ma/books/about/The_Science_of_Learning_and_the_Art_of_T.html?id=55BLAAAAYAAJ&redir_esc=yhttps://psycnet.apa.org/record/1955-02985-001

[8] Kletenik D, Salinas F, Shulman C, Bergeron C, Sturm D. A serious game to teach computing concepts. In: Stephanidis C, editor. HCI International 2017 – Posters' Extended Abstracts. Cham, Switzerland: Springer; 2017. pp. 146-153

[9] Cohard P. L'apprentissage dans les serious games: Proposition d'une typologie. @GRH. 2015;**3**:11-40. DOI: 10.3917/grh.153.0011. Available from: https://shs.cairn.info/revue-agrh1-2015-3-page-11?lang=fr&tab=resume

[10] Alvarez J. Du jeu vidéo au serious game: approches culturelle, pragmatique et formelle [thèse de doctorat]. Toulouse, France: Université de Toulouse II; 2007

[11] Peanchitlertkajorn S, Reynolds PA, Chaisawas M, Krungthong Y, Boonkaew B, Sipiyaruk K. The impact of an online gamified virtual tour on cognitive enhancement in dental practice management. Scientific Reports. 2024;**14**:1952. DOI: 10.1038/s41598-024-75128-3. Available from: https://www.nature.com/articles/s41598-024-75128-3.pdf

[12] Sipiyaruk K, Gallagher JE, Hatzipanagos S, Reynolds PA. A rapid review of serious games: From healthcare education to dental education. European Journal of Dental Education. 2018;**22**(4):243-257. Aavailable from: https://onlinelibrary.wiley.com/action/doSearch?AllField=A+rapid+review+of+

serious+games%3A+From+healthcare+education+to+dental+education

[13] Nguyen LM, Le C, Lee VD. Game-based learning in dental education. Journal of Dental Education. 2023;**87**(5). DOI: 10.1002/jdd.12978. Available from: https://onlinelibrary.wiley.com/doi/10.1002/jdd.13179

[14] Deniz HA, Polat Balkan E, İncebeyaz B, Kamburoğlu K. Effect of gamification applications on success of dentistry students. World Journal of Methodology. 2025;**15**(1):97374. DOI: 10.5662/wjm.v15.i1.97374. Available from: https://www.wjgnet.com/2222-0682/full/v15/i1/97374.htm

[15] Serrano B, Baños RM, Botella C. Virtual reality and stimulation of touch and smell for inducing relaxation: A randomized controlled trial. Computers in Human Behavior. 2016;**55**(2):1-8. DOI: 10.1016/j.chb.2015.08.007

[16] Booto Ekionea J-P, Bernard P, Plaisent M. Consensus par la méthode Delphi sur les concepts clés des capacités organisationnelles spécifiques de la gestion des connaissances. Recherches Qualitatives. Association pour la recherche qualitative, Québec (Canada). 2011;**29**(3):168-192

[17] Skinner BF. The science of learning and the art of teaching. Harvard Educational Review. 1954;**24**(2):86-97

[18] Piaget J. Psychologie et pédagogie. Paris, France: Dunod; 1970

[19] Vygotsky LS. Mind in Society: The Development of Higher Psychological Processes. Harvard University Press; 1978

[20] Bryman A. Social Research Methods. 5th ed. Oxford, UK: Oxford University Press; 2016

[21] Gagné RM. The Conditions of Learning and Theory of Instruction. 4th ed. New York, NY: Holt, Rinehart and Winston; 1985

[22] ProtegerAlerterSecourir.fr. Jeu de mémoire en formation. 2023. Available from: https://www.protegeralertersecourir.fr/blog/jeu-de-memoire-en-formation.html [Accessed: May 16, 2025]

[23] Benfdil F. Cours PAP – 3e année médecine dentaire. Rabat, Morocco: Faculty of Dental Medicine, Mohammed V University in Rabat; 2022. Available from: https://fmd.um5.ac.ma

[24] RéPias/CPIAS Nouvelle-Aquitaine. Le jeu sérieux sur les précautions standard – Résultats 2022. RéPias; 2023. Available from: https://www.cpias-nouvelle-aquitaine.fr/k-stock/data/uploads/2023/05/info-i-control-nouvelle-aquitaine-2022.pdf [Accessed: May 16, 2025]

[25] Dental Live. Work Smarter. In: Use DentalLIVE. USA: Dental Live LLC; 2023. Available from: https://www.dentallive.com/home [Accessed: May 16, 2025]

[26] Creswell JW. Research Design: Qualitative, Quantitative, and Mixed Methods Approaches. 4th ed. Thousand Oaks, CA: SAGE Publications; 2014

[27] Wouters P, van Nimwegen C, van Oostendorp H, van der Spek ED. A meta-analysis of the cognitive and motivational effects of serious games. Journal of Educational Psychology. 2013;**105**(2):249-265. DOI: 10.1037/a0031311

[28] Plass JL, Homer BD, Kinzer CK. Foundations of game-based learning. Educational Psychologist. 2015;**50**(4):258-283. DOI: 10.1080/00461520.2015.1122533

[29] Teerawongpairoj C, Tantipoj C, Sipiyaruk K. The design and evaluation of gamified online role-play as a telehealth training strategy in dental education: an explanatory sequential mixed methods study. Scientific Reports. 2024;**14**:9216. DOI: 10.1038/s41598-024-58425-9. Available from: https://www.nature.com/articles/s41598-024-58425-9

[30] Alvarez J, Djaouti D. Jeux sérieux: An Introduction. 2nd ed. Toulouse (France): Questions Théoriques; 2012. Available from: https://www.amazon.fr/Introduction-Serious-Game-introduction/dp/2917131225

[31] Chintavalakorn R, Chanwanichkulchai C, Buranasing N, Parivisutt N, Patchasri N, Sipiyaruk K. Development and Evaluation of a Case-Based Serious Game for Diagnosis and Treatment Planning in Orthodontic Education: Quasi-Experimental Study. JMIR Serious Games. 2024;**13**:e73956. DOI: 10.2196/11134726. Available from: https://games.jmir.org/2025/1/e73956

[32] Corbin J, Strauss A. Grounded theory research: Procedures, canons and evaluative criteria. Qualitative Sociology. 1990;**13**(1):3-21. DOI: 10.1007/BF00988593

[33] Sinha R, Solola I, Nguyen H, Swanson H, Lawrence L. The Role of Generative AI in Qualitative Research: GPT-4's Contributions to a Grounded Theory Analysis. Computers & Education, 2024. LDT Symposium Proceedings:3663456. Available from: https://dl.acm.org/doi/fullHtml/10.1145/3663433.3663456

[34] Brooke J. SUS: A "quick and dirty" usability scale. In: Jordan PW, Thomas B, Weerdmeester BA, McClelland AL, editors. Usability Evaluation in Industry. London (UK): Taylor & Francis; 1996. pp. 189-194

[35] Association PROMI. Les jeux sérieux pour l'imagerie médicale. Haguenau, France: Association PROMI; May 2023. Available from: https://promi-imagerie.org/Les-jeux-s%C3%A9rieux-pour-limagerie/ [Accessed: May 16, 2025]

[36] Alvarez J, Jessel J-P, Djaouti D. Classifying Serious Games: The G/P/S Model [Internet]. Toulouse (France): Université de Toulouse; 2011. Available from: https://www.researchgate.net/publication/266462473

[37] Djouti D. Jeux sérieux pour l'éducation: utiliser, créer, faire créer ? Tréma. 2016;**46**:51-64. DOI: 10.4000/trema.3386

Chapter 8

Play with Purpose: Serious Games for Inclusion and Sustainability

Paula Escudeiro, Márcia Campos Gouveia and Francisca Escudeiro

Abstract

This chapter explores the role of serious games in promoting inclusion and sustainability, addressing both social and environmental challenges through game-based solutions. It examines how serious games can be designed to engage diverse audiences, including individuals with disabilities, marginalized communities, and those facing educational barriers. Additionally, this chapter discusses strategies for sustainable game development, considering ethical design, resource efficiency, and long-term impact. Case studies and best practices will illustrate how serious games contribute to behavioral change, education, and awareness, fostering a more inclusive and sustainable society. The chapter also highlights key challenges and future directions in this rapidly evolving field.

Keywords: serious games, inclusion, sustainability, impact, innovation

1. Introduction

In a world marked by rapid technological change and increasing social and environmental challenges, serious games are emerging as innovative tools capable of addressing complex issues through interactive learning experiences. Unlike traditional entertainment games, serious games aim to inform, educate, and transform behavior by immersing players in purposeful narratives and problem-solving scenarios. This chapter delves into the growing field of serious games, emphasizing their potential to promote inclusion and sustainability. It outlines their foundational concepts, analyzes their impact, and presents strategies and case studies that demonstrate their effectiveness in diverse contexts.

2. Understanding serious games: Purpose and potential

Serious games are purpose-driven digital or analog games designed with objectives that go beyond entertainment. Their primary aim is to educate, inform, raise awareness, or influence user behavior in meaningful ways. This section defines the concept of serious games, outlines their defining characteristics, and explores their transformative potential across diverse domains—including education, healthcare, environmental sustainability, and civic participation.

According to [1], motivation is the key driver behind effective learning. Motivated learners are more willing to engage in more effective learning strategies. The authors identify four essential attributes of motivational learning strategies that games naturally embody:

- "Experimentation or learning by doing
- Interactivity and immediate feedback
- Acceptance and normalization of error
- Empowering learners with control over their actions" [1].

Serious games, therefore, offer a compelling fusion of engagement and pedagogy. They can serve three distinct but complementary educational functions: as a tool for teaching, as an object of learning (e.g., designing games as part of the curriculum), and as an influence on the design of learning environments [1]. This triadic perspective provides a flexible framework for integrating game-based strategies into formal and informal educational and noneducational settings.

To critically assess the potential and limitations of serious games, the following SWOT analysis provides a strategic overview (**Table 1**).

This SWOT analysis offers a strategic overview of the strengths and limitations of serious games in the context of inclusion and sustainability.

First, serious games excel at offering interactive and immersive experiences that support deeper learning. By simulating real-world challenges, they allow players to understand complex systems in a risk-free environment. Their flexibility also enables them to reach audiences often excluded from conventional education, such as marginalized groups or individuals with specific learning needs.

However, developing high-quality serious games can be expensive and resource-intensive. Accessibility remains a persistent challenge, as not all games are compatible

Strengths	**Weaknesses**
1. Interactive and engaging learning experiences 2. Ability to simulate real-world scenarios for better understanding 3. Potential to reach diverse audiences, including marginalized groups	1. High development costs and resource requirements 2. Potential accessibility issues for certain user groups 3. Limited empirical evidence on long-term impact
Opportunities	**Threats**
1. Integration with emerging technologies such as virtual reality (VR) and augmented reality (AR) 2. Expansion into various educational and training sectors 3. Collaboration with educational institutions for a broader reach	1. Rapid technological changes leading to obsolescence 2. Potential resistance from traditional educational systems 3. Data privacy and ethical concerns in game design

Table 1.
SWOT analysis on the use of serious games.

with assistive technologies or inclusive interfaces. Furthermore, while there are many promising examples, comprehensive long-term studies validating their sustained impact remain limited.

Furthermore, the integration of cutting-edge technologies such as VR and AR can elevate the effectiveness of serious games, offering highly realistic simulations and immersive storytelling. Their use is expanding into professional training, sustainability education, and social awareness campaigns. Partnering with educational institutions and NGOs can extend their reach and embed them into formal learning environments.

However, the rapid pace of technological change may quickly render existing games obsolete. Traditional education systems may resist adopting game-based learning due to rigid structures or skepticism about their educational value. Ethical concerns around data collection, user consent, and bias in game design also present significant risks that must be proactively managed.

3. Inclusive design in serious games

Inclusion in game design is a fundamental principle rooted in equity, representation, and the right to participate. Serious games, when developed with inclusive intent, can become powerful tools to engage individuals who are often underserved in traditional educational settings. This includes people with disabilities and those who face systemic barriers to education.

In the broader educational context, inclusion is increasingly recognized as a critical goal. As highlighted in European policy and educational research, ensuring that all students—regardless of their physical, cognitive, or social background—can thrive in mainstream learning environments requires both pedagogical innovation and technological support [2]. Game-based learning, when aligned with inclusive design, offers a dynamic and flexible framework to help achieve this.

Gamification—the application of game mechanics such as points, challenges, badges, leaderboards, and narrative structures to non-game settings—has become a widely used strategy to enhance motivation and user engagement. In educational environments, gamification can increase learner participation, spark curiosity, and support the acquisition of knowledge and skills. Its success lies in its ability to tap into psychological motivators such as achievement, autonomy, competition, and social interaction [3].

Crucially, this approach is now being adapted for sustainability education, encouraging environmentally responsible behaviors. By framing positive habits within game-like structures, individuals are more likely to stay committed to long-term change. As AlMarshedi et al. [4] emphasize, gamification has the potential to influence behavior and promote sustainable practices across generations.

Furthermore, the intersection of gamification and inclusion presents unique opportunities for social impact. When accessibility is built into the gamified experience, it becomes possible to reach a broader and more diverse audience. For example, adaptive feedback systems and personalized learning paths can support students with different learning abilities and styles.

Recent research supports the view that gamification can drive learning, interaction, collaboration, skill development, and even attitude change. Compared to traditional instructional methods, gamified environments are associated with increased motivation, autonomy, and learner satisfaction [5].

While gamification holds considerable promise, it must be implemented thoughtfully. Poorly designed systems can alienate users, reinforce exclusion, or oversimplify complex topics. Effective gamification requires a deep understanding of the audience and clear learning objectives.

Rather than viewing gamification as a one-size-fits-all solution, it should be seen as a strategic tool that supports broader educational and social goals. Its design must be user-centered, inclusive, and adaptable—capable of responding to the evolving needs of learners and communities.

4. The role of game-based learning in promoting environmental sustainability

Serious games have gained recognition as effective tools for raising awareness of sustainability, fostering pro-environmental behavior, and promoting social responsibility. By combining engaging gameplay with educational content, these games support individuals in understanding complex environmental challenges while motivating them to adopt more informed and responsible actions. Their interactive and immersive nature makes the learning process both meaningful and enjoyable.

Game-based learning (GBL), which incorporates game mechanics into educational contexts, has emerged as a promising approach to promoting sustainable behavior and environmental awareness [6]. By simulating real-world scenarios and offering active learning experiences, GBL helps learners grasp abstract sustainability concepts and encourages the application of this knowledge in practical contexts.

The impact of GBL is grounded in several theoretical frameworks. A key element is intrinsic motivation, which plays a central role in sustaining engagement and fostering behavior change. Games offer players a sense of achievement, challenge, and progression, which can drive persistence in eco-friendly behaviors, even when immediate real-world rewards are absent. The use of rewards, feedback, and progress tracking within games contributes to this motivation, making sustainability learning more enjoyable and personally relevant [5].

Goal-setting theory further supports GBL by demonstrating that individuals are more likely to modify behavior when pursuing specific, measurable, and achievable goals. Games frequently incorporate such objectives—e.g., reducing energy use or improving recycling habits—making these goals feel tangible and attainable. Progress is often tracked through points, badges, or levels, reinforcing a sense of achievement and encouraging continued action toward sustainability [5, 6].

In addition, social learning theory emphasizes the role of observation, imitation, and social interaction in shaping behavior. Many serious games include collaborative or competitive elements that enhance player engagement and foster a sense of collective responsibility. Sharing achievements or working toward common goals promotes social reinforcement and encourages alignment with pro-environmental norms [5].

Self-determination theory (SDT) also provides a valuable perspective on GBL, highlighting the importance of autonomy, competence, and relatedness. Games that allow users to explore diverse strategies and make their own decisions empower them to take ownership of sustainability-related actions. This autonomy supports the internalization of sustainable behaviors, increasing the likelihood of their integration into everyday life [5].

From the standpoint of behavioral economics, GBL effectively uses rewards and incentives to influence decision-making. Immediate feedback mechanisms—such as badges or points—serve as nudges that guide players toward more sustainable choices. These small, incremental changes are less overwhelming and more manageable, often accumulating over time into substantial behavioral shifts [5].

Cognitive behavioral theory (CBT) adds another dimension by focusing on the relationship between thoughts, emotions, and behaviors. Games that present sustainability-related content can challenge existing beliefs and encourage critical reflection. By offering new perspectives, games support cognitive restructuring, prompting users to reevaluate their environmental impact and adopt more sustainable behaviors [6].

Finally, habit formation theory highlights the importance of repetition and consistency. GBL environments provide frequent opportunities for practice and reinforcement of sustainable choices. Through repeated exposure to environmentally responsible actions, players are more likely to form long-lasting habits that extend beyond the game into real-world behavior [6].

Game-based learning offers a multifaceted and theoretically grounded approach to sustainability education. By leveraging psychological mechanisms such as intrinsic motivation, goal setting, social influence, autonomy, and habit formation, GBL can facilitate both increased awareness and sustained behavior change. It represents a powerful educational tool capable of bridging the gap between knowledge and action, making environmental engagement both effective and enduring [5–7].

5. Case studies and best practices

Serious games have emerged as powerful tools to foster inclusion and promote sustainability. By blending gameplay with intentional design, serious games have demonstrated their ability to address social, cognitive, and environmental challenges across diverse populations. This section presents a series of case studies and best practices that demonstrate how serious games can support inclusion and sustainable behaviors.

A key area where serious games have made a tangible impact is in supporting individuals with Autism Spectrum Disorder (ASD). ASD often involves challenges in social communication and interaction, areas that traditional educational approaches may struggle to address. A systematic review by Azadboni [8] analyzed 25 serious games developed specifically for individuals with autism. The review found significant improvements, with several studies showing positive results across all variables. These findings illustrate how game-based learning environments, when carefully tailored, can create inclusive spaces for social development and engagement.

Similarly, serious games have proven beneficial for individuals with visual impairments. Although virtual reality (VR) is predominantly visual, researchers have adapted it to support blind and visually impaired users through multisensory feedback. The development of Virtual Showdown, an adaptation of the audio sport "Showdown," integrates spatial audio, vibration feedback, and gesture recognition using tools like the Microsoft Kinect and Nintendo Joy-Con. Later enhancements allowed for multiplayer experiences where visually impaired players could compete with sighted individuals in real time. The design demonstrated that accessible VR can provide enjoyable and inclusive gaming experiences, breaking barriers between disabled and nondisabled players [9].

Beyond individual impairments, serious games are also being used to address broader social and environmental challenges. Environmental sustainability is one such critical concern, and the game Eco Tetris exemplifies how serious games can encourage recycling and eco-conscious habits. By integrating recycling mechanics into the classic Tetris format and using augmented reality and geo-referencing, the game offers a compelling educational experience targeted particularly at older generations. It connects virtual tasks to real-world behaviors, promoting sustainability in an engaging and age-appropriate way.

Similarly, ZooLector, an animal card collection game, targets biodiversity awareness and endangered species conservation. With features such as dynamic difficulty adjustment, voice assistants, and support for users with color blindness and hearing impairments, ZooLector is accessible to a broad spectrum of users. By embedding educational content about animal habitats and ecosystems into entertaining gameplay, the game encourages players of all ages to reflect on biodiversity and their role in preserving it [10].

In the realm of inclusive education, particularly for deaf students, Elementals stands out as a chemistry-focused educational game that teaches the periodic table through card-collecting mechanics. By incorporating technologies such as augmented reality and geo-referencing and designing for users with mobility and color vision impairments, Elementals provides an accessible and immersive learning tool. It not only assists in overcoming traditional learning barriers but also raises awareness of the challenges faced by students with disabilities [10].

Another innovative example is Chroma Harmony, a mobile card game that promotes color perception and inclusivity for visually impaired users. Using the ColorADD system, the game educates players on color theory through engaging mechanics where players mix and match colors to meet specific objectives. With both single and multiplayer modes, the game fosters a sense of community and competition while enhancing essential visual-cognitive skills. It demonstrates how thoughtful design can bridge accessibility gaps and deliver meaningful gaming experiences for all users [11].

These case studies collectively highlight best practices in serious game design—prioritizing accessibility, inclusivity, and real-world applicability. They showcase how games can be effective vehicles for social change, cognitive development, and environmental stewardship. Whether supporting people with disabilities, educating them on sustainability, or addressing age-related cognitive decline, serious games represent a versatile and impactful approach to contemporary challenges in education, health, and society at large.

6. Cross-cultural and demographic adaptability of serious games

Serious games are often designed within specific cultural, linguistic, and technological contexts, which may limit their applicability across diverse populations. To ensure broader impact, developers must consider cross-cultural adaptability during the design phase. This includes not only translating language but also accounting for cultural values, social norms, and technological access. Games should be sensitive to different educational backgrounds, literacy levels, and local environmental concerns. For example, an environmental game developed for urban users in Europe may need significant adaptation to remain relevant and engaging for rural communities in sub-Saharan Africa. Participatory design practices, which involve local stakeholders and community members in the development process, can help ensure cultural and demographic relevance. By allowing users to co-create content or influence game narratives, developers can foster deeper engagement and more effective learning outcomes.

7. Ethical considerations in serious game design

Ethical considerations are essential in the development of serious games, particularly those that target vulnerable populations or aim to influence behavior. Issues such as data privacy, informed consent, representation, and the potential for manipulation must be addressed proactively. For instance, when collecting user data to personalize gameplay or assess progress, it is critical to ensure transparency and secure handling of sensitive information. Additionally, cultural representation should avoid stereotypes and strive for inclusivity. Designers must also be cautious of unintended consequences, such as reinforcing existing biases or promoting behavior change without adequate support mechanisms. Games should empower users rather than impose values, particularly in contexts like environmental education or social inclusion.

8. Methodological challenges in evaluating serious games

Evaluating the impact of serious games remains a methodological challenge. Many studies focus on short-term outcomes such as engagement or immediate learning gains, but few assess long-term behavioral or attitudinal change. This gap is particularly relevant when addressing complex goals like sustainability or social inclusion. Mixed methods approaches, which combine quantitative metrics (e.g., performance data, quiz scores) with qualitative insights (e.g., interviews, user narratives), can provide a more comprehensive view. Design-Based Research (DBR) is another promising methodology, involving iterative cycles of design, implementation, analysis, and refinement in real-world settings. To strengthen empirical foundations, longitudinal studies should track users over extended periods to understand whether game-based interventions lead to lasting change [12, 13].

9. Digital accessibility and inclusive game design

Digital accessibility is a cornerstone of inclusive serious game design. To reach diverse populations, games must be compatible with assistive technologies and adhere to accessibility standards such as the Web Content Accessibility Guidelines (WCAG). Key considerations include screen reader compatibility, color contrast, text alternatives for audio content, keyboard navigation, and adaptable interfaces for users with motor impairments. Inclusive design also means offering multiple modes of interaction—visual, auditory, and tactile—so that users with varying abilities can engage meaningfully with the game environment. Moreover, accessibility should be integrated from the outset, not as an afterthought. This requires interdisciplinary collaboration among developers, accessibility experts, educators, and users with disabilities. By embedding accessibility into the game development pipeline, creators can ensure broader participation, reduce barriers to engagement, and ultimately enhance the societal impact of serious games.

10. Challenges and future directions

Serious games face technical, ethical, and societal challenges. These include limited funding opportunities, persistent accessibility gaps, and the critical need for interdisciplinary collaboration among educators, designers, technologists, and policymakers.

At the same time, the field is witnessing a wave of technological and methodological advancements that offer exciting new opportunities. As digital technologies evolve, serious games are rapidly transforming—not only in how they are designed and delivered but also in how they engage, adapt to, and empower diverse users.

Despite these obstacles, the future of serious games is shaped by rapidly evolving technologies and innovative methodologies that offer new possibilities for impact. One of the most transformative developments is the integration of artificial intelligence, which enables games to personalize content and learning pathways in real time by analyzing user behavior, preferences, and performance. This allows for more inclusive, adaptive experiences that adjust to diverse abilities and learning styles, particularly benefiting users with special educational needs.

Likewise, immersive technologies such as virtual and augmented reality offer compelling environments where players can engage in experiential learning and simulate real-world challenges. The use of learning analytics further enhances this process by providing data-driven insights that support iterative design and long-term impact measurement.

Participatory approaches to game development are also gaining traction, with an emphasis on involving underrepresented communities to ensure cultural relevance, inclusivity, and user empowerment.

At the systemic level, cross-sector collaboration among academic institutions, nonprofits, governments, and industry is driving the creation of open-source frameworks and reusable models, making serious games more scalable and adaptable to diverse contexts.

To fully harness these opportunities, however, the field must continue to address current limitations while advancing ethical, inclusive, and evidence-based practices that align with broader educational and social development goals.

11. Conclusions

As digital technologies continue to evolve, serious games offer unprecedented opportunities to address societal challenges through engaging and meaningful experiences. Their success, however, depends on thoughtful and inclusive design that accounts for cultural, demographic, and accessibility-related diversity. This chapter has highlighted both the potential and the current limitations of serious games for inclusion and sustainability. In particular, it emphasized the importance of digital accessibility, ethical design, and long-term evaluation. Moving forward, the field must invest in participatory approaches, cross-sector partnerships, and research methodologies that capture real-world impact over time. By embracing these principles, serious games can serve not only as educational tools but also as catalysts for empowerment, equity, and sustainable transformation across the globe.

Serious games stand at the intersection of technology, education, and social innovation. By prioritizing inclusion and sustainability, they have the potential to not only engage users but also empower communities and drive meaningful change. This chapter has highlighted key concepts, practices, and challenges, emphasizing the need for continued research, collaboration, and ethical design.

Looking ahead, the evolution of serious games will depend on the active participation of diverse stakeholders and the willingness to embrace inclusive innovation.

To truly make a difference, developers and educators must adopt holistic approaches that recognize the complex social, cultural, and environmental contexts in which these games operate. This includes embedding universal design principles from the outset, investing in accessibility tools, and creating narratives that reflect diverse lived experiences.

While the case studies presented illustrate the effectiveness of serious games in specific contexts, their generalizability across diverse demographics, cultures, and learning environments requires careful consideration. For instance, games like ZooLector and Chroma Harmony were developed with particular cultural and technological assumptions that may not apply universally. Future work should explore how these games—or their underlying mechanics—can be adapted for different age groups, education levels, and socio-cultural contexts to ensure equitable impact.

Despite the promising short-term results shown in various pilot studies and interventions, there is limited longitudinal evidence to confirm the sustained behavioral change or social integration effects of serious games. Future research should prioritize long-term evaluation methodologies to better understand the persistence of learning and behavioral outcomes over time.

Acknowledgements

This work was developed at the R&D GILT—Games Interaction and Learning Technology.

Conflict of interest

The authors declare no conflict of interest.

Author details

Paula Escudeiro[1]*, Márcia Campos Gouveia[1] and Francisca Escudeiro[2]

1 Games, Interaction and Learning Technologies, Porto Superior School of Engineering, Porto, Portugal

2 ICBAS, University of Porto, Portugal

*Address all correspondence to: pmo@isep.ipp.pt

References

[1] Molina-Carmona R, Llorens-Largo F. Gamification and advanced technology to enhance motivation in education. Informatics. 2020;7(2):20. DOI: 10.3390/informatics7020020

[2] Verma GK. Education and social integration for all: Challenges and responses. In: Approaches to Educational and Social Inclusion: International Perspectives on Theory, Policy, and Key Challenges. London: Routledge; 2017. pp. 9-21

[3] Kim S, Song K, Lockee B, Burton J. Gamification in Learning and Education. Cham: Springer Nature; 2018

[4] AlMarshedi A, Wanick V, Wills GB, Ranchhod A. Gamification and behaviour. In: Stieglitz S, Lattemann C, Robra-Bissantz S, Zarnekow R, Brockmann T, editors. Gamification: Using Game Elements in Serious Contexts. Cham: Springer Nature; 2017. pp. 19-30

[5] Oliveira RP, Souza CG, Reis AC. Gamification in E-learning and sustainability: A theoretical framework. Sustainability. 2021;**13**(21):1-20. DOI: 10.3390/su132111945

[6] Novo C, Zanchetta C, Goldmann E, de Carvalho CV. The use of gamification and web-based apps for sustainability education. Sustainability. 2024;**16**:3197. DOI: 10.3390/su16083197

[7] Oliveira RP, Souza CGd, Reis ACd, Souza WMd. Gamification in E-learning and sustainability: A theoretical framework. Sustainability. 2021;**13**:11945. DOI: 10.3390/su132111945

[8] Azadboni TT, Nasiri S, Khenarinezhad S, Sadoughi F. Effectiveness of serious games in social skills training to autistic individuals: A systematic review. Neuroscience and Biobehavioral Reviews. 2024;**161**:105634

[9] Aan H, Han S, Kim K. A multiplayer VR showdown game for people with visual impairment. Human-Computer Interaction. 2024. DOI: 10.1080/07370024.2024.2342961

[10] Escudeiro P, Gouveia MC, Escudeiro N. ZooLector: Raising awareness of biodiversity loss to all. In: 2023 IEEE Global Engineering Education Conference (EDUCON); 2023; Kuwait. New York: IEEE; 2023. pp. 1-5. DOI: 10.1109/EDUCON54358.2023.10125247

[11] Escudeiro P, Gouveia MC. Fostering inclusivity and creativity: A card game for color perception and inclusion. In: Proceedings of the 18th European Conference on Games Based Learning. Vol. 18. Denmark: Academic Conferences International, Reading, UK. Conference held at Aarhus University; 2024. pp. 1009-1013

[12] de Carvalho CV, Coelho A. Game-based learning, gamification in education and serious games. Computers. 2022;**11**(3):36. DOI: 10.3390/computers11030036

[13] Senka G, Tramonti M, Dochshanov AM, Jesmin T, Terasmaa J, Tsalapatas H, et al. Using a game to educate about sustainable development. Multimodal Technologies and Interaction. 2024;**8**(11):96. DOI: 10.3390/mti8110096

Section 4

Technological Innovations in Gaming

Chapter 9

Exploring the Effect of Size on Viewers' Perception of Augmented Reality Objects on Mobile Devices

Zhenan Tian, Martin Traunmueller, Petros Koutsolampros and Ava Fatah gen. Schieck

Abstract

Augmented reality (AR) has rapidly evolved and is increasingly being integrated into various industries, such as retail, education, and entertainment. One of the aims is to enhance the sense of reality by superimposing augmented digital objects onto the natural environment rather than replacing it. Therefore, integrating "realistically" digital AR objects with the physical environment becomes an essential factor for its success. Besides head-mounted displays, most AR applications run on mobile devices and take advantage of the widely distributed base of hardware, leading to user experience challenges due to scenery and augmentation distortion. While most current research on AR user experience addresses some aspects of user perception within optical see-through augmented reality, there is an existing gap in existing literature on the visual properties that affect user's perception of objects' size in AR experiences on mobile devices. To bridge this gap, this paper presents four experiments using an AR application that was developed on a mobile device and tested by two sets of participant groups. The experiments focused on four visual aspects of AR experiences that impact the perception of object size, including (1) background, (2) grouping of AR objects, (3) observing distance, and (4) observing perspective. The results show that grouping, the observing distance, and the observing perspective can affect the user's size perception of augmented objects, whereas the background on which the digital objects are superimposed has no such effect. This study advances knowledge on the effect of visual aspects on the perception of objects' size in mobile AR.

Keywords: human-centered computing, human-computer interaction (HCI), augmented reality, size perception, mobile device, user studies

1. Introduction

One of the essential qualities of augmented reality (AR) is its ability to enhance the sense of reality by superimposing augmented objects onto the natural environment, rather than replacing it [1]. In doing so, it is essential for the success of an AR application that its properties are represented correctly in their dimensions and scale, which is challenging to AR developers: While scenery and augmentations can become significantly distorted and partly abstracted, impacting a viewer's perception of virtual objects' size [2], the influencing factors are rooted not only in the technical equipment used but also in the perceptually correct enhancement [3].

Technological developments try to minimize such effects, for instance, by the introduction of wearable devices, such as head-mounted displays (HMDs) or smart glasses, by offering a rather stable technological framework presenting information directly in front of the user's eye. For example, a form of heads-up display is a retinal display that "paints" a picture directly on the sensitive part of the user's retina [4]. However, for everyday usage, HMDs show limitations due to their weight and narrow viewing angle compared to the human viewing angle [5]. Moreover, because each HMD device or smart glass has different design configurations and specifications in terms of its parts, users often perceive the same virtual object differently, depending on the AR device in use [3]. Meanwhile, mobile devices supporting AR, such as smartphones and tablets [6], are becoming more powerful and less expensive at a very rapid pace, leading to increasing popularity in real-world usage for AR applications: Alsop [7] outlined an estimated 1.7 billion mobile augmented reality (AR) users worldwide, a rise of 1.5 billion from the 200 million seen in 2015.

However, as most research has gained insight into the viewer's perception of an object's size in VR, depth perception, and exocentric distance in optical see-through AR and others, less is known about the user's size perception in AR applications on mobile devices. The four main variables that affect a user's size perception are the background, the object grouping, the observing distance, and the observing perspective [8], which are difficult to define, especially in a mobile setting. As boundaries between physical and digital increasingly blur due to the augmentation of digital information onto the physical world in human-computer interaction settings [9], it is necessary for a broad and successful AR adaptation to understand if and how a user's size perception in AR differs from reality.

This research hypothesizes that there is a particular size perception error when people view and observe AR digital objects through the mobile screen within a specific range, and the viewer's perception of the size of AR objects and actual objects is different. This error will change with the distance and the perspective of the AR objects on the screen. In order to test this hypothesis, we developed an AR mobile application that allows the user to generate simple 3D digital cubes and conducted four experiments based on four variables that impact size perception [8], as outlined above. We then examined the effect on viewer's size perception for augmented objects by (1) the AR background, (2) the grouping of AR objects, (3) the observing distance, and (4) the observing perspective. Next, we present the background and related work this research is based on, followed by the methodology applied to run the experiments and the results obtained. We conclude with an in-depth discussion and the conclusion of this work and give an outlook on future work.

2. Background

To explore the effect of visual factors on the viewer's perception of objects through AR technology, we need to understand the size of objects at the intersection between digital and physical environments. In the virtual reality environment, for instance, Thomas [2] has studied user perception of an object's size. The study showed participants' understanding and their perception of matching the size of two different-colored virtual objects. The study indicated that participants were able to perceive height and width very close to the target values. Murdoch [10] has studied brightness matching in optical see-through augmented reality. Bremers et al. [11] have discussed two user studies on depth perception, in particular on the perspective cue, and compared perception for different graphical representations of angles. The study indicated that graphical alterations of angles displayed on a screen resulted in more variation between individuals' angle size estimations. Peillard et al. [12] studied exocentric distance perception, i.e., the distance between two objects, neither of them being directly linked to the user, in optical see-through AR. The study suggested that two virtual objects are perceived closer to one another compared with two real objects. Fischer et al. [13] explored how different static visualization techniques influence users' ability to perform perception-based alignment in AR for breast reconstruction surgery, where surgeons must accurately identify the locations of several perforator blood vessels while planning the procedure. Diaz et al. [14] conducted two experiments using a perceptual matching task to understand how shading, cast shadows, aerial perspective, texture, dimensionality (i.e., 2D vs. 3D shapes), and billboarding affected participant perceptions of virtual object depth relative to real-world targets. This paper, unlike the studies mentioned above, addresses the use of mobile phones as a viewing tool and focuses on four visual aspects that affect the viewer's perception of a digital object's size.

2.1 Size perception of digital objects in AR

Augmented reality (AR) offers various situations in which users can visualize and interact to improve their experience and performance in completing actual tasks in everyday spaces [15]. However, with the increased utility and availability of AR technology, its usability aspect has started to draw much more attention lately in the research community [16]. One of the more important breakthroughs for AR vision technology is the size perception in the AR interface. Ahn et al. [16] studied the correct size perception of the augmented object for three representative AR displays. Their focus was more on finding out how people's vision of AR objects differed between devices, such as optical see-through HMDs and mobile devices. Shin et al. [17] have stated that it is necessary to resolve visual differences between different AR devices to obtain mixing consistency. Their focus remains on finding a balance of size perception and colors of augmented objects between different devices so that the size of virtual objects and colors seen by everyone is balanced between different AR devices. Rolland et al. [18] have investigated more about depth perception and size perception in AR from HMD, and the experiments carried out are based on 2D pictures. Thus, the user's size perception of 3D objects is not clearly defined either. Ling et al. [19] have carried out two experiments to explore the effect of the perspective projection, on a wall, on the sense of presence and space perception. They found that the way the digital space is presented is critical for the level of experienced presence and that the field of view, viewing mode, center of projection, and display critically affect the presence and the perceived layout in the digital projection. Peillard et al. [12] stated that, when using an HMD, people tend to perceive virtual objects located on the side farther than the objects located in front of them. Diaz et al. [14] stated that by using a perceptual matching task, people perceive the position of an AR object closer than a real-world object. Swan et al. [20] found a significant difference in distance estimation between the virtual object and the real object. Eggleston et al. [21] suggested that there was a difference in the participants' size judgments between VR and physical environments. Experiments by Luo et al. [22] were consistent across the participant population, and results showed that scene complexity and stereo vision could have a significant impact on user performance in virtual environments to make precise judgments on the size of virtual objects. Stefanucci et al. [23] employed size-judgment tasks to measure the perceived size of virtual objects displayed on a large screen monitor. They determined that the size of an object in the virtual environment is underestimated compared to an object in the real world. This difference was smaller when viewed in stereo. Thomas [2] has researched to explore the user's ability to judge the size of an object relative to a second object of a different color in the virtual environment. Kelly et al. [24] found that egocentric distances in virtual environments are frequently underestimated by up to 50% of the actual distances. In summary, many researchers have studied the size perception of objects in VR and the difference in size perception by the viewer between different AR devices, but to our knowledge, no one has focused on the effect of different factors on user size perception of AR on mobile phones. We believe it is necessary to investigate the effect of viewer's size perception of AR displays on the mobile device in-depth for its further widespread applications.

2.2 Size perception of physical 3D objects

Judging the sizes of objects accurately is necessary for organisms and machines to operate successfully in the world [25]. People's size perception of AR objects is also based on their basic size perception of real objects. People trust their intuition and feel that their perception is correct, but there is a cognitive bias that occurs when people are processing and interpreting information in the world around them, and this may affect the decisions and judgments they make [26]. Long and unreliable delays are involved in processing visual information in the retina, and ineluctably, such delays result in spatial errors [27]. One of the important factors in perceptions by people is the size perception of objects. The perceived size of an object depends on factors including: 1. the actual size of the object, 2. the distance of the object from the eye, 3. size constancy: This phenomenon results in objects of known size tending to appear constant in size regardless of their distance, and 4. perspective of the observer [8]. Because size constancy results in objects of known size tending to appear constant in size regardless of their distance [8], it will not be studied in this research. Gepshtein and Banks [28] have carried out experiments to estimate the distance between two parallel surfaces to explore the combination of vision and haptics in size perception. Peschel and Orquin [29] have studied surface size effects on visual attention. Foley [30] found that visual angles correspond closely to physical angles. A 3D object seen from different views forms quite different retinal images, and many different objects can form identical retinal images [31]. We extend this research and build on the study of people's visual size perception of objects in AR and focus on four visual aspects, including: 1. the background, 2. object size, 3. observing distance, and 4. observing perspective.

3. Methodology

To understand the viewer's size perception of AR objects in handheld mobile devices and how the viewer's size perception in AR differs from reality, we conducted a series of four experiments. All four experiments were built on the theory of the classical psychophysical method [32] and were designed to examine the effect of four aspects that were found to impact size perception by the viewer [8] in AR:

- Experiment 1 investigated the effect of environment, whether the AR context influenced viewer's visual judgments of size, and how much of the size variation from AR objects could be correctly observed by the average participant.

- Experiment 2 investigated the effect of grouping, viewer's visual size judgments of multiple AR objects.

- Experiment 3 investigated the effect of distance and whether there is a difference in the perception of an object's size between the actual and digital AR objects. If so, whether this difference is related to the observing distance between the object and the viewer.

- Experiment 4 investigated the effect of perspective—whether the viewer's size perception and the difference between AR objects and actual physical objects were related to the viewing perspective and angle.

At the end of each experiment, and finally, the results of the experiments were analyzed.

To conduct the following experiments, a Unity-based AR system was developed, allowing users to place digital objects on a mobile phone interface into the existing physical environment, using AR core[1], AR-Foundation[2], and a placement indicator asset[3].

The system interface consists of 4 sets of control buttons (**Figure 1**): According to "Cognitive Augmented Reality Cubes" that have been implemented throughout cognitive AR research [33, 34], the user is able to place a neutral white 30x30x30 cm AR cube by clicking the button in the upper left corner (**Figure 1, A**). Selecting the AR cube is marked by a green bottom edge to distinguish selected from unselected AR cubes. At the lower right corner of the interface, the user can rotate (B), scale (C), or delete (D) AR cubes. Furthermore, the user can touch the screen to move and drag the cube to its desired position.

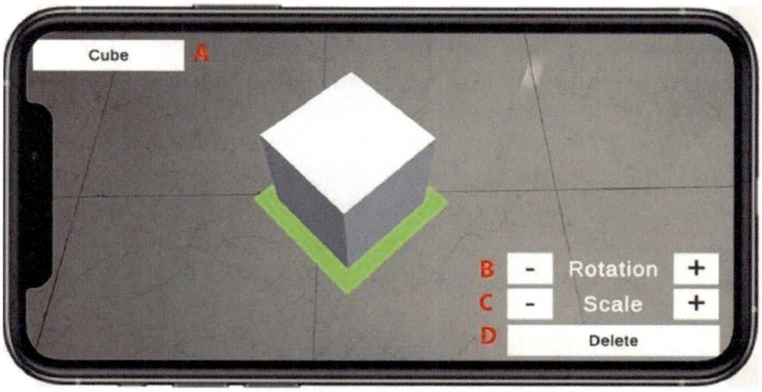

Figure 1.
AR application mobile interface: showing (A) cube placement button, (B) rotation button, (C) scale button, and (D) delete button.

---

1 Download and install directly from Unity's Package Manager.
2 Download and install directly from Unity's Package Manager.
3 Download from Github: https://github.com/fariazz/ARFoundationPlacementIndicator.

4. Experiments

To test our hypothesis, we conducted four experiments on the effect of the background environment (4.1), the object grouping (4.2), viewing distance (4.3), and viewing perspective (4.4) on the viewer's perception of AR objects' size. A total of 15 participants (10 males, 5 females, mean age 28.6 years) were recruited from the researcher's personal network to conduct Experiments 1 and 2, and a total of 30 participants (19 males, 11 females, mean age 28.6 years) were recruited to conduct Experiments 3 and 4. The experimental setup consisted of a Xiaomi Redmi Note 8 T mobile phone and a defined observation point from which participants conducted the AR experiments. At the beginning of each experiment, each participant was given information about the background of the experiment and was then guided to the observation point, the start of the AR experience.

4.1 Environment

In the first step, we examined how the environment influenced viewer's visual judgments of the AR objects' size and how much of the change in the size of AR objects was correctly observed by the participants. The experiment followed the psychophysics theory of the "method of limits" that indicated the sensory threshold by gradually increasing or decreasing the magnitude of the stimulus presented in discrete steps, hence gradually increasing the size difference until the participants noticed the difference [35]. To do so, we defined an "AR group" and a "control group" for the experiment. In the AR group (**Figure 2**, left), two AR cubes were placed on the ground at a distance of 2 meters from the observation point [18] on the AR operator interface of the handheld device: the left AR cube with the original size of 30x30x30cm and the right AR cube with 105% size. In the control group (**Figure 2**, right), the background of the two AR cubes was replaced with black, and all the other conditions stayed the same as in the AR group (**Figure 2**).

The experiment started with the first stimulus, a 5% size difference, i.e., an AR cube of 100% size and an AR cube of 105% size. Each participant was given 30 seconds to intuitively determine if there was a size difference between the two AR cubes or not. If the participant noticed a size difference, the participant was asked which of the cubes felt larger. If the participant did not notice a size difference, no further questions were asked, and the participant proceeded directly to the control group. After a 30-second break, participants were shown the control group experience, including the exact same situation just on a solid black background. The participant was also given 30 seconds to answer the same question as in the AR group. If all the participants had judged the AR cube size difference correctly at a 5% difference, the

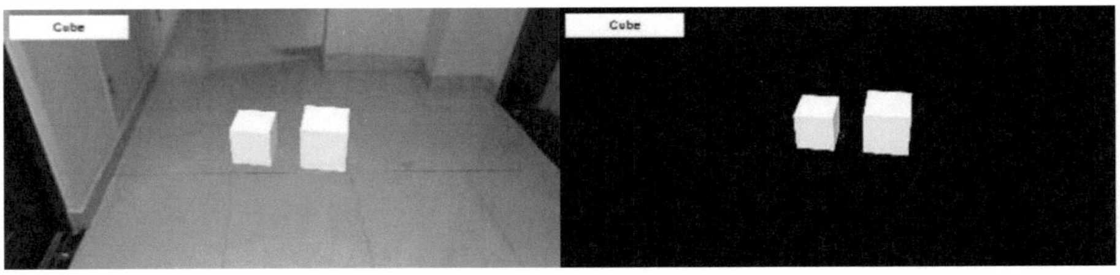

Figure 2.
Two AR cubes with a 10% size difference (2 meters away from observation point) - AR group (left), control group (right).

experiment would have ended. Otherwise, the experiment was repeated by increasing the cube size difference by 2.5% [2] each time until all the participants could correctly judge the two cube sizes. The whole experiment took about 2 minutes per participant.

4.2 Grouping

Next, we examined people's visual size judgments of multiple AR objects by employing the psychophysics measure "just-noticeable difference," which states the just-noticeable difference (JND) is not a fixed quantity but rather depends on how intense the stimuli are being measured [36]. We placed three AR cubes at 2-meter distances, starting with 5% size differences: one in original size, one with a 5% size decrease (95% of original size), and one with a 5% size increase (105% of original size), according to Weber's Law [37]. These three cubes were placed on the ground in parallel, and the order in which they were presented to participants was random (**Figure 3**).

First, the participant was asked at the observation point if a size difference exists between these three AR cubes. When the participants noticed a difference, they were asked to select three objects from large, medium, and small. When the participant did not notice a difference, the experiment ended for that participant.

Suppose that at 2 meters, everyone was able to arrange the objects in the correct size; the experiment was no longer conducted by enlarging the object gap but by increasing the distance to 4 meters instead, to test the effect of distance on the group. In these cases, whenever someone could not identify the size difference between three AR cubes, the 5% difference in size was increased to 7.5%, and the experiment was repeated at 2 meters. Size differences increased by 2.5% each time until all participants aligned the three objects correctly. The 4-meter experiment was then conducted for verification. The whole experiment took about 2 minutes per person.

4.3 Viewing distance

Next, we examined whether there was a difference in viewer's size perception between a physical object and an AR object and whether it was related to the distance of observation. In this experiment, five AR cubes were visualized that looked the same as the actual, physical cube, only differing in size. The selection of AR cube

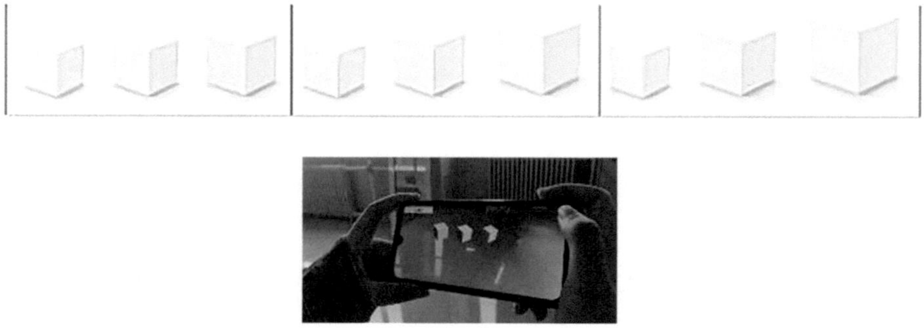

Figure 3.
AR Cubes with 5, 7.5, and 10% size intervals (above, from left to right) and as shown on the mobile interface during the AR experience (below).

quantities was based on one of the principal paradigms to explore the capacity of spatial attention, which has been the multiple objects tracking task. Subjects can track a subset of up to five objects [38]. The interval of the cube's size change was set at 10% according to Experiments 1 and 2, resulting in five AR cubes with 80% size, 90% size, 100% size, 110% size, and 120% size. They were arranged side by side and equally spaced on the interface of the mobile phone, placed on the ground at the same angle as the physical cubes (**Figure 4**).

Figure 4.
Real cube and AR cube with the same size (left) and AR cubes with four different sizes, the interval of variation is 10% (right).

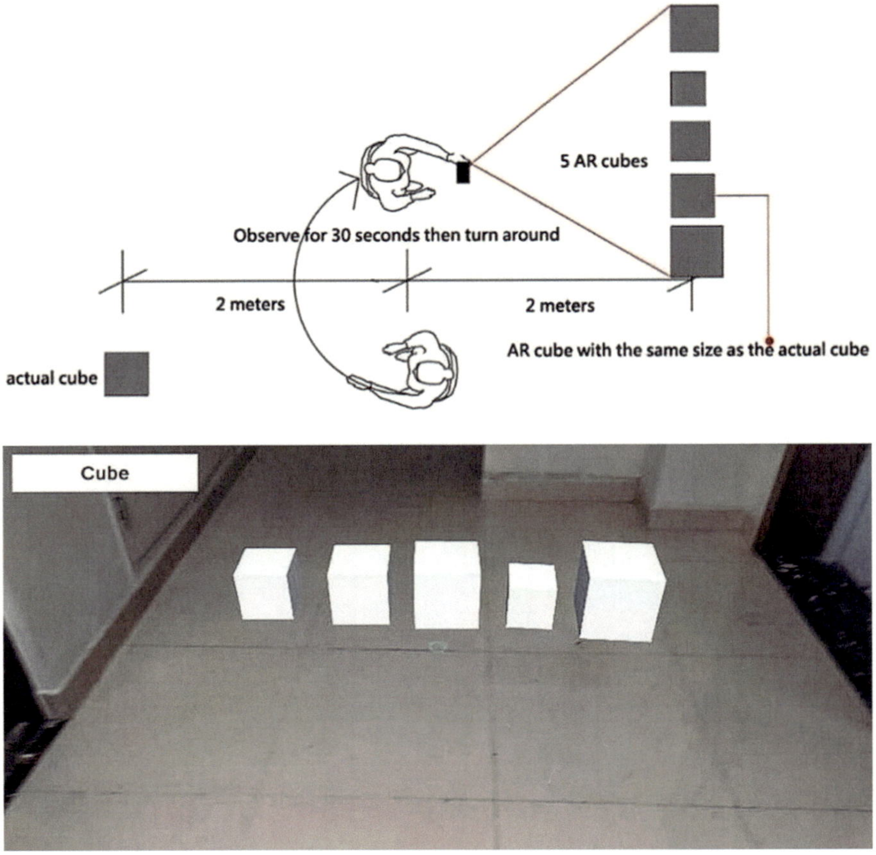

Figure 5.
Experimental procedure (above), and during AR experience (below).

This experimental setup consisted of two distances as control groups to detect the effect of different distances on human size judgments of AR objects [39]. Each participant was asked to look at the physical cube from the observation point for 30 seconds. Then, the participants were asked to turn around, hence not being able to see the physical cube. After a 30-second break in between, the five AR cubes were then shown to participants in the AR application at a 2-meter distance from the observation point on the screen, one of which was the same size as the actual cube. The order of the five AR cubes was randomly displayed. Each participant was then asked to choose an AR cube of the same size as the physical cube shown. When all participants have completed the experiment at 2 meters, they move on to the next experiment at 4 meters, following similar conditions. The whole experiment took about 3 minutes per participant (**Figure 5**).

4.4 Viewing perspective

Finally, we examined how participants' different observing perspectives would affect viewer's size judgments of AR objects. In this experiment, five AR cubes were visualized to look the same as the physical cube, only with a different size. Similar to Experiment 4.3, the interval of the cube's size change was set at 10% according to Experiments 1 and 2, resulting in five AR cubes with 80% size, 90% size, 100% size, 110% size, and 120% size. Cubes were arranged side by side and equally spaced on the interface of the mobile phone, placed on the ground at the same angle as the physical cube (**Figures 6** and 7).

Taking [40] as a reference, we set up two angle experiments, one of which was done with a 90-degree angle. The other experimental setting was at an angle of 45 degrees [16]. Participants were first asked to stand at the observation point and to observe the actual cube at 45° to the left, 2 meters away from the observation point. Then, they took a 30-second break, after which they were asked to turn around and pick out the AR cube on their phone screen that matched the size of the actual cube they observed. Next, the same experiment was conducted 2 meters from the observation point, 45° to the right. This was followed by the same experiment with 2 meters from the observation point, 90° to the left, and 2 meters from the observation point, 90° to the right. All conditions were the same for each experiment, except for the angle of observation. This whole experiment took about 3 minutes per participant.

Figure 6.
AR cubes at 45° (left) 2 meters away from observation point.

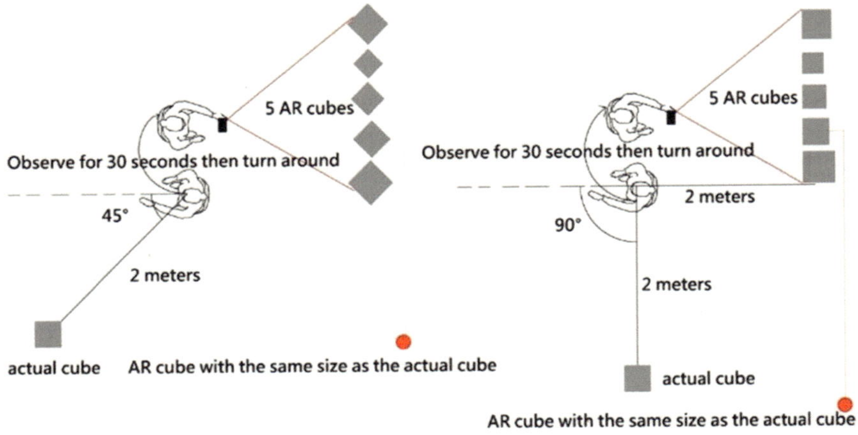

Figure 7.
The steps of the experiment at the 45° and 90° directions.

5. Results

5.1 Environment

The collected data were analyzed using a one-way ANOVA. When the size difference between two objects was 5%, the majority of participants (80%) were not able to accurately judge the size difference between AR cubes with the natural environment background, and almost half of the participants (46.7%) were not able to accurately judge the size difference when the background was black. Nevertheless, when the size difference between objects increased to 7.5 and 10%, the same number of participants could not identify the size difference between AR cubes on a physical or black background (26.7% at 7.5% increase and 7% at 10% increase), as shown in **Figure 8**.

These findings indicated that the size differences between AR objects could affect people's size judgment ($p < 0.05$); however, no significant effect between AR

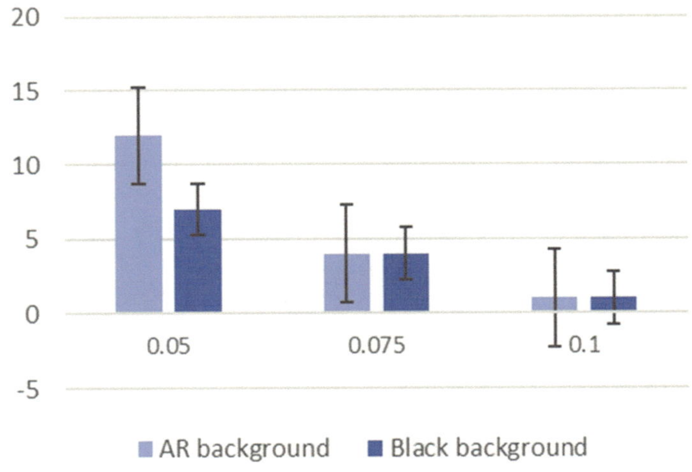

Figure 8.
Number of participants who cannot correctly determine the sizes of two cubes.

background and black background was found (p = 0.677). This outcome suggests that a realistic background does not affect people's misjudgment of the size of AR objects; hence, the effect of the background behind the AR objects can be ignored in the subsequent experiments.

5.2 Grouping

Our findings from Experiment 2 indicated that when there were three AR cubes grouped, all participants (100%) were able to tell that there was a size difference between these three AR cubes compared to the situation when there are only two AR cubes: results showed that at a difference of only 5% in the size of each cube, all people were able to identify the largest cube, but only about a third (31%) of the participants could fully distinguish the size difference between the three AR cubes. When the size difference between three AR cubes increased to 7.5%, the proportion of the participants who could distinguish the size difference increased to 86.7%. When the size difference between the cubes increased to 10%, all participants (100%) could identify the largest and smallest cubes correctly (**Figure 9**). Then the experiment was repeated at 4 meters [39], which also proved that all participants (100%) could identify the largest and smallest cubes correctly.

These results revealed that on mobile devices, people are able to identify the largest AR objects, but there was a certain amount of error (69% at a 5% size difference and 13.3% at a 7.5% size difference) in determining which one is the smallest. Furthermore, even when the size difference between AR objects is small, such as 5%, one can still distinguish the largest of them. However, it is easy for people to confuse the smallest and middle-sized objects, which decreases as the difference in the size of the objects increases. Besides, when the size difference between AR objects is large enough, such as 10%, people were able to recognize the difference in size between all AR objects 100% of the time. The result from this experiment is an essential prerequisite for subsequent experiments.

5.3 Viewing distance

The data collected from Experiment 3 were analyzed by ANOVA. At 2 meters, a third (33.3%) of the participants chose the correct AR cube that was the same size as the physical cube. A minority of the participants (10%) chose an 80% decreased-size

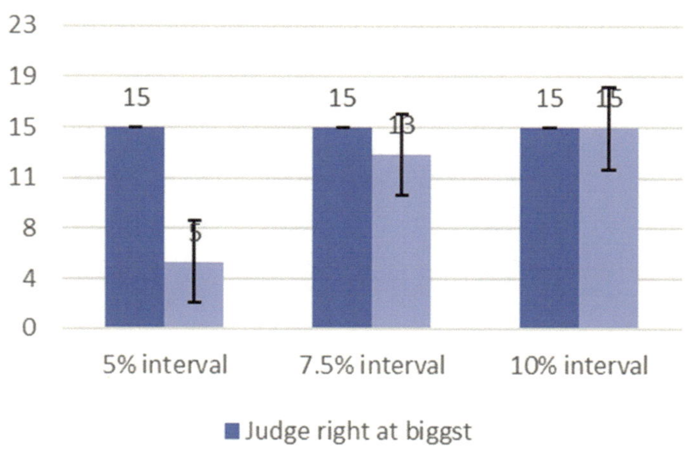

Figure 9.
Number of participants who have made the right choice.

AR cube, 16.7% of the participants chose the 90% decreased-size AR cube, 23.3% of the participants chose a 110% increased size AR cube, and 16.7% of the participants chose the 120% increased size AR cube. At a 2-meter distance, 40% of participants underestimated the size of the AR cubes, and 26.7% of participants overestimated the size of the AR cubes. At 4 meters distance, almost half of the participants (46.7%) made the correct choice, 3% of participants chose the 80% decreased-size AR cube, and 20% of participants chose the 90% decreased-size AR cube; over a quarter (26.7%) of participants chose the 110% increased size AR cube, and 3% chose the 120% increased size AR cube. At a 4-meter distance, almost a quarter (23%) of participants overestimated the size of the object, and almost a third (30%) underestimated the size of the object. The distance from the observing point was found to significantly influence the participant's judgment of the object's size ($p < 0.05$) (**Figure 10**).

These results suggest that the probability of people judging AR digital objects to be the same size as physical objects increases, and the probability of underestimating the size of objects decreases when observing distance increases. The margin of error that people choose tends to be more than a 10% difference in size.

5.4 Viewing perspective

According to our findings, the comparison between the angle on the left and the angle on the right shows that there is not much difference in people's choices (**Figure 11**) (The correct size was selected by 20% of participants at 45 degrees from either the left or the right, by 40% of participants at 90 degrees from the left, and by 37% of participants at 90 degrees from the right). Whether at 45° or 90°, participants made similar choices when looking at the left or right side. However, when comparing the 45° and 90° angles, it becomes clear that the angle of observation dramatically influences the final choice made by the participants. For instance, at 45°, a total of 5% of the left- and right-hand observations resulted in a choice of an 80% decreased-size AR cube, 22% in a 90% decreased-size AR cube, 20% in the original (100%) size AR cube, 45% in a 110% increased size AR cube, and 8% in a 120% increased size AR

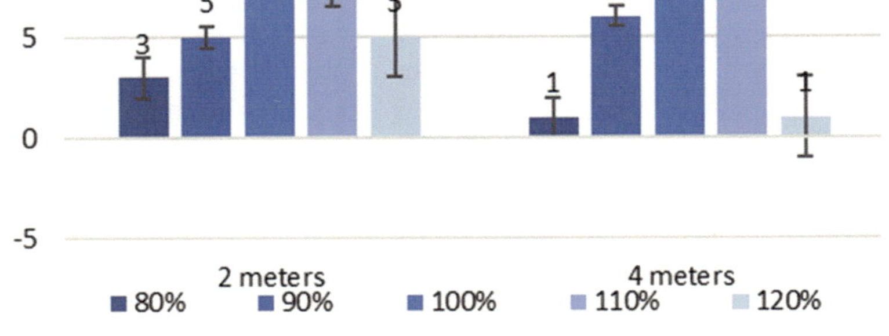

Figure 10.
All types of choices that participants made.

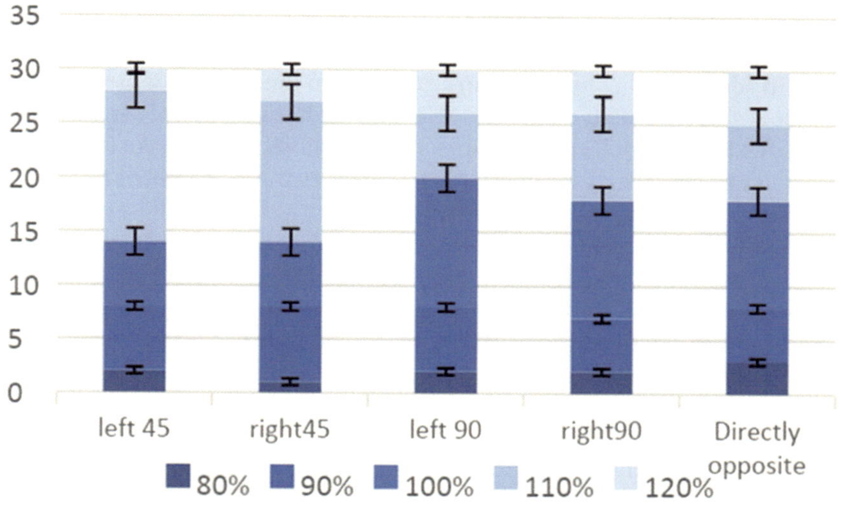

Figure 11.
Comparison of participants made decisions from different perspectives.

cube. This means that a total of 53% of people underestimated the size of the AR cubes, and 27% overestimated the size of the AR cubes after viewing the actual cube at 45°. When viewed at 90°, left-sided and right-sided viewing resulted in a total of 6% of participants selecting an 80% decreased-size AR cube. Eighteen percent of participants selected a 90% decreased-size AR cube. Thirty-eight percent of participants selected the original (100%) size AR cube, 24% of participants selected a 110% increased size AR cube, and 14% of participants selected a 120% increased size AR cube. This means that a total of 38% underestimated the size of the AR cubes, and 24% overestimated the size of the AR cubes after viewing the actual cube at 45° (**Figure 11**).

These results indicate that more participants made correct judgments (18%) at 90° from the observing point than at 45° from the observing point. However, regardless of whether people were viewing at 45° or 90° from the observing point, a much larger proportion of participants underestimated the size of AR objects if they misestimated the size. Hence, the angle at which an object is viewed does affect one's judgment of the size of AR objects ($p < 0.05$).

6. Discussion

This paper evaluated people's size perception of AR objects and how they differ from the size perception of natural objects. Addressing this problem requires both the development of effective evaluation methods and an understanding of what visual information might contribute to differences between virtual displays and the natural world [23]. Accordingly, a methodology was developed to explore the effect of different factors on people's perception of size through four experiments. The results from the experiments will be discussed below.

6.1 Background and the size of AR objects

Results from Experiment 1 showed that a real environment that is overlaid by digital objects has barely any impact on people's size perception of augmented objects.

Consequently, the location might make a difference to the AR context, but wherever people start using AR applications, it will not affect their perception of the size of the AR object. In addition, the difference in size between multiple AR objects does affect people's visual size judgment of the AR objects. When there are only two same basic AR geometries on the mobile device's screen, most subjects will make the wrong size comparison when the size difference between these two AR geometries is within a small interval. Furthermore, an increasing number of subjects will be able to correctly discriminate the gap between the sizes of the disparate objects. When the size difference between the two AR objects reaches a certain level, such as 10% in this experiment, essentially all subjects can judge it correctly, meaning that a 10% difference in volume size can be used as a threshold for discriminating two AR objects' size differences. In addition, when there are only two AR objects to compare, whatever the objective result may end up being, people subjectively feel that it is a straightforward matter to judge the object's size.

Nevertheless, when the number of objects increases, even if only one object is added, people subjectively believe that it becomes more difficult to judge the difference in size between more objects. This may conclude that even if the difference in size does not change, simply increasing the number of AR objects can make it more difficult to judge people from a subjective point of view. For example, when the size of three AR objects is being judged. Regardless of the difference in size between the objects, participants will be able to tell that the three objects are not the same size, unlike when two objects are judged; some participants think two AR cubes were the same size. This indicates that when there are more references to the same kind of AR object, people are more likely to notice differences in size. Almost all people can tell which is the largest object at any size difference between the AR cubes, but when the difference between the three objects is not large enough, it is easier to misjudge the size of the smallest and middle volumes. That is, with a constant size difference, as more AT objects were compared, people were often able to judge the largest object correctly. However, a greater number of objects did not help people to identify the relatively small object. Therefore, when many of the same AR objects are present simultaneously, the ability of the user to recognize the size of the relatively smaller AR objects is weaker.

Besides, results from Experiment 3 showed that there was a difference in the perception of the AR object's size on mobile devices compared to physical objects. In most cases, people tend to underestimate the size of AR objects that are the same size as physical objects (the same shape). At the same time, a relatively small number of people tended to overestimate the size of an AR object of the same volume as an actual object (the same shape). Some people will underestimate the size of AR objects, and some people will overestimate the size of AR objects within a specific range of size differences, and the needs of each group of people should not be ignored. Moreover, in both experiments, regardless of the number of objects being compared, 10% was a basic threshold at which all people were able to identify differences in object size correctly. It is also to provide a little help for people to build AR applications in the future: what is the smallest interval of size difference from AR objects that people will not distinguish wrongly?

6.2 Distance from observing

The distance of the AR object to the person is the distance from the location where the AR object is located to the human eye, not the distance from the human eye to the phone screen. Experiment 3 indicated that the distance of an AR object to the human eye does affect one's judgment of its size. Only 33% of participants made the right choice at 2 meters, while when the distance increased to 4 meters, the correct rate increased to 46%, a 13% increase in correctness. At 2 meters, the proportion of people who made a choice at 80% size and 120% size is 27%, while at 4 meters, this error rate was only 6%, a rate reduction of 19%. With the choice at 90% and 110%, the proportion was 40% at 2 meters and 47% at 4 meters. Therefore, it can be concluded that if the distance at which people look at AR objects is increased, it can improve people's ability to identify the size of AR objects that are the same as real objects. Furthermore, when the distance is increased, the size difference interval at which people's judgment errors are made gradually decreases, gradually moving closer to being within the 10% size interval. Similarly, from Experiments 1 and 2, a 10% size difference of objects is the threshold of observation. The closer the AR object is to the screen, the greater the error in judging the object's size, and there will also be more people choosing objects with larger size errors.

6.3 Perspective from observing

Experiment 4 showed that the angle of observation does influence people's visual size judgment of AR objects. However, the left side and the right side do not influence people to make different judgments. When combined with the findings from Experiment 3 at 2 meters, it is clear that sideways orientation does not have a significant effect on one's observations because the proportions of the various choices for the two sides at 90° are very close to the selection of those observed head-on in Experiment 3.

When observing at 45°, only 20% of participants made the right choice. In comparison, when the viewing angle was adjusted to 90°, the ratio of participants who made the right choice was approximately 38%, an 18% increase in the correct rate. Besides, at 45°, approximately 43% would underestimate the size of the AR object. When people viewed objects at an off-diagonal angle, more people misjudged the size of the object, and those who misjudged tended to underestimate the size of the AR object. At the entire 90° observation range, from frontal to lateral, the correctness of one's judgment of the size of the AR object decreases as one's point of observation deviates from the forward 90° and begins to shift to the lateral direction. Participants have the lowest probability of making the correct choice when viewing from the observation point at 45°. When people misjudge the size of an AR object, this error tends to be more within the 10% size range.

6.4 Limitations

Having gained insights into how people's size perception of AR objects can differ due to the discussed variables, we are aware that this work is limited by several factors. Firstly, using one type of mobile device that has been used for all experiments, the experiment and its AR representation are bound to the device's technical specifications and screen size properties. While experiment measurements were not taken on other models of mobile devices (such as a tablet), this leaves question marks on the effect of screen size and the device's performance. Secondly, the interface design and its user interaction (UX) have not been further evaluated in this work, while having the potential to impact the AR experience for the viewer, which might affect their decision-making. Furthermore, while aiming to include a high diversity of people demographics from various social backgrounds, the situation this work was conducted in—during a global pandemic affecting especially the recruitment process—led to a limitation in recruitment, as most of the participants share similar work backgrounds that might affect the outcome.

7. Conclusion and future work

With many of us now at home during a global pandemic, AR is a tool that can help us transform our immediate surroundings into learning, work, and entertainment spaces [41]. The development of AR is still in its early stages, and there is still more potential for the future, which can bring reality and virtual environments closer together.

This multifaceted research intends to bridge the existing gap with its focus on the visual factors that impact the perception of the size of AR objects on mobile devices. Thus, experimental studies have been conducted on many aspects that affect people's visual size perception in AR, such as AR background, groups of AR objects, observing distance, and observing perspective. First of all, the natural environment behind the AR object does not interfere with the people's size judgment of the AR object itself. Secondly, there is a specific error in people's size perception of the AR objects on mobile device screens. When the size difference interval between AR objects is within 10%, some people will misjudge the size of AR objects. In terms of the extension to AR applications, such as AR games or AR furniture arrangement, if the same AR objects appear in the AR apps, the size difference between them is within 10%, which may cause people not to recognize the difference between them. Thirdly, people's perception of AR objects is not the same as physical objects in real life. Regardless of the conditions, most people tend to underestimate the size of AR objects. However, a certain number of people will overestimate the size of AR objects. People's perception of AR objects bias tends to occur in the 10% range. A 10% size difference from AR objects is a clear cut-off point where people can clearly distinguish volume size between AR objects. Nevertheless, when many objects are present simultaneously, it is subjectively more challenging to distinguish between them in terms of size. At the same time, people's size judgment of AR objects is also related to observing distance and angle. When the observation conditions are the same and only the observation distances differ, one has a greater probability of being able to judge the true size of an AR object when the observation distance is greater. When the observation conditions are the same and only the angle of observation differs, one is more likely to misjudge the size of an AR object when the angle is 45° to the point of observation. The conclusions of these experiments lead to recommendations for the design of future AR experiences and the application interface design. For instance, before people start with the AR experience officially, people are given a simple AR object size test to get a bias in people's size perception of AR objects. Depending on their tendency to judge, some adjustments are made to the overlay of the AR interface with natural objects to achieve a better visual effect.

This research has studied the difference between static AR objects and actual objects. However, in real-life environments, when people use AR applications with their phones or pads, in most cases, AR applications present dynamic images, and AR objects have more than simple geometric shapes. Lastly, the study of user's size perception for dynamic AR objects and complex forms of AR objects would be worthy of future investigations.

Author details

Zhenan Tian, Martin Traunmueller, Petros Koutsolampros and
Ava Fatah gen. Schieck*
Bartlett School of Architecture, University College London, London, UK

*Address all correspondence to: ava.fatah@ucl.ac.uk

References

[1] Billinghurst M, Grasset R, Looser J. Designing augmented reality interfaces. ACM Siggraph Computer Graphics. 2005;**39**(1):17-22

[2] Thomas BH. Examining user perception of the size of multiple objects in virtual reality. Applied Sciences. 2020;**10**(11):4049

[3] Kruijff E, Swan JE, Feiner S. Perceptual issues in augmented reality revisited. In: 2010 9th IEEE International Symposium on Mixed and Augmented Reality (ISMAR 2010); 13-16 October 2010; Seoul, Korea. New York: IEEE; 2010. pp. 3-12

[4] Itoh Y, Klinker G. [DEMO] INDICA: Interaction-free display calibration for optical see-through head-mounted displays based on 3D eye localization. In: Proceedings of the IEEE International Symposium on Mixed and Augmented Reality (ISMAR 2014); 10-12 September 2014; Munich, Germany. New York: IEEE; 2014. pp. 345-346

[5] Maimone A, Yang X, Dierk N, State A, Dou M, Fuchs H. General-purpose telepresence with head-worn optical see-through displays and projector-based lighting. In: Proceedings of the IEEE Virtual Reality Conference (VR 2013); 16-20 March 2013; Orlando, FL, USA. New York: IEEE; 2013. pp. 23-26

[6] Craig AB. Mobile Augmented Reality. In: Craig AB, editor. Understanding Augmented Reality. Oxford: Elsevier; 2013. pp. 209-220. DOI: 10.1016/B978-0-240-82408-6.00007-2

[7] Alsop T. Global mobile augmented reality (AR) users 2019-2024. 2021. Available from: https://www.statista.com/statistics/1098630/global-mobile-augmented-reality-ar-users/

[8] Kaiser P. The Joy of Visual Perception [Internet]. 2005. Available from: https://www.yorku.ca/eye/thejoy.htm [Accessed: 2025-06-22]

[9] Raisamo R, Rakkolainen I, Majaranta P, Salminen K, Rantala J, Farooq A. Human augmentation: Past, present and future. International Journal of Human-Computer Studies. 2019;**131**:131-143

[10] Murdoch M. Brightness Matching in Optical See-through Augmented Reality. 2020

[11] Bremers A, Yöntem A, Li K, Chu D, Meijering V, Janssen C. Perception of Perspective in Augmented Reality Head-up Displays. International Journal of Human-Computer Studies. 2021;**155**:102693. DOI: 10.1016/j.ijhcs.2021.102693

[12] Peillard F, Argelaguet J, Normand A, Lécuyer A, Moreau G. Studying Exocentric Distance Perception in Optical See-Through Augmented Reality. In: 2019 IEEE International Symposium on Mixed and Augmented Reality (ISMAR 2019); 14-18 October 2019; Beijing, China. New York: IEEE; 2019. pp. 115-122

[13] Fischer M, Leuze C, Perkins S, Rosenberg J, Daniel B, Martin-Gomez A. Evaluation of Different Visualization Techniques for Perception-Based Alignment in Medical AR. In: 2020 IEEE International Symposium on Mixed and Augmented Reality Adjunct (ISMAR-Adjunct 2020); 9-13 November 2020; Virtual Conference. New York: IEEE; 2020. pp. 45-50

[14] Diaz M, Walker D, Szafir A, Szafir D. Designing for depth perceptions in augmented reality. In: 2017 IEEE International Symposium on Mixed and Augmented Reality (ISMAR). 2017. pp. 111-122

[15] Müller L, Aslan I, Krüßen L. Advances in computer entertainment. GuideMe: A Mobile augmented reality system to display user manuals for home appliances. In: Reidsma D, Katayose H, Nijholt A, editors. Lecture Notes in Computer Science. Vol. 8253. 2013

[16] Ahn J, Ahn E, Min S, Choi H, Kim H, Kim G. Size Perception of Augmented Objects by Different AR Displays. 2019

[17] Shin K, Kim H, Lee J, Jo D. Exploring the effects of scale and color differences on users' perception for everyday mixed reality (MR) experience: toward comparative analysis using MR devices. Electronics. 2020;**9**(10):1623. DOI: 10.3390/electronics9101623

[18] Rolland J, Gibson W, Ariely D. Towards quantifying depth and size perception in virtual environments. Presence: Teleoperators and Virtual Environments. 1995;**4**(1):24-49. DOI: 10.1162/pres.1995.4.1.24

[19] Ling Y, Nefs HT, Brinkman WP, Qu C, Heynderickx I. The effect of perspective on presence and space perception. PLoS One. 2013;**8**(11):e78513

[20] Swan JE, Singh G, Ellis SR. Matching and reaching depth judgments with real and augmented reality targets. IEEE Transactions on Visualization and Computer Graphics. 2015;**21**(11):1289-1298. DOI: 10.1109/TVCG.2015.2459895

[21] Eggleston RG, Janson WP, Aldrich KA. Virtual reality system effects on size-distance judgements in a virtual environment. In Proceedings of the IEEE 1996 Virtual Reality Annual International Symposium (VRAIS '96), 30 March – 3 April 1996; Santa Clara, CA, USA. New York: IEEE; 1996. pp. 139-146

[22] Luo X, Kenyon R, Kamper D, Sandin D, DeFanti T. The effects of scene complexity, stereovision, and motion parallax on size constancy in a virtual environment. In: Proceedings of the IEEE Virtual Reality Conference (VR 2007); 10-14 March 2007; Charlotte, NC, USA. New York: IEEE; 2007. pp. 139-146

[23] Stefanucci JK, Creem-Regehr SH, Thompson WB, Lessard DA, Geuss MN. Evaluating the accuracy of size perception on screen-based displays: Displayed objects appear smaller than real objects. Journal of Experimental Psychology: Applied. 2015;**21**(3):215

[24] Kelly JW, Donaldson LS, Sjolund LA, Freiberg JB. More than just perception–action recalibration: Walking through a virtual environment causes rescaling of perceived space. Atten. Percept. Psychophys. 2013;**75**(7):1473-1485. DOI: 10.3758/s13414-013-0503-4

[25] Maruya A, Zaidi Q. Mental geometry of three-dimensional size perception. Journal of Vision. 2020;**20**(8):14-14

[26] Cherry K. What is cognitive bias?. 2020. Available from: https://www.verywellmind.com/what-is-a-cognitive-bias-2794963

[27] Schlag J, Schlag-Rey M. Through the eye, slowly; delays and localization errors in the visual system. Nature Reviews Neuroscience. 2002;**3**(3):191-191

[28] Gepshtein S, Banks MS. Viewing geometry determines how vision and

haptics combine in size perception. Current Biology. 2003;**13**(6):483-488

[29] Peschel AO, Orquin JL. A review of the findings and theories on surface size effects on visual attention. Frontiers in Psychology. 2013;**4**:902

[30] Foley JM. The size–distance relation and intrinsic geometry of visual space: Implications for processing. Vision Research. 1972;**12**:323-332

[31] Ittelson WH. Ames Demonstrations in Perception: A Guide to their Construction and Use. Princeton: Princeton University Press; 1952

[32] Strasburger H. Software for Visual Psychophysics: An Overview. 2020

[33] Shahid H. Pictorial Cube: An Augmented Reality Application for 3D Visualization of Learning Objects. 2021

[34] Boletsis C, McCallum S. Augmented Reality Cubes for Cognitive Gaming: Preliminary Usability and GameExperience Testing. 2016

[35] Gescheider G. Psychophysics: The Fundamentals. 3rd ed. 1997

[36] Schacter DL, Gilbert DT, Wegner DM. Psychology. 2nd ed. 2010

[37] Gustav TF. Elemente der Psychophysik (Elements of Psychophysics). 1860

[38] Pylyshyn ZW, Storm RW. Tracking multiple independent targets: Evidence for a parallel tracking mechanism. Spatial Vision. 1988;**3**(3):179-197

[39] Isoyama N, Sakuragi Y, Terada T, Tsukamoto M. Effects of augmented reality object and texture presentation on walking behavior. Electronics. 2021;**10**:702

[40] Erkelens CJ. Perception of perspective angles. Perception. 2015;**6**(3):2041669515593022

[41] Papagiannis H. 3 ways augmented reality can have a positive impact on society, COVID-19. In: World Economic Forum. 2020

Chapter 10

Internet-of-Things Integration: Sensor-Driven Gameplay on WowCube

Nikola Peric, Marats Kicikovs and Maxim Filin

Abstract

The WOWCube® is an interactive 2 × 2 cube screen that combines a physical puzzle with digital interactive gaming. It embeds 24 high-resolution screens across eight magnetically linked modules, each containing its own microcontroller, communication ports, battery, and sensors. The device exemplifies a transreality gaming object: Players manipulate the physical cube (twisting faces, tilting, tapping, or shaking), while the cube's software updates the virtual game state across all screens. This chapter explores how the WowCube's sensor suite (a 6-axis IMU with gyroscope and accelerometer) and connectivity (Bluetooth, custom docks) enable integration with Internet-of-Things (IoT) systems and external game engines. We discuss the WowCube's hardware/software architecture, illustrate sensor-driven gameplay mechanics (e.g., using tilt and shake as inputs), and describe examples of IoT integration *via* a Raspberry Pi "DIY Dock". We also consider WowCube modules as AR-friendly building blocks (e.g., assembling modules into interactive maps for augmented reality experiences). Finally, we outline how independent developers can use the open Software Development Kit (SDK) and Application Programming Interface (SDK/API) to treat the cube as an external controller or item display in engines like Unity or Godot. This chapter aims to demonstrate the WowCube's unique blend of tangible interaction and connectivity, offering new possibilities for IoT-enhanced gaming and mixed-reality applications.

Keywords: WowCube, tangible user interface, Internet of Things, transreality puzzle, sensor-based gaming, augmented reality, game control mechanisms, integrated systems

1. Introduction

The age of the Internet of Things (IoT) is breaking down the barriers between the physical and virtual worlds [1]. Sophisticated smart devices are now able to interact with each other seamlessly *via* networks, and mixed and augmented reality (AR/MR) interfaces blend virtual information with the physical context [1]. In this transreality paradigm, gaming and entertainment are able to combine physical objects with software; a relevant example is a games console that also acts as a physical game. The WOWCube® is a striking example, acting as a transreality puzzle: A 2 × 2 handheld cube with full-color displays on every side [2, 3]. Manipulation of the cube's parts (in a similar way to a Rubik's Cube) changes the digital game state on each side in real time. Osipov and Nikulchev state, "We have developed a novel WOWCube device, which combines properties of a puzzle and a computer video game and is a so-called 'transreality puzzle'" [3]. In contrast to traditional static puzzles, the "winning combinations and game strategy are specified in software and depend on the game loaded to the console" [2]. Thus, the system represents a tangible user interface paradigm: Physical manipulation of the cube (rotation, tilting, and tapping) is the input method for the embedded software **Figure 1** [2].

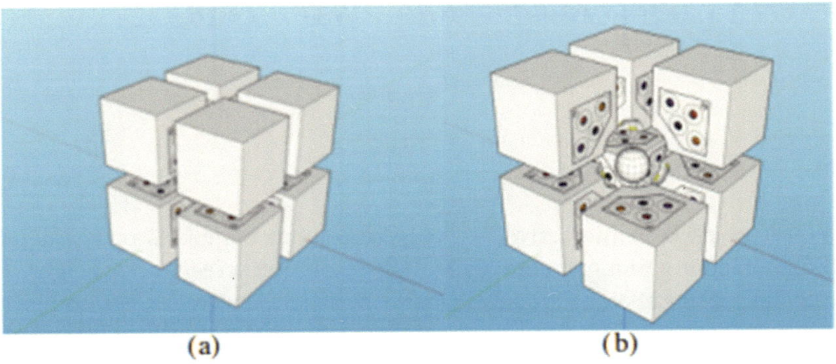

(a)

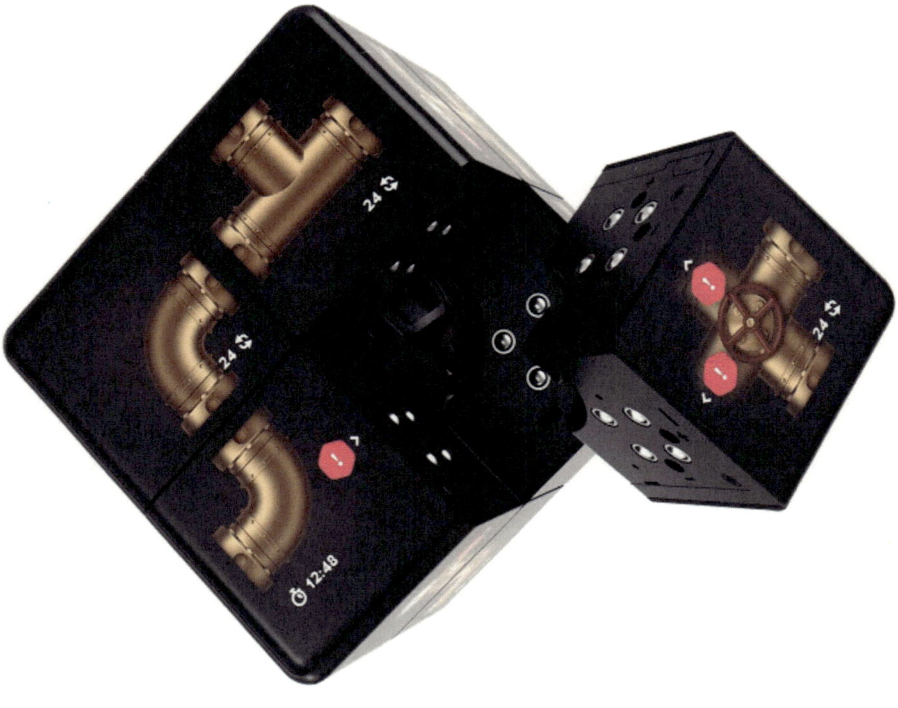

(b)

Figure 1.
The WowCube is a 2 × 2 tangible gaming console with 24 color screens (six faces per layer) [2, 3]. It uses physical rotations and sensor inputs to control video games in a mixed-reality fashion.

The WowCube's 2 × 2 cube exterior is decked in a galaxy pattern and rests on a desk, which is reflective of its design for full-screen puzzle immersion.

The WowCube's hardware includes eight identical cube modules, each with its own low-power microcontroller, battery, and wireless radio [2, 4]. Internal magnetic connectors carry power and data between modules so that the assembly functions as one integrated system [2, 4]. Each external face sports a 240 × 240 TFT LCD, and the device uses an on-cube operating system (CubiOS) to coordinate games across modules [2, 4]. In gameplay, "objects can literally move from one module to another" *via* the inter-module linkages [4].

The WowCube marries mechanical puzzle play with interactive graphical interfaces: Users solve levels by twisting the cube, and the game visuals respond by moving characters or items across the cube's faces. As an entertainment platform, it targets STEM learning and cognitive training, but from a systems standpoint, it exemplifies a tightly coupled physical/digital device [2, 3].

In this chapter, we discuss how WowCube's integrated sensors and connectivity enable its integration within the Internet of Things (IoT) environment. We first outline the cube's architecture and sensors (§2), then explore sensor-driven interaction (§3)—for example, using tilt, impact, and motion as input modalities for games. Section 4 discusses integration with IoT: Connecting the WowCube to external devices (robots, home appliances, and networks) *via* accessories such as the Raspberry Pi DIY Dock [5]. Section 5 considers the WowCube modules as external controllers and augmented reality (AR) devices, with novel applications within game engines like Unity or Godot, as well as physical markers in the context of augmented reality games [5]. We ground these discussions in quotes from WowCube's technical documentation and relevant academic literature [4–6].

2. The WowCube hardware and software framework

The WowCube system consists of eight separate cube modules that stick together magnetically, thus creating a stable 2 × 2 secure configuration [2, 4]. Each module measures 70 × 70 × 70 mm and weighs 385 g [4], and contains:

a. an energy-efficient SoC microcontroller;

b. three 240 × 240 IPS LCD panels (one on each external face of the module);

c. a built-in battery (420 mAh per module, ~3360 mAh total) [4];

d. Bluetooth 4.2 + BLE for wireless communication [4]; and

e. onboard sensors. The specs sheet lists "Sensors: 6-axis IMU (Gyro + Accelerometer)" [6, 7], indicating each module can detect its orientation and motion in 3D space.

The cube lacks any exterior buttons or touch-sensitive input devices, but instead, interaction is managed through regulating the cube along with its sensors based on sources [2, 6], the overall system design can be summarized as follows: "WOWCube is a mechatronic game console... controlled by changing the mutual position of the sections... Each outer side of each section has a 240 × 240 TFT

Figure 2.
WowCube module cross-section. Each module (a "cubicle") has three external displays (240 × 240 TFT LCDs), a battery, SoC, and three internal faces with magnetic connectors (for data/power) [2, 4].

display... The microcontrollers draw on-screen graphics, define game mechanics, and enable interaction of neighboring sections through serial connections" [2]. **Figure 2** illustrates the internal "smart connector" groups of a single section that allow the exchange of power and data between the modules. The connectors are based on small magnetized spheres to provide electrical contact on the contact of the modules [4], and thus allow the distributed software to keep the modules synchronized during rotation. The operating system, named CubiOS, runs across all eight modules, hence forming a decentralized application where game data and logic are shared across the modules, while the output is split across several screens. Moreover, an open Software Development Kit (SDK) and Application Programming Interface (API) have also been provided to enable developers to create applications on this 8-module platform [4].

In summary, the WowCube platform is an embedded cyber-physical system combining: Low-power microcontrollers, wireless communications, and an IMU (gyroscope+accelerometer) for sensing [6]. This sensor suite is crucial for its IoT integration and gameplay (next sections). The presence of Bluetooth and a modular connectivity bus means the cube can interface not just with itself but with external controllers or hosts. For example, each module's data bus can connect to a Raspberry Pi through a specialized dock (Section 4), and the SDK allows linking the cube to game engines or other software [4].

3. Sensor-guided gameplay and interaction

The WowCube's gameplay revolves around tangible manipulation, but the integrated IMU sensors further enrich control. By design, tilting, tapping, and shaking are native inputs. The official documentation instructs that to navigate menus, "you should tilt the cube" to move a cursor highlight [4].

Initiation of the game or selection of an application requires the action of "double-tapping (light knock) the cube on any of its faces." [4] This is internally tracked using an accelerometer such that variations in tilt lead to changes in orientation that prompt software reaction; nevertheless, an instantaneous rise in acceleration (impact) on two opposite faces signals the double-tap feature. The user also has the ability to shake the cube to trigger global commands: performing three shakes.

The main menu is entered again [4]. The inputs used—tilting, tapping (impact), shaking—are now core sensor-based inputs on the WowCube.

In addition, some games may incorporate continuous motion or angles. For instance, a racing or flying game could map the cube's pitch/roll (from the gyro) to steering input. Osipov et al. note that the WowCube "has accelerometer, or display sensors, or any other sensors to control the gameplay," though they emphasize that the primary control remains the rotation of sides [3]. In practice, third-party apps (using the SDK) often treat the IMU readings like a 6-DOF game controller. Gyro drift and responsiveness must be managed in software, but they allow intuitive interactions: For example, tilting the cube forward could accelerate a car, or twisting it could turn a character.

Sensor-driven inputs make the WowCube games more kinesthetic than traditional video games. They engage fine motor skills and spatial reasoning—users must physically rotate the cube to manipulate onscreen elements. This aligns with research on tangible interfaces improving cognitive tasks [2]. Moreover, leveraging sensors ties the device into the broader IoT/AR vision: The cube is not a static replica of a puzzle but a smart object that can sense and react to its environment [1, 3]. In essence, every physical motion becomes an IoT-like signal broadcast by the cube to its own system or to other systems.

4. IoT connectivity and external integrations

The WowCube's communications and accessories enable it to join external IoT ecosystems. By default, each cube connects *via* Bluetooth 4.2/BLE, allowing it to pair with PCs or mobile devices. More powerfully, the company provides a DIY dock station based on Raspberry Pi, explicitly to "connect the world of WOWCube Systems to the world of Raspberry Pi" [5]. In practice, this dock is a small 2 × 2 board that mates a Raspberry Pi's GPIO to the cube's magnetic connector bus. Developers can attach sensors, actuators, or network interfaces to the Pi, while the WowCube is inserted on top. This turns the cube into an IoT "controller" or display. For example, one could attach a Pi camera or environment sensor, send its data into a WowCube app, or conversely send cube gestures to control a home device *via* the Pi.

Figures 3 and **4** show the WowCube DIY Dock components [5]. The Pi (**Figure 3**) runs Linux and the WowCube's SDK example servers, while the shield (**Figure 4**) maps the cube's contacts to the Pi's pins. Through this, almost any IoT service becomes accessible to the cube. For instance, one could code a WowCube game to trigger a drone launch when a puzzle is solved, or use cube motions to adjust smart lights. The creative tools page notes: "Do you want to connect the cube to something unusual – IoT, robots, drones, watering systems, etc.? Everything is possible with a DIY dock station" [5]. This explicitly invites IoT integration.

It is significant that the WowCube is provided with an open development environment. The Software Development Kit (SDK), written in C/C++ and using UDP networking, along with the application programming interfaces (APIs), enables the execution of WowCube logic on different platforms [4]. Thus, a game engine executed on a personal computer is able to receive sensor information broadcast from the cube or send instructions to its display screens. For example, a developer can make an application in Godot or Unity that maps the cube's tilt and taps to virtual actions, and

Figure 3.
Raspberry Pi computer. This standalone circuit board operates in the WowCube "DIY Dock Station" for bridging the cube to Internet of Things peripheral devices [5].

at the same time, render graphics either on the cube or on the personal computer. The cube can be used as a smart peripheral; its displays can present extra game viewpoints, such as an "item board" or map, while main gameplay happens on the PC. The cube could also display sensor data from an Internet of Things (IoT) network in real time. The WowCube documentation explicitly states that it provides an "open API and SDK to enable independent developers to develop their own applications" **Figure 5** [4].

In summary, WowCube's IoT capabilities stem from two elements: (1) built-in comms and sensing (Bluetooth + IMU) for wireless link and gesture capture, and (2) hardware docks/SDK that bridge to external devices. These allow WowCube to function either as an IoT-enabled controller (sending sensor-based commands outward) or an IoT-informed display (receiving external data and showing it across its 24 screens).

DOI: http://dx.doi.org/10.5772/intechopen.1011908

(a)

(b)

Figure 4.
Printed circuit board PCB of the Do-It-Yourself Dock "Shield." The adapter board allows interfacing of the module bus of the WowCube with a Raspberry Pi [5].

4.1 AR integration using MergeEDU

In a practical application of augmented reality integration, the WowCube has been effectively combined with the MergeEDU platform as a physical augmentative controller and display for augmented reality visualizations. For instance, in presentations

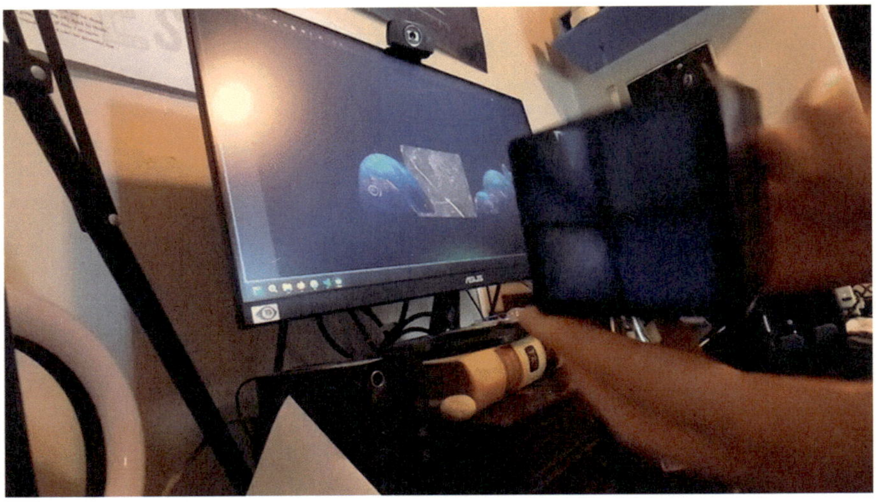

Figure 5.
Shows the WOWCube being used as an input device in the Godot game engine to send commands for movement.

involving Merge's augmented reality app, the WowCube was used to move and rotate a digital globe overlay in accordance with the physical movement of the cube **Figure 6** [8].

These practical applications demonstrate the WowCube's ability to interact with spatial augmented reality systems, not just as a theory, but as an effective learning device.

4.2 Practical applications of board games

Beyond video games, the WowCube has also seen use in physical board game implementations. In one project, single modules were employed as dynamic character tiles displaying player statistics, health, or identities on the screen. Players could rotate modules to change orientation or trigger in-game effects.

These modules illustrate the WowCube's value as a smart IoT object that bridges physical and digital play areas **Figure 7**.

4.3 Demonstrating neural input (MEG device)

In a first-of-its-kind experimental setup, the WowCube was demonstrated to respond to input from a brain-machine interface. A subject connected to a MEG device [9] was able to manipulate aspects of the cube with brain signals, opening new possibilities for accessibility and cognition-based IoT interaction. This proof-of-concept experiment showcases the system's support for nontraditional input techniques **Figure 8**.

5. WowCube as game controller and AR display

Apart from its built-in games, the WowCube is also an input and display peripheral for other third-party platforms. Its wireless, modular design allows it to be compatible with typical game engines. For example, developers working with Unity or Godot can think of each of the cube's faces as a user interface tile or heads-up display (HUD), and map cube movements to game controls. The WowCube game jam community has seen it used as an external controller with custom engine projects. While official examples for Godot are

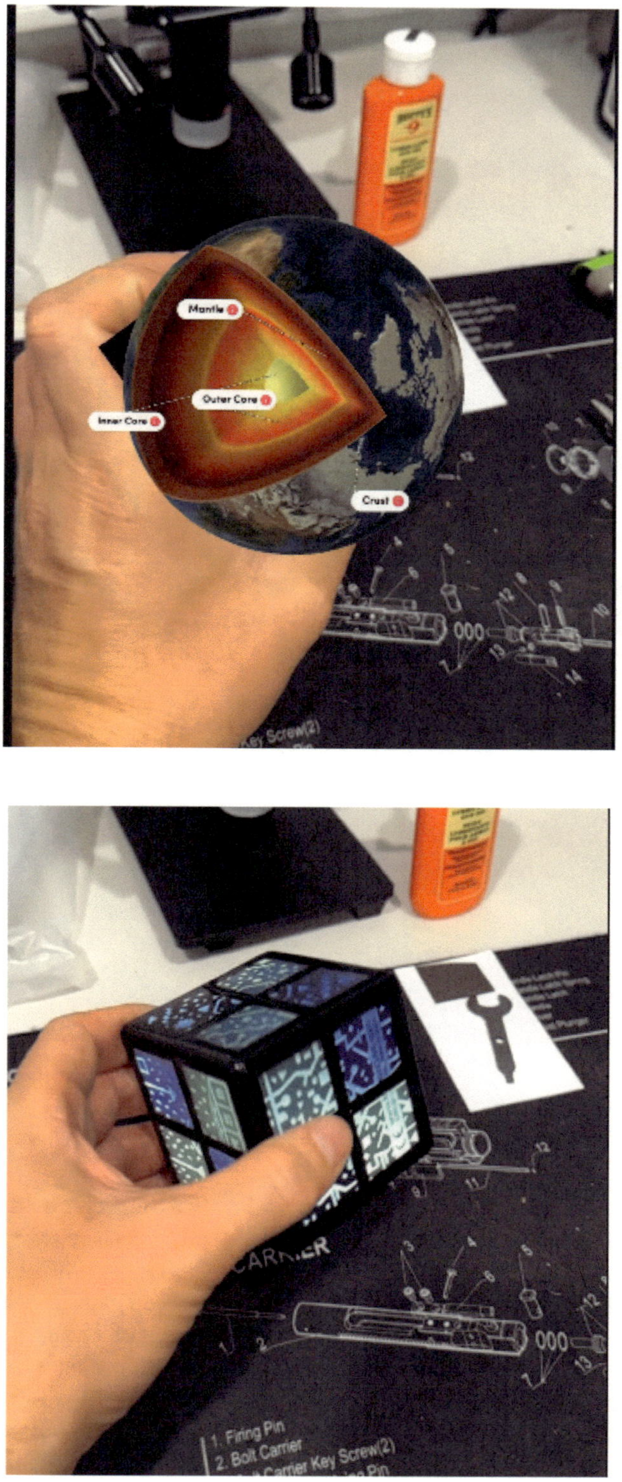

Figure 6.
AR GLOBE application running on the WOWCube® system. Screenshots show the augmented reality interface, where the physical rotation of the WOWCube manipulates a virtual globe in real time. The system demonstrates spatial interaction between tangible input and digital content [8].

Figure 7.
Dynamic character modules are used in a physical board game powered by the WOWCube® system.

Figure 8.
Neural control of the WOWCube® via MEG interface. The figure depicts a subject using magnetoencephalography (MEG) to control the WOWCube system [9].

lacking, the principle is still clear: Since the cube's Software Development Kit (SDK) communicates over UDP/Bluetooth Low Energy (BLE), it can interface with any engine that can handle network or Bluetooth inputs. Furthermore, independent projects have already demonstrated the WowCube being used to control off-screen games, such as driving a car by tilting the cube. These creative uses highlight the Internet of Things (IoT) aspect: After all, the data and visual output from the cube are just network packets and images, usable for external systems.

In addition, the WowCube modules have the potential to be reconfigured for augmented reality (AR) and novel geometric uses. The WOWBlock accessory ("Standard blocks allow connecting cube modules to create an alternative geometry" [5]) enables the creation of walls, panels, or bespoke shapes using these modules. It is possible to arrange the modules into either a planar surface or an irregular shape, thus acting as interactive AR markers. For instance, when the AR camera of a game engine detects the unique pattern of screens, virtual objects can be bound to those same physical points. Then, each module's screen could display a piece of a larger map or offer contextual details. This evolved concept turns the cube from an individual unit into a modular AR map. As noted by Kim et al., the use of AR with the Internet of Things (IoT) entails the ubiquitous combination of physical and digital spaces [1]. The WowCube's ability to form configurable surfaces fits into this concept of "AR-IoT": The physical cube modules are effectively turned into smart pixels in the real world **Figure 9**.

In summary, the WowCube can work alongside classic controllers at the same time. **Figure 10** illustrates conventional gamepads, which mainly rely on button

Figure 9.
Illustrates the disassembly of the WowCube into individual modules and then organized in a flat plane, where it is being utilized as a modular augmented reality (AR) map. Each module is a dynamic display tile that can interact with virtual objects via *physical arrangement.*

Figure 10.
Classic game controllers. Those devices can be supplemented with the multi-screen, sensor-integrated interface of the WowCube in order to enable hybrid (IoT) gaming [1].

presses; adding a WowCube complements the input options. For example, in a multiplayer game, classic controllers can be used for movement, and the WowCube can be an interactive puzzle or stat display. Contemporary trends in IoT game design favor "embodied interaction," where body gestures or object movements are used as game inputs [1], a space where the WowCube shows remarkable prowess. By combining timeless and IoT-style input techniques, designers can create more immersive interactions.

In a recent game jam [10], WowCube was successfully integrated with the Godot engine to act as a motion-based controller. The developers used its built-in IMU and SDK to map cube tilts and rotations to the game's movement and interaction controls, demonstrating how WowCube can function as an external, networked input device for third-party engines like Godot, Unity, Unreal, or even custom engines. This showcases the potential for growth beyond its use as a standalone console for internal games.

6. Technical issues and concerns

The WowCube's technical specs impose some limits. Each module's microcontroller has limited RAM/flash (e.g., ~192 kB RAM [2]), so game code must be efficient. Screen resolution per face (240 × 240) is low by modern standards, so graphics are pixellated. The cube's inertia means very fast flips can cause missed sensor readings; debouncing algorithms are needed to avoid false double-taps. Its Bluetooth 4.2 link offers modest bandwidth, so wireless control of the cube (e.g., streaming an external app to the cube's screens) is lower-performance than local apps. These constraints mean that IoT usage is typically event-driven or low-bandwidth (e.g., sending sensor values or static images).

Another challenge revolves around synchronization of multiple modules. While data sharing is made easier by the WowCube's operating system, new applications of Internet of Things (IoT), namely, assigning each module an augmented reality (AR) target status, will need to solve small differences in alignment of displays, as well as latency in data transmission while rotating modules. Continuous data streaming is facilitated by magnetic connectors when modules are connected [4]; nevertheless, connections can momentarily be disrupted while components rotate, potentially creating delays in communication amidst complicated movements. The system does contain data-buffering capabilities that will enable continued data transmission without interruption once regular connectivity is resumed. Notably, the WowCube's firmware has been designed such that "when two modules are close enough, their neodymium magnetic balls bind to each other which seals contact and the transferring of data between the modules," [4] thus minimizing data loss.

Despite these issues, the WowCube has demonstrated robustness in mixed configurations. The modular OS is even agnostic to cube size: "it does not matter if it is a 2 × 2 or 3 × 3 model cube... the operating system will be able to manage and control how the cubes in the device interact" [4]. This suggests future IoT games could involve larger WowCube arrays. The current challenge for developers is content creation: Each game must consider eight displays and six degrees of motion freedom. The open SDK and community examples help, but designing "sensor-driven" IoT gameplay requires multidisciplinary creativity (electronics, game design, AR frameworks).

6.1 Packet size and bandwidth limits

WowCube defines a maximum transmission packet size of 28 bytes (#define MAX_PACKET_SIZE 28), equivalent to 224 bits, which constrains real-time data streaming and high-resolution content updates. Developers must utilize compact data formats and often rely on a utility like save.inc for compression.

To illustrate, the following chart compares typical data types and their feasibility over a single packet **Table 1**.

6.2 Memory and processing bottlenecks

Each WowCube module is equipped with a low-power SoC microcontroller that has limited RAM (around 192 KB) [6] and flash memory. While sufficient for simple games and sensor-driven input, this constrained memory has its limits:

Game code must be extremely optimized, utilizing as few large buffers, assets, or real-time render operations as necessary.

Audio processing is minimal, with the only supported waveforms being small. (wav 16-bit Signed PCM @ 22,050 Hz, mp3 CBR and VBR @ 32 kHz, 44.1 kHz, and 48 kHz from 24 kbps to 192 kbps).

Complex physics simulations, AI, or procedural generation must be offloaded to other systems (e.g., *via* Bluetooth/UDP) or dealt with using light-weight approximations.

Additionally, with a resolution of only 240 × 240 per screen, full-frame high-resolution imagery or video streaming is quite impractical [6].

Developers should use:

- Condensed assets
- Tile-based graphics
- Utilize delta updates instead of complete redraws.

The constraints seen in the development of the WowCube mirror those seen in embedded systems or retro handheld consoles, creating a unique blend of game development and microcontroller engineering **Table 2**.

Data type	Size (bytes)	Fits in one packet?	Notes
Boolean flag	1	✓ Yes	Simple game states
RGB color (1 face)	3	✓ Yes	For visual effect updates
3-axis IMU reading	6	✓ Yes	Accelerometer input
4 × 4 sprite frame	16–20	✓ Yes (compressed)	Minimal animations
8 × 8 sprite frame	64	X No	Must be split across packets
Game HUD update	~100	X No	Potentially laggy *via* BLE
Full-screen update (240 × 240)	~57 KB	XX No way	Must use delta rendering only

Table 1.
Data types used in WOWCube communication and their transmission feasibility over BLE packets.

Platform	RAM	Screen resolution	Wireless	Features
WowCube module	192 KB	3 × 240 × 240 IPS LCD (per module)	Bluetooth 4.2 BLE	Sensor input, magnetic connectors, CubiOS
ESP32	320–520 KB	External (*via* SPI or Endpoint)	Wi-Fi + BLE	Low-power dual-core SoC, widely used in IoT
Arduino mega	8 KB	External	None	Basic microcontroller, no native display
Raspberry Pi 4	1–8 GB	HDMI (full HD)	Wi-Fi + BT	Full OS, desktop-class apps, USB/HDMI/GPU

Table 2.
Comparison of various IoT hardware platforms in relation to the WOWCube.

6.3 Physical durability and stress testing

The WowCube platform has undergone extensive physical stress tests [11], including high/low temperature exposure (+75°C to −40°C), vibration, salt/dust resistance, and electrostatic discharge (ESD). According to statements from the CEO, upcoming crash tests are planned to validate structural integrity under impact.

These trials confirm that the WowCube hardware is being engineered not only for gameplay but for use in demanding or educational physical environments [6].

7. Conclusion

The WowCube exemplifies a connected, tangible gaming platform at the intersection of IoT and AR. Its 6-axis sensors (gyro+accelerometer) enable novel gameplay controls, for example, using tilt, tap and shake as input—while its modular, wireless hardware and SDK allow it to interface with other devices and software. By adding a Raspberry Pi dock, one can extend the WowCube's reach to any IoT gadget (robots, sensors, home systems) [3]. In mixed-reality contexts, WowCube modules can serve as dynamic physical screens or markers for AR overlays [1, 5]. As an example, developers have integrated the cube with game engines (Unity, Godot) to use it as an external controller or multi-view display. This chapter has outlined the technical underpinnings and integration scenarios of the WowCube, supported by the literature on pervasive gaming and tangible interfaces [1, 2]. The WowCube's design illustrates the way that physical manipulation and built-in sensors can transform a normal puzzle into an IoT-enhanced gaming device, offering a blueprint for future interactive hardware.

Author details

Nikola Peric[1*], Marats Kicikovs[2] and Maxim Filin[3]

1 Independent Researcher, Belgrade, Serbia

2 Independent Researcher, Riga, Latvia

3 CubiOs Inc., Sarasota, Florida

*Address all correspondence to: nikolaperic27.np@gmail.com

References

[1] Kim K et al. The augmented reality internet of things: Opportunities of embodied interactions in Transreality. In: Nee A, Ong SK, editors. Springer Handbook of Augmented Reality. Cham: Springer; 2023. pp. 797-829. Available from: https://link.springer.com/chapter/10.1007/978-3-030-67822-7_32

[2] Osipov IV et al. Gamification device WowCube: Design and program environment. In: Proc. Psychology and Education - ICPE 2018. Vol. 5. No. 11. London, UK: European Proceedings of Social and Behavioral Sciences (EpSBS). 2018. Available from: https://www.europeanproceedings.com/article/10.15405/epsbs.2018.11.02.55

[3] Osipov IV, Nikulchev E. WOWCube puzzle: A transreality object of mixed reality. In: Arai K et al. editors. Future Technologies Conference (FTC) 2018. Advances in Intelligent Systems and Computing. Vol. 881. Cham, Switzerland: Springer; 2019. pp. 29-41. Available from: https://www.researchgate.net/profile/Ilya_Osipov2/publication/328408975_WOWcube_Puzzle_A_Transreality_Object_of_Mixed_Reality/links/5beb5f9192851c6b27bd0801/WOWcube-PuzzleA-Transreality-Object-of-Mixed-Reality.pdf

[4] WOWCube Inc. Technical Description – WowWiki. WowCube Community Wiki; 2024. Available from: wiki.wowcube.com

[5] Cubios Inc. Creative Tools – WOWCube® Entertainment System. Sarasota, FL; 2025. Available from: wowcube.com/tools

[6] Cubios Inc. Technical Specifications – WOWCube® Game System. Sarasota, FL; 2025. Available from: wowcube.com/specs

[7] Osipov IV et al. Development of a gaming application for a customized eight-processor device with a tangible Interface. Procedia Computer Science (Amsterdam, Netherlands). 2021;**186**:777-786. Available from: https://www.sciencedirect.com/science/article/pii/S1877050921010632

[8] Filin M. WOWCube Renders a Globe in AR. Sarasota, FL: YouTube; 2025. Available from: https://youtube.com/shorts/ooUQ5cHUn0g?si=Y5CQ_luhp1-SoWN4

[9] Tukmanov A. Controlling WOWCube with Brainwaves (MEG). Sarasota, FL: YouTube; 2021. Available from: https://www.youtube.com/watch?v=ay71NIbpOWg

[10] WOWCube Game Jam Entry. Moon Whispers. itch.io; 2025. Available from: https://itch.io/jam/wowcube-game-jam/rate/3684495

[11] Filin M. Sacrifice in the Name of Science! .... LinkedIn. Sarasota, FL; 2021. Available from: https://www.linkedin.com/posts/maxfilin_wowcube-activity-6836000386869006337-cyBZ